Massacre in Mexico

MASSACRE IN MEXICO

Elena Poniatowska

TRANSLATED FROM THE
SPANISH BY HELEN R. LANE
UNIVERSITY OF MISSOURI PRESS
Columbia and London

To Jan
1947–1968

Originally published under the title *La Noche de Tlatelolco*.
Copyright © Ediciones Era, S.A. Avena 102, Mexico 13, D.F. Mexico.
English translation copyright © The Viking Press, Inc., 1975.
This edition reprinted by arrangement with Viking Penguin, a division
of Penguin Books USA Inc.
University of Missouri Press, Columbia, Missouri 65201
Printed and bound in the United States of America
All rights reserved
5 4   04 03 02 01 00

Acknowledgment: Acuff-Rose Production, Inc. and House of Bryant:
For lyrics from "Bye Bye Love" written by Boudleaux & Felice Bryant.
© 1957 Acuff-Rose Publications, Inc.

Library of Congress Cataloging-in-Publication Data

Poniatowska, Elena.
    [Noche de Tlatelolco. English]
    Massacre in Mexico / Elena Poniatowska ; translated from the
  Spanish by Helen R. Lane
       p.   cm.
    Translation of: La noche de Tlatelolco.
    Reprint. Originally published: New York : Viking, 1975.
    ISBN 0-8262-0817-7
    1. Students—Mexico—Tlatelolco—Political activity. I. Title.
  LA340.T55P613   1992
  378.1'981—dc20   91-20343
                                                          CIP

♾™This paper meets the requirements of the
American National Standard for Permanence of Paper
for Printed Library Materials, Z39.48, 1984.

Contents

Acknowledgments

We wish to thank Rosario Castellanos for her poem, which was written especially for this book.

The poems by José Emilio Pacheco, José Carlos Becerra, Juan Bañuelos, and Eduardo Santos were the first protests by writers following the example set by Octavio Paz.

Margarita García Flores, who was Press Secretary of the University of Mexico during the events of 1968, was kind enough to lend us a number of her valuable bulletins, *Noticias Universitarias,* distributed by the General Information Office of the National University of Mexico.

Finally, we wish to thank all those who gave us their names and their testimony.

E.P.

Introduction

The Student Movement of 1968 and the brutal government repression that brought it to an abrupt end deeply disturbed the Mexican people. A political, social, and moral crisis ensued that has not yet been resolved. Elena Poniatowska's book *Massacre in Mexico* is not an interpretation of these events. It is something that far surpasses a theory or a hypothesis: an extraordinary piece of reporting, or, as she calls it, a "collage" of "voices bearing historical witness." A historical chronicle—but one that shows us history before it has congealed and before the spoken word has become a written text. For the chronicler of an era, knowing how to listen is even more important than knowing how to write. Or better: the art of writing implies previous mastery of the art of listening. A subtle and difficult art, for it requires not only sharp ears but also great moral sensitivity: recognizing, accepting the existence of others. There are two breeds of writers: the poet, who hearkens to an inner voice, his own; and the novelist, the journalist, and the historian, who hearken to many voices in the world round about them, the voices of others. Elena Poniatowska first made a name for herself as one of Mexico's finest journalists, and shortly thereafter she was widely hailed as the author of starkly dramatic short stories and highly original novels, worlds governed by an offbeat brand of humor and fantasy in which the boundaries separating ordinary everyday reality from the eerie and unexpected become fuzzy and blurred. In both her writings as a journalist and her works of fiction, her language is closer to oral tradition than to classic literary Spanish. In *Massacre in Mexico* she uses her admirable ability to listen and to reproduce what others have to say to serve the cause of history. Her book is a historical account and at the same time a most imaginative linguistic tour de force.

   Massacre in Mexico is a passionate testimony, but not a biased one. It is a passionate book because cold objectivity in the face of injustice is a form of complicity. The passion that suffuses all her pages, from first to last, is a passion for justice, the same burning ideal that inspired the students' demonstrations and protests. Like the Student Movement itself, *Massacre in Mexico* upholds no particular thesis and puts forward no hard and fast ideological line; on the contrary, it is a book whose underlying rhythm, at times luminous and lyrical and at others somber and tragic, is the rhythm of life itself. The mood at the beginning is one of joyous enthusiasm and euphoria: on taking to the streets, the students discover the meaning of collective action, direct democracy, and fraternity. Armed with these weapons alone, they fight repression and in a very short time win the support and the loyalties of the people. Up until this point, Elena Poniatowska's account is the story of the civic awakening of an entire generation of young people. This story of buoyant collective fervor soon takes on darker overtones, however: the wave of hope and generous idealism represented by these youngsters breaks against the wall of sheer power, and the government unleashes its murderous forces of violence; the story ends in a bloodbath. The students were seeking a public dialogue with those in power, and these powers responded with the sort of violence that silences every last voice raised in protest. Why? What were the reasons behind this massacre? Mexicans have been asking themselves this question since October 1968. Only when it is answered will the country recover its confidence in its leaders and in its institutions. And only then will it recover its self-confidence.

   As with all historical events, the story of what took place in 1968 in Mexico is a tangled web of ambiguous facts and enigmatic meanings. These events really happened, but their reality does not have the same texture as everyday reality. Nor does it have the fantastic self-consistency of an imaginary reality such as we find in works of fiction. What these events represent is the contradictory reality of history —the most puzzling and the most elusive reality of all. The attitude of the student leaders and that of the government, for instance—to cite just two examples. From the very beginning the students demon-strated a remarkable talent for political action. Their immediate discovery of direct democracy as a method of bringing new life to the movement while at the same time keeping it in close touch with its primordial source, the Mexican people as a whole; their insistence on holding a public dialogue with the government, in a country accustomed to wheeling and dealing between various power-figures behind the scenes and secret string-pulling by corrupt, conniving leaders in high government circles; the modest and moderate nature of the students' demands, which might be summed up in the word *democratization*, a heartfelt aspiration of the Mexican people ever since 1910—all of this was evidence both of the students' maturity and of their instinctive political wisdom. But while these virtues and talents were quite obvious on the tactical level, they seem to evaporate from the moment that we hear the students begin to ponder the perspectives that lie ahead for the Movement, its goals, and its import within the twofold context of the history of Mexico and the current world situation. In place of tactical and strategic realism, what we find at this juncture are empty formulas, rigid programs, dogmatic oversimplifications, vacuous high-flown phrases and slogans. Almost all these young people thought that they were participating in a movement that in reality was quite different from the one that they were actually participating in. It was as though the Mexico of 1968 were a metaphor of the Paris Commune or the attack on the Winter Palace: Mexico was Mexico, and yet also another time and another place—another reality. The theatrical drama that they were writing in the pages of history was not the same one that they were reading. Their acts were real; their interpretations were imaginary. A number of them were persuaded that there was a direct connection between the railway workers' movement in 1958 and their own movement ten years later; but they thereby failed to see the difference in objectives and tactics and above all the different class structures involved in the two movements, and hence did not appreciate the entirely different significance of these two episodes. Others were quite certain that the middle-class Student Movement would be followed by worker and peasant movements: history as a relay race. But the Mexican working class failed to snatch up the torch held out to them: it proved as indifferent as the working classes in the countries of the West and in the United States to similar appeals and similar hopes of changing the system.

The attitude of the Mexican government was even more disconcerting—and even less forgivable. It proved to be unbelievably blind and deaf. But both its blindness and its deafness stemmed from its inability to face up to what was happening. It was not that our government officials were blind and deaf; it was simply that they refused to see or to listen. In their eyes, acknowledging the mere existence of the Student Movement would have been tantamount to self-betrayal. The Mexican political system is founded on a single implicit, immutable belief: the President of the Mexican Republic and the official government Party are the incarnation of the *whole* of Mexico. Accustomed as they are to delivering only monologues, intoxicated by a lofty rhetoric that envelops them like a cloud, our presidents and leaders find it well-nigh impossible to believe that aspirations and opinions that are different from their own even exist. It is they who are the past, the present, and the future of Mexico. The Institutional Revolutionary Party is not a majority political party: it is Unanimity itself. The President is not only the highest political authority: he is the incarnation of all of Mexican history, Power itself in the form of a magic substance passed on from generation to generation in unbroken succession, from the first *Tlatoani* down through the Spanish viceroys to each president as he takes office. Unlike the Hispanic and Latin American pattern of dictatorship by *caudillos,* Mexican authoritarianism is legalistic, and the roots of this legalism are religious in nature. This is the real explanation of the terrible violence visited upon the students. The military attack on them was not only a political act; it also assumed the quasi-religious form of *chastisement from on high.* Divine vengeance. Exemplary punishment. The morality of a wrathful God the Father Almighty. This attitude has profound historical roots; its origins lie in the country's Aztec and colonial past. It can be traced back to a kind of petrification of the public image of the head of the nation, who ceases to be a mere man and becomes an idol to be worshiped. It is yet another expression of the *machismo,* and above all of the pre-eminence of the *father* in the Mexican family and in Mexican society. . . . In a word, in the Mexico of 1968, men once again made history with their eyes blindfolded.

I have always considered it necessary to look back to our colonial history in order to have even a partial understanding of the Mexico of today. By so doing, we will not, of course, find the answer to all our questions. But since the world of New Spain is the immediate antecedent of the world we live in today, our colonial past enables us to establish certain parallels with our present. In the case of the events of 1968, how can we help but be reminded of the so-called "disturbances of 1692"? The similarities between these two chapters in our history are, as we shall see, no less significant than their differences.

The end of the seventeenth century was a relatively felicitous era in our country's history. While Spain was falling into a more and more profound political and social torpor that was to last for nearly two centuries, New Spain was prospering. For the most part, peace reigned throughout this immense territory, with only sporadic disturbances in the provinces and occasional uprisings by brave Indians in the far north of the country, which was still not completely under the control of the authorities in the capital. Thanks to the remarkable development of agriculture, and even more particularly of mining, a class of wealthy "creoles" (that is to say, descendents of Spaniards who had been born in Mexico) had come into being and was flourishing. An ambitious, enterprising, devoutly religious class eager to flaunt its prosperity: thanks to its generous contributions, splendid civic and religious buildings were erected, lining the streets of every city in the country. This colonial culture reached its apogee in the second half of the seventeenth century, and among the many remarkable talents it produced were two outstanding figures: Sor Juana Inés de la Cruz, a poetess whose genius is recognized the world over, and the historian and mathematician Carlos de Singuenza y Góngora. It is not surprising that the inhabitants of New Spain should regard Mexico City as "the head and capital of the American continent," as Singuenza y Góngora himself described it, and call it, out of a sense of pride not unlike that of Bostonians a century and a half later, "the new Rome." Foreigners were equally impressed by the city, and even as late as the dawn of the nineteenth century Baron Alexander von Humboldt wrote, ". . . no city on the New Continent, including those in the United States, possesses scientific centers as large as those in Mexico . . . or as many beautiful buildings, which would not look at all out of place in the most elegant streets of Paris, Berlin, or Saint Petersburg." Creole society saw its own splendor and solidity reflected in its churches and palaces: gold altars and gilded salons, heavy cement foundations and walls of stone. This society nonetheless turned out to be more fragile than the monuments it erected.

In 1692 a shortage of corn caused an uprising among the common people—Indians, mestizos, and even impoverished creoles—and for the first time in its colonial history Mexico City was the scene of serious disturbances as the poorer classes rioted in the streets. This act of bold defiance took the government by surprise, for it was not accustomed to seeing its authority challenged. The people raided the storehouses, poured into the main square of the city, burned the official archives, and threatened to set fire to the very seat of Spanish colonial power, the Viceroy's palace. The rioting had turned into something more than a protest against the scarcity of corn and taken on subversive political overtones. Once the authorities had recovered from their initial shock, they unleashed pitiless forces of repression that cast a dark shadow over the waning years of the seventeenth century in Mexico. The golden dream of the Viceroyalty ended in a sudden blaze of fire; in its glaring light colonial society discovered its other half, its hidden face: an Indian, mestizo face, an angry, blood-spattered face. Heretofore, civil disturbances had been limited to local rebellions in the provinces, and the uprisings in the north were seditious acts by tribes not yet subjugated, not yet evangelized and converted to Christianity. The riots in Mexico City, however, revealed a rift that ran through the very heart of Mexican society. The testimony of Singuenza y Góngora, who witnessed these distur- bances, is as impressive as Elena Poniatowska's: "Hordes of men came rushing down that street where I was standing (and down all the others that led into the public squares). The Spaniards had un- sheathed their swords, but they stopped in their tracks for the same reason that kept me standing there as though rooted to the spot: because the blacks, the mulattos, and all the raggle-taggle plebes were shouting: 'Death to the Viceroy and all his henchmen!' And the Indians: 'Death to the Spaniards who are eating up our corn!' And exhorting each other to bravely enter the fray, since there was no Cortez on the scene this time to conquer them, they stormed into the plaza to join the others and throw rocks. 'Hey, you sisters!' the Indian women shouted to each other in their own toungue, 'let's join in this battle with happy hearts, and God willing, we'll be rid of the Spaniards, so it doesn't matter at all if we die without making a last confession. This is our country, isn't it? So what are these Spaniards doing here anyway?' "

Almost all historians regard these riots of the year 1692 as a forerunner of the battles for Independence a hundred years later. I do not know, however, whether anyone has noted one thing which to me is the most characteristic feature of this entire chapter in our history. The uprising of 1692 was a rebellion against the power of the Viceroy and Spanish domination; this revolt, however, was not really a revolutionary act, but an instinctive explosion. Its negation contained no element of affirmation. It would be fruitless to study this revolt in depth in the hope of discovering any sort of idea on the part of these rebels as to what Mexican society should be like once the power of the Viceroyalty had been done away with. A return to the world antedating the Spanish Conquest was impossible: it had been completely destroyed, along with its princes and its priests, its gods and its pyramids. Another world had been built upon its ruins: those rebelling against the Viceroy shouted their protests in Spanish, and worshiped the same God as their oppressors. None of the principles, neither of the two universalisms—the Spanish Empire and Roman Catholicism—that had served as the cornerstone of colonial society could serve as a principle of reform. Colonial society suddenly found itself trapped in a blind alley: there was no solution available within the religious, philosophical, and political constructs that served as its foundation. There was an irreconcilable contradiction between the Catholic-monarchic universalism and the particularism of the Indians and mestizos who had risen up in rebellion. Or to put it more precisely: the solution lay not *within* but *without* the ideology of New Spain. Yet another century was to go by before Mexicans would begin a slow, hesitant, timid search for the principles of another sort of universalism and attempt to apply these principles to our reality —with very little success, moreover.* These principles borrowed from

---

* The difficulty that the Hispanic and Lusitanian countries have experienced and are continuing to experience in their effort to adopt democratic principles and adapt them to their own situation ought to be the central concern of historical and social studies in Latin America, Spain, and Portugal. But this has not been the case at all, and however incredible it may seem, we still do not know why democratic institutions have not proved viable in the majority of our countries. There is a great deal of talk about our economic underdevelopment, and in recent years this underdevelopment and our dependence have been used as convenient excuses for all our failings and shortcomings. I do not deny that underdevelopment and dependence do indeed exist in our countries, but I also note that very few people have troubled to ponder the question as to whether or not there is any relation between this underdevelopment and our political life. The modernity of a country cannot be measured solely, or even primarily, in terms of the number of factories and machines it possesses. The most essential criterion is the degree of development of intellectual and political criticism. Doubtless the poverty of our scientific and philosophical tradition has the same origin as our shallow democratic tradition. Our history is as rife with *caudillos* as the waters of the Gulf of Mexico are infested with sharks.

abroad were those of the Enlightenment as they had taken shape in the
two revolutions that served as a model for the independence movements in Spanish America: the French and American Revolutions.

There are unquestionably certain similarities between the disturbances in Mexico in 1968 and those in 1692. In both cases there was a
sudden awakening from a dream, from the illusion of genuine
prosperity and social harmony. Around 1950 the groups holding the
reins of power in the economic and political sphere—including the
majority of technicians and many intellectuals—began to feel a certain
sense of self-satisfaction at the progress that had been made since the
consolidation of the post-Revolutionary regime (1930): political stability; uninterrupted economic development despite a high rate of
population growth; impressive completed public-works projects; the
birth of a sizable middle class; the increased number of jobholders and
the rise in the standard of living of the working class; and finally, as in
the seventeenth century, an over-all atmosphere of peace and calm, as
though each and every sector of the population were in perfect
agreement, from labor leaders to bankers and members of the higher
echelons of the institutionalized Revolution to the proconsuls of the
big international corporations. In 1690, creole society saw itself
reflected in its baroque palaces and its convents and its private
schools; in 1960, the post-Revolutionary society saw its image in its
factories, its ranches, its Hollywood-style mansions, and its colossal
monuments commemorating glorious Revolutionary victories and
Revolutionary heroes. It would be unfair, however, to compare the
baroque art of the seventeenth century, which even in its most
deliriously extravagant flights of fancy was an exquisite art, with the
megalomaniacal style of post-Revolutionary Mexico, conceived and
executed in the very best tradition of Stalinist art. There was no lack of
praise of our country on the part of foreigners. The most resounding
tribute paid us was that by President Kennedy, who unhesitatingly
proclaimed that the Mexican regime was a model for all of Latin
America. The heirs of our revolutionaries had at last received
Washington's benediction. But it represented a posthumous triumph
for the Mexican Revolution. In reality, our poor Revolution had long
since been the victim of a twofold takeover: it had been co-opted
politically by the offical government Party, a bureaucracy that is
similar in more than one respect to the Communist bureaucracies of
Eastern Europe, and it had been co-opted economically and socially

by a financial oligarchy that had intimate ties to huge American corporations.

In 1968 this apparent consensus fell to pieces, and the other face of Mexico was suddenly revealed: a generation of angry young men and women and a middle class which bitterly opposed the political system that had ruled the country for forty years. The disturbances of 1968 suddenly brought to light the deep split within that area of Mexican society that might be described as the developed sector, within that predominantly urban sector, that is to say, which includes almost half the population of the country and which in the last few decades has undergone a more and more rapid progress of modernization. But the crisis within the Mexico that is modern and developed assumed even more dramatic and crucial proportions when the Student Movement bared what lay concealed behind it: the other Mexico, the Mexico in rags and tatters, the millions of desperately poor peasants and the masses of the underemployed who emigrate to the cities and become the new nomads of our day—nomads wandering about the urban desert.

As in 1692, the 1968 movement lacked any sort of precisely defined ideology. Unlike the uprising in 1692, it was not a movement of the lower classes but of students, the middle class, and intellectual groups. As in 1692, though for different reasons, it was a direct expression of the general dissatisfaction of the country as a whole. A deep dissatisfaction in the face of the paralysis of the political system that had taken root after the violent phase of the Mexican Revolution had come to an end (the PRI was founded in 1929); and a deep dissatisfaction as well at the turn taken by the social program of the revolutionaries, which had degenerated into a policy of "development" that had benefited only a small minority. This is why the summons to "democratize" the country immediately gained the support of the majority of the population belonging to the urban sector. As in 1692—though again for very different reasons—it was political demands that became the prime concern. But it is that very fact which betrays the major difference between the disturbances of 1692 and those of 1968: whereas the principles on which colonial society was based could provide no answer to the crisis of 1692, the principles on which present-day Mexican society is founded are capable of providing, if not a solution, at least the beginning of a solution, to our problems. "Democratization" is far from being the final solution, naturally, but it is the right path to follow in order to examine our problems in public, discuss them, propose solutions to them, and organize ourselves politically so as to ensure that these solutions are effectively implemented. Those who are impatient must be reminded what development in the form of a sort of forced march imposed on a people by bureaucratic socialism has meant in the past and continues to mean today: such artificially speeded-up development has been achieved only at the cost of immeasurable physical suffering and moral degradation. The creation of a democratic tradition in Mexico is just as important and just as urgent a problem as economic development and the struggle to achieve genuine equality.

In 1968 the Mexican political system was plunged into crisis. Seven years have since gone by, and we still have not succeeded in creating an independent democratic movement that can offer any real solutions for the enormous problems confronting our country. The spontaneous and healthy negation of 1968 has not been followed by any kind of affirmation. We have proved incapable of drawing up a coherent and viable program of reforms and of creating a national organization. The truth of the matter is that the primary beneficiary of the events of 1968, and very nearly the only beneficiary, has been the regime itself, which in the last few years has embarked upon a program of reforms aimed at liberalizing it. It would be morally wrong to ignore these reforms or minimize their importance; but at the same time it would be an untruth to maintain that they are all that is required. No, the real remedy is not to be found in a reform from the top downward, but rather from the bottom upward, a reform strongly backed by an *independent* popular movement. What must be done is to create an alternative altogether different from the PRI, something that thus far the traditional opposition parties in our country have been unable to accomplish. An intellectual paralysis has overtaken the Mexican left, at present the prisoner of simplistic formulas and an authoritarian ideology that is even more pernicious than the bureaucratic sclerosis of the PRI and the system that concentrates political power in the hands of a president who is a mere party appointee. As for the right: for a long time now the Mexican bourgeoisie has had no ideas—only self-interests. For all these reasons, the "democratization" that the students were seeking in 1968 continues to be a legitimate demand and a pressing task. It is absolutely essential for any attempt at genuine reform in Mexico. Democracy may be roughly defined as that free arena in which criticism takes place. But criticism of others must be accompanied by self-criticism. To communicate with others, we must first learn to communicate with ourselves. Those groups that are eager for change in Mexico should begin by taking steps in the direction of their own democratization, that is to say, making free criticism and debate the practice within their own organizations. And what is more: they should examine their own consciences and criticize their own attitudes and ideologies. There are hosts of arrogant theologians and stubborn fanatics among us: their dogmas are as resistant to change as stone. The intellectual regeneration of the left will be possible only if it sets aside many of its ironclad formulas and humbly *listens* to what Mexico is really saying—what our past history and our present are saying. If it does so, it will regain its political imagination. If not, will our country be obliged to wait, as in 1692, for yet another century?

—Octavio Paz

Taking to the Streets

> PEOPLE, UNITE, DON'T ABANDON US, PEOPLE, UNITE, PEOPLE, DON'T ABANDON US, PEOPLE, UNITE.
>
> —*Banners at the demonstration of*
> *August 18, 1968*

They are many. They come down Melchor Ocampo, the Reforma, Juárez, Cinco de Mayo, laughing, students walking arm in arm in the demonstration, in as festive a mood as if they were going to a street fair; carefree boys and girls who do not know that tomorrow, and the day after, their dead bodies will be lying swollen in the rain, after a fair where the guns in the shooting gallery are aimed at them, children-targets, wonder-struck children, children for whom every day is a holiday until the owner of the shooting gallery tells them to form a line, like the row of tin-plated mechanical ducks that move past exactly at eye level, click, click, click, "Ready, aim, fire!" and they tumble backward, touching the red satin backdrop.

The owner of the shooting gallery handed out rifles to the police, to the army, and ordered them to shoot, to hit the bull's-eye, and there the little tin-plated creatures were standing, open-mouthed with astonishment and wide-eyed with fear, staring into the rifle barrels. Fire! The sudden blinding flash of a green flare. Fire! They fell, but this time there was no spring to set them up again for the next customer to shoot at; the mechanism was quite different at this fair; the little springs were not made of metal but of blood; thick, red blood that slowly formed little puddles, young blood trampled underfoot all over the Plaza de las Tres Culturas.

These youngsters are coming toward me now, hundreds of them; not one of them has his hands up, not one of them has his pants around his ankles as he is stripped naked to be searched; there are no sudden blows, no clubbings, no ill treatment, no vomiting after being tortured; they are breathing deeply, advancing slowly, surely, stubbornly; they come

3

round the Plaza de las Tres Culturas and stop at the edge of the square, where there is a drop of eight or ten feet, with a view of the pre-Hispanic ruins below; they walk on toward me again, hundreds of them, advancing toward me with their hands holding up placards, little hands, because death makes them look like children's hands; they come toward me, row on row; though they are pale, they look happy; their faces are slightly blurred, but they are happy ones; there are no walls of bayonets driving them off now, no violence; I look at them through a curtain of raindrops, or perhaps a veil of tears, like the one at Tlatelolco; I cannot see their wounds, for fortunately there are no holes in their bodies, no bayonet gashes, no dum-dum bullets; they are blurred figures, but I can hear their voices, their footsteps, echoing as on the day of the Silent Demonstration; I will hear those advancing foot-steps all the rest of my life; girls in mini-skirts with their tanned young legs, teachers with no neckties, boys with sweaters knotted around their waists or their necks; they come toward me, laughing, there are hundreds of them, full of the crazy joy of walking together down this street, our street, to the Zócalo, our Zócalo; here they come; August 5, August 13, August 27, September 13; Father Jesús Pérez has set all the bells of the cathedral to ringing to welcome them, the entire Plaza de la Constitución is illuminated; there are bunches of *cempazúchitl* flowers everywhere, thousands of lighted candles; the youngsters are in the center of an orange, they are the brightest burst of fireworks of all. Was Mexico a sad country? I see it as a happy one, a marvelously happy one; the youngsters are marching up Cinco de Mayo, Júarez, the Reforma, the applause is deafening, three hundred thou-sand people have come to join them, of their own free will, Melchor Ocampo, Las Lomas, they are climbing up through the forests to the mountaintops, *Mé-xi-co, Li-ber-tad, Mé-xi-co, Li-ber-tad, Mé-xi-co, Li-ber-tad, Mé-xi-co, Li-ber-tad, Mé-xi-co, Li-ber-tad.*

E.P.

I didn't "join" the Student Movement; it had been an intimate part of my life for a long time. What I mean is, I'm from Poli; * I live in a house there; that's where my pals, my neighbors, my work are. . . . My kids were born there. My wife is from Poli, too. The Movement has been very close to our hearts for many years. It's not a whim of the moment, or a joke or "good vibes," or anything like that. That's not what it is at all. It's a question of fighting for everything we believe in, for the things we've always fought for, things that our fathers and our fathers' fathers fought for before us. . . . We come from working-class families, people who have always worked hard for a living.

> *Raúl Álvarez Garín, theoretical physicist, ESFM; † professor at the National School of Biological Sciences of the IPN; CNH ‡ delegate; prisoner in Lecumberri*

Mé-xi-co—Li-ber-tad—Mé-xi-co—Li-ber-tad—Mé-xi-co—
Chant at demonstrations

I joined the Student Movement simply because one day the *granaderos* § turned up at the INBA ‖ with police dogs and chains and hauled everybody off to jail. And the INBA hadn't even come out and said whether it supported the Movement or not! (I'm

---

* Instituto Politécnico Nacional (The National Polytechnic Institute [IPN], Mexico City).
† Escuela Superior de Físico–Matemáticas (School of Theoretical Physics at the IPN).
‡ Consejo Nacional de Huelga (National Strike Committee).
§ The riot police.
‖ Institute Nacionale de Bellas Artes (the National Institute of Fine Arts).

5

rather inclined to think it didn't, right?) This arbitrary invasion made many of us actors and actresses aware of what was happening, and we decided to join the students and help them, *really* help them, not just march arm in arm in demonstrations or yell at the top of our lungs in meetings. . . . So then we formed an actors' brigade.

Margarita Isabel, actress

PEOPLE UNITE—PEOPLE UNITE—PEOPLE UNITE
Chant at demonstrations

The decision confronting us was not whether to join the Movement but whether to get out of it or stay in it. We had a rather good idea what was going to happen from the very beginning—we suspected, quite rightly, that repression, mass arrests, and clubbings were in the offing—so we had a choice. We could either "go underground," meaning buy a plane or a train ticket or whatever and get out, or stay in the city and wait and see what would happen. . . . We were all in our schools, Raúl in Theoretical Physics, I in Philosophy, and we were already involved in student affairs. The concrete problems in my school, for instance, were: a preparatory program for working-class students, flunk-outs, freeing Vallejo,* the curriculum and other academic problems, the independence of the School of Psychology, etc. I was elected president of the student body in 1967, but now I'm just an ordinary alumnus. . . . Everything changed after the twenty-sixth of July. . . . I'm not the same now; we're all different. There was one Mexico before the Student Movement, and a different one after 1968. Tlatelolco is the dividing point between these two Mexicos.

Luis González de Alba, CNH delegate from the
Faculty of Philosophy and Letters, UNAM; †
prisoner in Lecumberri

---

* Demetrio Vallejo, leader of the railway union, imprisoned from 1959 to 1970 for leading an illegal strike. (Translator's note.)

† Universidad Nacional Autónoma de Mexico (Autonomous National University of Mexico).

"Going underground" means doing nothing.

Gilberto Guevara Niebla, CNH delegate from the
Faculty of Sciences, UNAM; prisoner in
Lecumberri

I think that repression was responsible for the effectiveness and the importance of the Student Movement. More than any political speech, the very fact of repression politicized people and led the great majority to participate actively in the meetings. It was decided that classes would be suspended in each school, and that was what got us to thinking about forming brigades and action committees in each department. The members of the brigades were students who engaged in all sorts of activities, from collecting money to organizing "lightning meetings" in the streets, in the most isolated working-class districts. Mass demonstrations were one of the most effective political weapons of the Movement.

Carolina Pérez Cicero, student at the Faculty of
Philosophy and Letters, UNAM

Mexico had never seen such huge and such enormously enthusiastic spontaneous demonstrations as the ones organized by the students. There was one demonstration, in support of the Cuban Revolution, some years ago, but it was not nearly as wide in scope. The Student Movement really shook Mexican society to its foundations, and that's why the government began to be so afraid of it.

Félix Lucio Hernández Gamundi, CNH delegate
from ESIME,* IPN; prisoner in Lecumberri

At most, fifteen thousand demonstrators took part in the marches in Mexico City. But six hundred thousand people, from every walk of life, and young people in particular, gathered to show their support. When have we ever seen anything like that? How could the government put up with something like that? It had every reason to go off its nut.

Salvador Martínez de la Roca ("Pino"), of
the Action Committee of the Faculty of
Sciences, UNAM; prisoner in Lecumberri

---

* Escuela Superior de Ingeniería Mecánica y Eléctrica (School of Mechanical and Electrical Engineering).

They couldn't stand the thought that a veritable multitude, between three hundred and six hundred thousand people, had marched down the principal streets of Mexico City, the Paseo de la Reforma, Juárez, Cinco de Mayo, bearing banners and placards that made fun of the "principle of authority." They were forced to put down the student protest undermining the status quo, the PRI,* fake labor unions, and leadership by "mummies."

> *Eduardo Valle Espinoza ("Owl-Eyes"),*
> *CNH delegate from the National School of*
> *Economics, UNAM; prisoner in Lecumberri*

By marching through the streets, we were more or less avenging all the students in the provinces who had been the victims of repression before our turn came: the students of Puebla, Tabasco, Chihuahua, Sinaloa, Guerrero, Sonora, and in a certain sense, the victims of oppression in Morelia, Hermosillo, and Monterrey.

> *Ernesto Hernández Pichardo, student at the*
> *National School of Economics, UNAM*

DON'T SHOOT, SOLDIER: YOU'RE ONE OF THE PEOPLE TOO

Banner at the August 27 demonstration

Mexico today has a population of forty-eight million, scattered over a territory of two million square kilometers. Its rate of population growth is 3.6 per annum (at any rate that is what Dr. Loyo tells us), and since this rate of growth increases every year, there will be ninety million people in our country in 1990. Seventy per cent of them will be under twenty-three years of age.

I mention this because I believe that young peasants, workers, and students are facing a very dim future, since job opportunities are being created for the benefit of special interests rather than society as a whole. We are continually told, "You are the future of the country." But we are constantly denied any opportunity to act and

---

* Partido Revolucionario Institucional (Institutional Revolutionary Party, the official Mexican government party).

participate in the political decisions that are being made today. . . .
We want to and ARE ABLE TO participate today, not when we are
seventy years old. . . .

pr̶e̶s̶e̶n̶t̶

Gustavo Gordillo, *CNH delegate from*
the National School of Economics, UNAM

> **PEOPLE, DON'T ABANDON US—PEOPLE, UNITE!**
> *Chant at the August 13 demonstration*

I didn't join the Movement; I was part of it from the day I was born.
It's my medium, the very air I breathe, and to me the Movement
meant protecting my home, my wife, my children, my comrades.

Ernesto Olvera, teacher of mathematics at
Preparatory 1,* UNAM; prisoner in Lecumberri

> **FREE-DOM FOR POLITICAL PRISONERS!**
> **FREE-DOM FOR POLITICAL PRISONERS!**
> *Chant at the August 13 demonstration*

The 1968 Student Movement was not suddenly born that same year;
it did not come about by spontaneous generation. Countless revolutionary political organizations and important student groups had
previously made the same demands. In Mexico freedom for political
prisoners is a demand that goes back as far as political imprisonment itself. The same is true of the fight to do away with Article
145, which establishes penalties for "social dissolution," and the
fight to do away with the *granaderos*. The 1968 Movement took up
all of these demands and not only pressed for the six reforms on its
list but also became the spokesman for the reforms most urgently
sought by Mexican students, workers, and intellectuals.

In many parts of the country, students had previously led the entire nation in protest movements whose general tenor was very much
like that of the 1968 Movement. The most important movements of

---

* University high school.

this sort were those in Puebla in 1964, Morelia in 1966, and Sonora and Tabasco in 1967. Moreover, the demonstrations in support of Cuba, Vietnam, and the Dominican Republic mobilized large groups of students, particularly in Mexico City, and the awareness of the oppression of other peoples greatly raised their level of political consciousness and their awareness of their own strength. This was quite evident in the student protests in Morelia during 1962 and 1963; the movement for university reform in Puebla in 1962; the UNAM strike in 1966; the frequent student strikes for economic and academic reforms in various parts of the country (in particular in the rural normal schools); the student movement in the School of Agronomy in Ciudad Juárez, Chihuahua, which was supported by the other schools of agronomy and by the students of the IPN, and many other student protests.

I do not believe that these protests are isolated incidents. On the contrary, I believe that after the national strike in April 1956 there was a sharp escalation of student protest movements. The Teachers' Movement in 1958, the Railway Workers' Movement in 1958–1959, and the demonstrations in support of the Cuban revolution all contributed to this process, which reached its peak in 1968. Doubtless the Student Movement has hopes that workers and peasants will carry on the struggle.

> *Pablo Gómez, student at the National School of*
> *Economics, UNAM; member of the Communist*
> *Youth; prisoner in Lecumberri*

Every year the "fish,"* the little fishes, organize two demonstrations that are always the same: one for Cuba and another for Vietnam. They gather in front of the Teatro Xola or go to the Juárez Hemiciclo, let out a few shouts and a few *vivas* and a very few *mueras*, hold up three banners, and at eight o'clock sharp the demonstration ends, as punctually as it began; they fold their banners, put away their placards, and go back home. That's all they ever do! I can't imagine why they keep doing the same old stuff!

> *Salvador Martínez de la Roca (Pino), of the*
> *Action Committee of the Faculty of Sciences, UNAM*

---

* Members of the Communist Party (PC) are often called this in Mexico because *"los PCes"* is pronounced the same as *"los peces,"* the fish. (Translator's note.)

> DIA-LOGUE—DIA-LOGUE—DIA-LOGUE—DIA-
> LOGUE—DIA-LOGUE—DIA-LOGUE—DIA-LOGUE
> *Chant at the August 13 demonstration*

The railway workers were alone in 1958. We aren't.

Luis González de Alba, of the CNH

> PEOPLE, OPEN YOUR EYES!
>
> *Street poster*

The conflict is very different from the one in May in France. In Mexico there were practically no demands for changes in the schools and universities, only political petitions: freeing the political prisoners, abolishing the *granaderos,* firing the mayor of the city [*sic*], the head of the security police. . . .

Can we really talk about solid democratic traditions when in fact there is only one political party? When candidates of any other party are not seated in either house of the legislature· or only a few are seated to give the appearance of an opposition? And what can we say of the solid tradition of the *tapado,* the next presidential candidate whose name is kept a secret by the president in office and his advisors till the very last minute and then announced through the official Party, the PRI? Everyone in Mexico knows that in the space of just a few weeks, the *tapado,* who often has been a complete unknown up until then, suddenly becomes the most talented, the most capable man imaginable; his portrait begins to appear on every wall, on all the billboards, on lampposts draped in the colors of the national flag, on neon signs—full-face, profile, half-profile; his monogram, the initials of his name are painted on every fence, they are carved more or less indelibly into the sides of mountains: scars, stigmata defacing the land. Millions of pesos are wasted on this sort of propaganda to hoodwink the ignorant and gullible masses into believing that the candidate proposed by the PRI has exceptional virtues. What can opposition parties do in the face of this sort of enslavement of the masses, these astronomical expenditures? Either join the other side, or carry on a very modest campaign, a few speeches that blow away in the wind. . . .

These political tricks, these trappings are what have disgusted young students who find every door closed to them and all the jobs set aside for politicians of the PRI, unless they "fall in line" and "get on the bandwagon."

> *Professor M. Mayagoitia, letter to*
> *Le Monde, Paris, October 7, 1968*

WE DON'T WANT OLYMPIC GAMES! WE WANT A REVOLUTION!
Chant by students at a number of meetings

DOWN WITH MUMMIES!
Student slogan

There is no doubt that students at the University and the IPN, with their disturbances in the streets and their rowdy behavior in their schools, gave the police every reason to intervene. There were many holdups by students. Public warnings and threats of possible punishment had come to have no effect at all. Discipline inside the schools was practically nil. The student "victory" that forced Rector Ignacio Chávez to resign had obviously brought on a tense and demagogic atmosphere within the National University that forced the authorities to covertly adopt the policy of "Agree that the student is right, even though he's not." Many of us remember how a member of the Supreme Court, who was also acting president of the Board of Regents of the University, Attorney José Caso Estrada, referring to the group of "fossils" * and gangster-like student leaders at the University, declared that historically the victors (the loser was Rector Chávez) always carry off the spoils. And the spoils in this case turned out to be control of the University. The new authorities

---

* "Professional students," who spend years at the University without getting a degree—often political agitators. (Translator's note.)

were all in favor of catering to the students' demands. University Reform was looked upon as a panacea, and the sorcerers' apprentices heated up their test tubes and their cauldrons, concocted their magic mixtures, announced that the University would be run democratically with the participation of the student body, called on these young people to help decide on the curriculum, plans for improvement, and appointments of teachers and directors. They even went so far as to raise the question "Why not have a student as rector?" Any sort of disciplinary rules were automatically regarded as bad pedagogy. We would have to be understanding and sympathetic and kowtow to these young people whose possible faults or feelings of confusion were due only to the sins and the bewilderment of their elders. We would have to pay for our sins like good Christians. The hour of repentance had come. Fathers have the sort of sons they deserve. *Mea culpa, mea culpa, mea culpa.*

Gerardo Hernández Ponce,
teacher at Preparatory 2, UNAM

My father keeps telling me what a good son *he* was and all that. . . . And then I start thinking, "Good Lord, am I some strange sort of creature, or neurotic, or what?" Grownups are so anxious to set exemplary standards for us that they make themselves out to be absolutely perfect, abstract models we should imitate, and bang! that's the end of any communication between us. I get to thinking, "Jeez, to hear my old man talk, he did everything right, and I'm doing everything all wrong!" That's why I can't communicate with him, no matter how hard I try. When my old man begins with that business of "When I was your age . . ." I feel like going off to bed.

Gustavo Gordillo, of the CNH

Young people are angry. They have a right to build the world they live in. They have every reason to be angry. We must humbly admit that this is so, because that is one way of remedying our defects and shortcomings. Our traditions are bad; our attitude toward life couldn't be worse. We have fathered a rebellious, misunderstood generation of young people, who have no free choice as to the sort of present and future they would like to have. We older people ought to become young in heart again, beg these youngsters to accept us, dye our gray hair and cover up our wrinkles with cosmetics, get in on the action, try out this new dance step and do our best to hide the fact that it leaves us panting. Show them that we understand, that we're sorry, and above all do what we can to maintain our position with them, or better yet, improve it. Our deepest, most heartfelt desire is to be popular with young people, to be accepted by them. We *must* succeed in doing this, but the question is how.

Pedro Tamariz, teacher at the Erasmo
Castellanos Quinto School

Hey there, you with the long hair, didn't I put money in your collection box for a haircut?

Juan López Martínez, father of a family

Everybody shuts himself up in his own little world. Adults look on anything young people do as an attack on their principles and their moral code. That's the reason behind their illogical hostility toward long hair. What does long hair have to do with decency or whether a kid's good or bad? I like having long hair, but that doesn't mean I'm a homosexual or feminine or who knows what all. Adults try to make the length of your hair the one measuring rod of your sexual normality or your moral decency.

Gustavo Gordillo, of the CNH

My old man and my old lady regard their principles as immutable.

Gabriela Peña Valle, student at the Faculty
of Philosophy and Letters, UNAM

Why do you wiggle your behind like that? What's more, you don't know how to sit properly. I'd sooner die than wear a skirt like that.

Mercedes Fernández de Cervantes,
mother of a family

A hundred and fifty pesos for a skirt like that! And it's not even twenty inches long!

Elsa Treviño de Zozaya, mother of a family

Why don't you just go around stark naked?

Sofía Arrechiga de Toscano, mother of a family

Enrollment at the National University and the Polytechnical Institute is snowballing. The number of students in both institutions is already much larger—proportionally—than in any other part of the world. The standard of work accomplished in these institutions is discouraging, for both the quality and the quantity couldn't possibly be any lower.

There is, of course, no single, clear-cut cause for this situation—which has gotten no better and in fact is getting worse all the time. The reasons are both numerous and complex, and if I list a few of them, it is not with the intention of indicating their relative importance, nor do I maintain that they are the only ones: prostitution as a public activity and an effective means of controlling the government, workers, and peasants; bad students and worse teachers; the passivity and the lack of exemplary models of behavior within the family; the lack of attractive political parties that would promote independent points of view in public life; social inequalities with scandalous extremes of wealth and poverty; an inexorable colonial dependence that deeply influences, debases, and distorts every aspect of our development; the extremely painful image of an overall international situation that is chaotic, unjust, and bloody.

In short, a complex state of affairs where nothing is clear-cut, where the few positive forces are slow-moving and inadequate. Hopes that continually come to nothing, because a painful, ever present, desolating reality brands our souls with its stigmata. This has been, and continues to be, the daily bread of young and old. What can we expect of our young people? What do we dare demand of them? What are we older people giving and receiving?

The 1968 Student Movement in Mexico admittedly lost its bearings, and the sudden violent turn it took seemed disproportionate to the street incident that gave rise to it. But which of the rest of us knew where we were heading? What do we have to offer and what are we seeking? If we do not find the right road soon, we must face up, in all honesty, to one fact at least: tragedies such as that on October 2 in the Plaza de las Tres Culturas in Tlatelolco will blindfold us even more, and the lack of hope will lead to more bloodshed still.

Pedro Ramírez Arteaga,
professor of philosophy,
University of Hermosillo, Sonora

My folks are pompous asses, and so are my teachers.

> *Vera Pomar Bermúdez, student*
> *at the School of Dentistry, UNAM*

The only time I get along well with my parents is when we go to the movies, because nobody talks then.

> *Victoria Garfias Madrigal,*
> *student at the Faculty of*
> *Engineering, UNAM*

You see now why I'm a hippie.

> *Eduardo Parra del Río, hippie*

I'm delighted by young people today—their fashions, their songs, their freedom, their lack of hypocrisy, their way of looking at love and living it. I prefer the Beatles to Beethoven. How can I explain the difference between John Lennon's "I, Me, Mine" or Paul McCartney's "The Fool on the Hill" and the romantics of my day? I spent my entire youth sitting on Augustín Lara's * white brocade sofa, with my tiny foot, as slender as a needlecase, resting on a little cushion; the boys sang "Mujer, mujer divina" in my ear, and you wouldn't believe how bored stiff we were. I don't know what I would have given to have them say to me, "See you later, alligator, after while, crocodile," instead of humming, "You've become timid and fearful," and I only wish that when we broke up we'd have merely said,

> *Bye bye love*
> *Bye bye happiness*
> *Hello loneliness*
> *I think I'm gonna cry.*

> *Luz Fernanda Carmona Ochoa,*
> *mother of a family*

We had no spirit at all; "I'd like to but I can't" was our motto; when we liked a boy we pretended we didn't; we spent our days fretting, exchanging little notes, gossiping, playing footsie under the table,

---

* Writer of sentimental Mexican popular songs. (Translator's note.)

putting on an act, telling the boys "hands off," making "deals" not worth two cents. We did everything on the sly and it seems to me that's how I lived my whole life, on the sly, getting what I wanted in secret, the way a little girl steals jam from the cupboard, hurriedly closing the door, terrified that somebody might have seen me. . . . That's why I like the way young people live now; the life my daughter leads seems a thousand times better to me than the one I led. I know my daughter doesn't lie to me.

Yvonne Huitrón de Gutiérrez,
mother of a family

I come from a working-class family. My parents are too tired at night to talk about anything. We eat and go to bed. The people I talk to are my pals at night school.

Elpidio Canales Benítez, messenger
boy at Ayotla Textil

My folks don't even talk to each other. Nobody says much around our house. Why would they talk to us?

Hermelinda Suárez Vergara, operator
at Esperanza Beauty Salon

We've got a television set at home.

Rodolfo Nieto Andrade, student
at Vocational 1,* IPN

Communicate with my old man and my old lady? Are you kidding?

Javier Garza Jiménez, student at the
Faculty of Political Sciences, UNAM

At Poli I never heard expressions like "mummies," "squares," people "on the right wave length," and so on. Nobody ever talked about the "sandwich" generation, our parents' generation, crammed in between their children and their own parents like a slice of head cheese. Maybe they use that kind of language at the UNAM, but it seems more like the jargon of intellectuals or small groups hankering to be part of the Movement, to be "in." When we

---

* Vocational high school.

talk among ourselves at Poli, we use the crudest sort of language, bricklayers' language.

Raúl Álvarez Garín, of the CNH

We foresaw the clubbings and the mass arrests, we more or less expected to be thrown in jail, but we didn't foresee that some of us would be murdered.

Gilberto Guevara Niebla, of the CNH

During the Movement, when there was one violent incident after another, many comrades suddenly disappeared, bunches of them were thrown in jail, there were fewer and fewer meetings, lots of people dropped out, there were tanks and bayonets all over the place—this was after the attack on the Santo Tomás campus, the bloodiest and most frightening incident before Tlatelolco. The students took their wounded to the School of Medicine so they wouldn't be hauled off to jail and the *granaderos* and soldiers would go away; I was terribly down in the dumps that day. All of a sudden the thought came to me, "What in the world am I doing here?" . . . I'm lying there on the bed, looking at the ceiling, and suddenly I decide that I don't give a damn whether there's going to be a dialogue with the government or not, whether anybody starts spouting absurd arguments against it, whether they fire Cueto * and free the prisoners or not. You're far away right now, and you have no idea what's happening here; I could be with you, I could be like you, devoting my whole life to my profession, concentrating on one tiny little area that I would be thoroughly familiar with, poring over the latest research and the most recent findings published in the professional journals. . . . I felt that day that those areas in my life that had been most important to me in the last few years were falling to pieces.

Luis González de Alba, of the CNH

A fine thing, setting their dogs on us like that! All because we want what's guaranteed in the Constitution, the right to protest, the chance for everyone to go to school, an end to the sort of poverty I see in the towns my mom takes us to visit.

---

* The Mexico City Chief of Police.

After what happened at Tlatelolco, me and my buddies are going
to carry sticks and stones around with us, and if we come across a
granadero or a soldier by himself, we'll let him have it!

Rodolfo Torres Morales, eleven years old,
in his first year of junior high school

To me, the most horrifying thing was realizing that such a thing
was possible in a civilized country: Tlatelolco, killing people, irra-
tional behavior, throwing people in prison, but on the other hand, I
also realized how many sources of strength a woman has when she
loves a man.

Artemisa de Gortari, mother of a family

It's sad to have to die so young! If you hadn't been an agitator and
gotten mixed up in all this, you'd be free and not have a care in the
world right now!

An Army officer, to the CNH delegate from the
Chapingo School of Agriculture, Luis Tomás
Cervantes Cabeza de Vaca, at Military Camp 1

**MEXICO—FREEDOM—MEXICO—FREEDOM—MEX-
ICO—FREEDOM—MEXICO—FREEDOM—MEXICO**
Chant at the August 13 demonstration

I'm from the UNAM, where they talk in a pedantic in-group jargon.
If you're a university student, you're one of the elite. I'd hung
around with boys whose fathers worked for my father ever since I
was a kid, and when I began working in the brigades I could make
myself understood, but I soon noticed that when guys from the Faculty of Political Sciences, Paco Taibo for instance, came in contact
with working-class people, in the beginning especially, they would
talk to them about the class struggle, the means of production in the
hands of the bourgeoisie, the class in power, and all that stuff, and
nobody understood them. There was no communication. As a matter of fact, there was a wall of mistrust between them. The same
thing happened with the students from Humanities. The girls from
Philosophy would come back from the brigade meetings looking

as cute as hell and with a big smile on their face and say, "Comrades, we went to see the workers today! It was really great, really exciting! We passed out handbills: 'Come on, you workmen, take one, here you are, my good fellow.' " And the workers would say: "What the hell do those girls think they're doing?" The workers looked on us students as clowns of some sort, if not downright asses. Then I noticed that the language began changing, or rather, that we were discovering a common language, and that's what pleased me most about the whole Movement. . . . Little by little working-class people began to teach us how to talk like them and the way they applauded showed us we understood each other. We began to learn about Mexico and its sad realities. This was an everyday experience in the brigade. Once we went to a market out by Ixtapalapa to pass out handbills. Later it came my turn to speak, and when I finished, a little old lady, a really old one, gave me a couple of pesos tied in a handkerchief or a little rag. I was terribly touched, and gave her money back to her because she needed it more than we did, but I'll remember her little wrinkled hand, that crumpled handkerchief, her withered old lady's face peering up at me for the rest of my life. . . . Another time, those of us from Theoretical Physics and Sciences held a meeting in Xochimilco. All of us were deeply touched by the people's response. We drew a crowd of six thousand!

Salvador Martínez de la Roca (Pino),
of the Action Committee, UNAM

We decided to do the only thing we know how to do: play-act. We said, "We're going to try to explain to people what the Movement stands for, what the students want, what the six points are; we're going to show them that we're neither vandals nor savages." How? By acting. Those of us in the group from the Theater of Fine Arts made up our minds from the start: "We can't stand on the sidelines with our arms folded. We have to help publicize the Movement." So we went to La Lagunilla, to the Merced, to Jamaica and all the other public markets, and we also organized brigades to visit public squares and parks, two or three factories (very few, however), and cafés and restaurants, and once we got there we'd simply start talking with people. We would also get on buses and streetcars and trolleys and start talking together in loud voices so people would hear us. We organized encounters—*happenings,* you know what I mean? I'd go up to a newspaper stand, for example, and ask for a newspaper, and just then a very "square," very middle-class matron, wearing earrings and a little pearl necklace, the sort of *señora* who does the marketing herself every two weeks, would come by— another one of the Fine Arts actresses.

She'd buy a paper at the newsstand too, and then turn to me, as though commenting on something she'd seen in the paper she'd just bought, and say, "Those crazy students are born trouble- makers. Just look at this, will you? When there are so many Mex- icans like me, people who simply want to live in peace and quiet and not make trouble for anybody! What in the world do those students want? They just want to stir up a fuss, that's all! I'm cer- tain they're Communists—they must be to act like that!"

I'd stand there in my boots and my mini-skirt listening to her, and then suddenly I'd turn to her and burst out, "Listen, *señora,* you're going to have to explain what you mean, because what you're saying is nonsense. What are you trying to insinuate?"

I'd say this very loudly, and the other actress would raise her voice too, till finally both of us would be shouting at each other at the top of our lungs. A crowd would gather, because everybody's curious when they see two people having a violent argument, right? And we'd go at it so hot and heavy that everybody in the crowd was sure we'd come to blows—and sometimes that's exactly what happened! Our audience wouldn't say anything at first, but then suddenly, without even realizing it, they'd begin to take sides and some man in the crowd would say, "Listen, *señora,* this young lady is right, you know, because you don't even know what the stu- dents' six demands are. They're this and this and this . . ."

And the man wouldn't be one of us actors either!—just someone passing by who'd stopped to listen because he had a personal inter- est in the student problem for one reason or another. Then we'd talk to this comrade who didn't even know he was one of us, and lots of times the bystanders who spoke up were much more politi- cally aware and could argue much more convincingly than we could. The crowd would almost always end up siding with me and the "snob" would have to take to her heels: "You dried-up old maid, shove off, what do you know about it, you tottering old wreck"— and the poor actress would light out with her tail between her legs.

She really thought exactly as we did, but she was the willing martyr
of the "happening" we staged.

Margarita Isabel, actress

You know what? The brigades were the very core of the Movement.
People went to the demonstrations because of the brigades. Why
did everyone follow the students' lead? Because of the brigades,
because before the demonstrations we handed out leaflets on the
buses and trolleys, in the markets, the big department stores, the
workshops, on the corners where we held "lightning meetings,"
scattering to the four winds the minute we smelled a *granadero* coming. . . . Man, how I remember the brigades!

Salvador Martínez de la Roca (Pino),
of the Action Committee, UNAM

I began to work in the Movement in August. I made friends with
the CNH representative of Vocational 7, and was appointed head of
a brigade of sixteen kids: ten boys and six girls: the Che Guevara
brigade, a real mother of a brigade! We painted slogans on walls,
we held "lightning meetings," we collected contributions on buses,
in the streets, in the markets. I hardly ever went to Vocational 7, I
was always somewhere else, with the brigade. No, I'm not a student, but I'm young; I was a clothing vendor, but the Student
Movement, the six demands, the possibility of putting an end to
the police repression and the arbitrary power that affects all our
lives appealed to me. The first time we held a meeting was in the
big market at Tacuba. We drew a crowd of three thousand people,
and since the headquarters of the Ninth Police Precinct is right
across the street, we were attacked by the cops and all the market
vendors stepped in and armed themselves with sticks and stones
and heads of lettuce and tomatoes to help fight them off. We were
terribly touched.

Antonio Careaga García, clothing vendor

We made the streets ours when we entered the Zócalo on Tuesday,
August 13, because that violated a taboo. . . . They all said we'd
never get as far as the Zócalo.

Salvador Martínez de la Roca (Pino),
of the Action Committee, UNAM

> **CHE-CHE-CHE-GUEVARA—CHE-CHE-CHE-GUE-VARA—CHE-CHE-CHE-GUEVARA—CHE-CHE-CHE-**
> *Chant at the August 13 demonstration*

A demonstration without police is a peaceful demonstration.
> *Manifesto published in* El Día, *August 12, 1968,*
> *signed by the CNH and the Coalition of Secondary*
> *and College Teachers for Democratic Freedoms*

We had already marched in a demonstration from the south to the center of the city, and another from the north to the center of the city. Now—in this third demonstration—our goal was the very heart of the life of the country: the Zócalo. We had to take over one of the most imposing public squares in the world (even de Gaulle had been impressed by it!) and raise our voices in protest beneath the balcony, the very balcony where the President of Mexico presents himself for public adulation on historic occasions. We had to give voice to our indignation, hurl any and every insult we could think of at this paternalistic figure, this giver of life, the great Tlatoani, our papa, God. Why not? We could not forget that they had destroyed the Puerta de San Idelfonso with their bazookas—beautiful four-hundred-year-old, living, wondrously carved wood—we could not forget that they had occupied schools, that they had clubbed students, teachers, and bystanders alike; we could not forget that they had taken over the universities of Michoacán, Puebla, Sonora, and Tabasco, and flatly rejected the demands of Sinaloa, Durango, Nuevo León. . . . For the first time an indignant crowd, a multitude of citizens, aware of their rights, were making their voices heard.
> *Luis González de Alba, of the CNH*

> **WE TEACHERS CONDEMN THE GOVERNMENT FOR ITS TERROR TACTICS**
> *Banner of the Coalition of Secondary and College Teachers*
> *for Democratic Freedoms at the August 13 demonstration*

PEOPLE UNITE—PEOPLE UNITE—PEOPLE UNITE—
PEOPLE UNITE—PEOPLE UNITE—PEOPLE UNITE
Chant at the August 13 demonstration

MEXICO—FREEDOM—MEXICO—FREEDOM—MEX-
ICO—FREEDOM—MEXICO—FREEDOM—MEXICO
Chant at the August 13 demonstration

BOOKS YES—BAYONETS NO
Placard at the August 13 demonstration

YOU DON'T TAME PEOPLE, YOU EDUCATE THEM
Placard at the August 13 demonstration

The August 13 demonstration was about to take place; all of Mexico City knew what was going on and knew the demonstration was going to take place because the brigades had spread the word. The demonstration was the greatest political victory we had won thus far. We had estimated that fifty thousand people would turn out, and two hundred fifty thousand gathered in the Zócalo. At this meeting, the CNH summed it all up in the words "We shall return to the Zócalo; twice as many of us as are here today." This statement meant that those of us in the brigades had our work cut out for us. We would have to labor long and hard; but the brigades immediately increased in size. Groups of two hundred to four hundred students were formed very soon thereafter. Teachers joined us and supported us, as they had already begun to do in the past, and this made us feel both more confident and more responsible. This is how we organized in the schools: when the meetings ended, we gathered together in three classrooms and planned where each brigade would meet; we passed out boxes to collect money and the handbills the brigades needed. I might point out that at that point we were passing out approximately six hundred thousand handbills and taking in a thousand to two thousand pesos a day. Moreover, we were not the only ones who spoke in the "lightning meetings"; we also invited the man in the street to have his say. As usual, the language of the people was clear-cut, frank, and firm: they were with us. This was the golden age of the Movement—from the twelfth to the twenty-seventh of August. One time a guy who was making a nuisance of himself in a "lightning meeting" on the Avenida Juárez gave a speech. I had hold of his belt and was trying to drag him away, but he went on and on: "I'm all for the Movement, because it's human," and all kinds of nonsense like that. I didn't pay much attention, because I can't abide fancy speeches. When we finally got him down off the roof of the bus— we'd been standing on top of it addressing the crowd—I said to him, "Now that you've had your say and spouted all that nonsense, cough up a hundred pesos." And he did.

Salvador Martínez de la Roca (Pino), of
the Action Committee, UNAM

COME OUT ON THE BALCONY, LOUD-MOUTH—
COME OUT ON THE BALCONY, LOUD-MOUTH—
COME OUT ON THE BALCONY, LOUD-MOUTH
Slogan or provocative insult shouted by the crowd
at the August 13 demonstration in the Zócalo,
attended by an estimated crowd of two hundred
and fifty to three hundred thousand people

When the demonstration on the thirteenth ended, people poured down all the adjoining streets, boys and girls folding banners between them as though they were bed sheets, putting placards away, and climbing into buses from their schools, already jammed full, returning to their guard posts on the rooftops, to sandwiches passed around at three or four o'clock in the morning, to tacos hurriedly wolfed down at a place on Insurgentes, to hot coffee, laughter, the happiness of having won a victory. We were all overjoyed. . . . I don't know why they turned off the street lights. We came back from the Zócalo in darkness and went down Juárez and the Reforma with nothing but car headlights to show us the way. . . . It was

marvelous! A dream! We laughed till our sides ached, passing on all
the jokes and funny remarks we'd heard.

Luis González de Alba, of the CNH

It seems to me that if the president, despite the hostile slogans, the
insults, the violence, the cries of down with this or that, had come
out on the balcony and confronted the crowd, he would have divided the demonstrators and won over a great number of them.
Young people are much more docile than we think, and a gesture
such as that would have impressed them. Here in Mexico gestures
are always very important: the hand offered in friendship, the flag
at half-mast, and so on. But he failed to appear on the balcony. I am
convinced to this day that the president's advisors are his worst
enemies.

Leonor Vargas Patrón, teacher in a normal school

Instead of saying that he bears no rancor in his heart and was unaf-
fected by all the insults, wouldn't it have been better if he'd come
out on the balcony and addressed the students?

Alicia Sarmiento de Gómez, mother of a family

After being with a brigade all day long, it amused me and angered
me to return to CU* and attend a meeting where various factions
argued endlessly with each other and members of the Movement
took five hours to reach an agreement on some hairsplitting resolution. We went out in brigades and did our damndest to get the
working class to support us. The theorists didn't go out and work
with the brigades; all they did was shut themselves up and waste
their time kidding around for hours on end. They kept talking, for
instance, about the political prisoners. Those of us who were active
in the brigades were beginning to understand what being political
prisoners meant when they started persecuting us even though we
weren't doing anything illegal. . . . All of us who just wanted to
get something done were friends: Poli, UNAM, Chapingo. But in
the CNH, it was a mess: the Maoists, the Trotskyists, the Spartacists, the Communists were all at each other's throats! I was just

---

* Ciudad Universitaria (University City).

another activist, and I'm sure all of us would have agreed to a dialogue with almost anybody, but that was not the position of the
CNH, which refused to negotiate with any functionary who had
anything at all to do with repression! It was as though everybody in
the government was an agent of repression! In the meetings, there
were speeches over an hour long about Althusser, Marx, and Lenin,
but the speakers never once got around to talking about what interested us: *What are we going to do tomorrow?* Pure bullshit! They
were beaten from the start because they were theoreticians and
spent all their time explaining why the government would refuse to
grant the students' six demands. There are all sorts of factions at
UNAM. There are lots of students in the Faculty of Political Sciences, a really dumb school, who side with the PRI. They're convinced they're going to be diplomats, deputies, and maybe even
president of the country. Don't just promise me something, serve it
up to me on a platter! In the Law School, everybody's a potential
president. In their first years at the University they seem very revolutionary, but they're just showing off; they spout all sorts of fancy
language about technocracy, the humanization of science, art-
science-technology-for-the-benefit-of-the-people, and all that kind
of crap. They appear to be Leninist-Marxists to the core in those
years, but when it comes right down to it they're nothing but mea-
sly bureaucrats, because they aren't going to solve the concrete
problems of the country in the School of Economics or Law or Political Sciences or Philosophy or Letters or Humanities. . . . Leaders
with that kind of background kept running off at the mouth, and I
felt like really beating the shit out of them because it seemed to me
that they were a minus quantity in the Movement.

Salvador Martínez de la Roca (Pino),
of the Action Committee, UNAM

I live in Ciudad Sahagún and commute to school every day in a
second-class bus: Mexico City—Teotihuacán—Otumba—Apan—
Calpulalpan and all the other lines between. I leave home at five
o'clock in the morning so as to be at Vocational 1, the one on the
corner of Peluqueros and Orfebrería, at seven. My folks give me
twelve pesos a day for bus fare, five to get to school and five to get
home—because a first-class bus costs six-fifty—plus two pesos to

get around here in the city. I first found out about the Student
Movement when I couldn't take my final exams in math, physics,
chemistry, electronics workshop, design, and technology and all my
other subjects, and I was hopping mad because I knew all the material very well. There was a strike on! And they closed the school. I
thought I'd soon be back in school—all this happened in the second
week in August—but my dad wouldn't let me come in from Sahagún: "Those kids are rebels!" he kept saying. My old man had
heard on the radio that the whole thing was a mess. He wouldn't
give me my carfare to school and that was all there was to it. All my
friends went to the meetings at Vocational. Two kids in my class—
the second year at Vocational—were killed and as I remember four
of them were thrown in jail, among them Luna, who told us afterward that they'd all been brutally clubbed. . . . My dad told me,
"I've worked too hard for my money for you to waste it running
around the streets in the city!" He works in the National Railway
Car factory.

> Andrés Montaño Sánchez, student of Physical-
> Mathematical Sciences, Vocational 1

It's not likely that the government will meet our demands. The government has always said, "Don't put pressure on us and we'll meet
those demands that seem reasonable." That's precisely what they
told the physicians in 1965: "Go back to your hospitals, take care of
your patients—it's criminal not to take care of sick people—and
since you're justified in asking for higher salaries, when you're
back at your posts we'll give you your raise." The doctors went
back to the hospitals, and what happened? The leaders were thrown
in jail, they lost their pay, there were mass reprisals, police sur-
veillance, and stricter control over the hospitals. Vallejo? If he gives
up his hunger strike, they may let him out. The hunger strike that
began in December of '69 at Lecumberri? If they don't go on with it,
the prisoners jailed for the disturbances in 1968 will probably get
out. But no pressure, you understand. The government can't be
pressured, the government won't grant a single one of the demands
if there are meetings, demonstrations. . . . Just be patient, and
then maybe . . . perhaps . . . possibly . . . The government is
always generous to anyone who patiently bides his time. . . . Isn't
that what those who want a political career are always told? Wait it

out, my friend . . . you'll just have to put up with it . . . be patient, be patient. . . .

Isabel Sperry de Barraza, grade-school teacher

The Government of the Republic is most willing to meet with the representatives of teachers and students at the UNAM, the IPN, and other educational institutions connected with the present problem, in order to exchange views with them and acquaint itself directly with their demands and suggestions, with the aim of definitely resolving the conflict that our capital has experienced in recent weeks, a conflict which in fact has affected the lives of all its inhabitants to some degree.

Luis Echeverría, Secretary of Internal Affairs,
August 22, 1968

NOTICE TO THE PUBLIC

The two hundred and fifty thousand students and teachers who have gone on strike in support of our six-point petition have been notified of the step taken by the Executive to resolve this conflict that is so grievously affecting the entire country, and particularly those of us who are students and teachers.

We trust that there will be no further attempt to sidestep the public dialogue that we have insisted on from the beginning, and that the Executive will appoint those officials that it considers competent to carry on this dialogue with the sole recognized representatives of students and teachers: the National Strike Committee and the Coalition of Secondary and College Teachers for Democratic Freedoms, respectively.

It is incumbent upon the Government of the Republic to solve this problem as rapidly as possible, and in order to do so it must set a place, a date, and a time for these talks to begin. Our sole condition is that they be held in public. [Many technological schools of the IPN, among them the second, third, fourth, sixth, and seventh; Vocational Schools 1, 2, 4, etc.; many schools of the UNAM; the Iberoamerican University, La Esmeralda, the Conservatory, the Carlos Septién García School of Journalism, the Mexican Dance Academy of the INBA, and the University of Veracruz signed the above statement.]

El Día, *August 23, 1968*

Can a telephone call be considered a public dialogue?
Five-hour discussion during a meeting of CNH
rank-and-file members in the Auditorium of
Philosophy and Letters, UNAM

DIA-LOGUE—DIA-LOGUE—DIA-LOGUE—DIA-
LOGUE—DIA-LOGUE—DIA-LOGUE—DIA-LOGUE
Chant at demonstrations

The government has been talking to itself for fifty years now.
Roberto Escudero, CNH delegate from the Faculty
of Philosophy and Letters, UNAM

During the meetings the delegates from the University felt it their duty to politicize those from the IPN. They explained certain philo-sophical tendencies, revolutionary tactics, and methods of per-suasion. They didn't talk about the next demonstration—they talked about Lenin, Marcuse, the Sino-Soviet quarrel, imperialism, and other subjects that so tried the patience of the majority of the delegates that they were on the verge of downright rebellion. The delegates from the IPN wanted their demands satisfied, that and nothing else, and those from the University, those from Humanities in particular, wanted to prove that the government was rigid and reactionary and that the task of the CNH was to make the Student Movement see this reality and face up to it.
Gustavo Gordillo, of the CNH

I had nothing to do; I went to my room, got undressed, and picked up a book to read for a while. The bed was too soft and I couldn't get warm for quite a while because I couldn't find my damned pajamas. I opened *One-Dimensional Man* and got as far as page five. *Eros and Civilization* had been a terrible bore, and now I had to read another of Marcuse's books, all because Díaz Ordaz had happened to mention "the philosophers of destruction." . . .
Luis González de Alba, of the CNH

Let's be just a little bit concrete.

> *Petition by the theoretical physicist Raúl*
> *Álvarez Garín, of the IPN, who despaired of ever*
> *seeing an end to the interminable disquisitions of*
> *the UNAM delegates from Humanities, Political*
> *Sciences, and Law*

"Why did you get home so late night before last?"

"Because we were painting slogans."

"Where?"

"On the Palacio . . ."

"On the Palacio de Hierro? *"

"No, that wasn't where."

"Well, what Palacio then?"

"On the Palacio."

"You mean the Palacio Nacional? †"

"Yeah."

"Good heavens! You're stark raving mad! You might get killed! What's the matter with you? You're out of your minds!"

"We're immortal. . . . And besides, we planned the whole thing very carefully—the time, who was going to be the lookout, the getaway car with the motor running, how much paint we'd need—you forget, old girl, we're experts at painting slogans."

"I can't believe it. Who told you to do that?"

"Oh, various people."

"And what did you do last night? You got home very late again. . . ."

"Oh, we went to the Capri last night. . . ."

"To the Capri? What for?"

"Just for a joke. The place is a tomb—a bunch of corpses sitting around pretending to have a good time, like skeletons clinking glasses and rattling their bones, and a lousy show that's as old as the year one. We were with three other studs, and Oswald, Javier, and I sneaked out without paying our share of the bill. They were such asses they deserved it."

---

* A big department store.
† The Capitol building.

"Oh, Jan, youngsters are getting killed and disappearing without a trace, really serious things are happening, and one night you go out painting slogans and the next you go to the Capri and skip out without paying the bill. What's the matter with you kids? You're plain out of your minds. . . ."

"No, old girl, that's how it is. We get vibrations!"

Jan Poniatowski Amor, student, Antonio Caso
Preparatory School

On November 17, 1968, a nineteen-year-old student—Luis González Sánchez—was killed by a police officer who had caught him painting Movement propaganda on a wall near the freeway.

Excélsior, November 18, 1968

I never really thought of Zapata as a student symbol, an emblem. Zapata has become part of the bourgeois ideology; the PRI has appropriated him. Maybe that's why we chose Che as our symbol at demonstrations from the very first. Che was our link with student movements all over the world! We never thought of Pancho Villa either. His name never even crossed our minds!

Claudia Cortés González, student at
the Faculty of Political Sciences, UNAM

CHE-CHE-CHE-GUEVARA—CHE-CHE-CHE-GUE-VARA—CHE-CHE-CHE-GUEVARA—CHE-CHE-CHE-

Chant at demonstrations

When the U.S.S.R. invaded Czechoslovakia, my head swam. Who could I believe in now?

Óscar Hidalgo Estrada, student at the
Faculty of Law, UNAM

BOOKS YES, GRANADEROS NO

Banner at the Silent Demonstration, Friday,
September 13, 1968

We had to take over the Zócalo; we had to deconsecrate the Zócalo—and we did, three times.

Salvador Martínez de la Roca (Pino), of the Action Committee, UNAM

THE AGITATORS ARE IGNORANCE, HUNGER, AND POVERTY

Banner at the Silent Demonstration, Friday, September 13, 1968

When the Movement began, the five schools that appeared to be the most radical were Political Sciences, Economics, Philosophy, The College of Mexico, and Chapingo. . . . In the CNH, we called them the *acelerados.** . . . But it was the delegates from Poli who turned out to be the real *acelerados.*

Gustavo Gordillo, of the CNH

In physics, everything is subject to further proof. No theory is ever the final word. And you kids keep spouting a thousand and one things as though they were absolute truths: "We're waging revolution," "The working class is with us"—pure crap that nobody believes. . . . You people in the CNH are screwing everything up.

Salvador Martínez de la Roca (Pino), of the Action Committee, UNAM

The Movement was widely supported, especially among the middle class, because the students, especially those at the University, come for the most part from middle-class families.

Francisco Rentería Melgar, economist

Workers in the biggest labor unions in the country could give us strong support, and we trained our batteries on them. The members of the brigades were given daily orders to "make contact with the working class," but the minute we approached them, we came up against the stone wall of union corruption, which prevented us

---

* Speed demons, fast movers, ultra-radicals.

from mobilizing the workers. So we made plans to remedy this situation and help the workers organize independent unions.

Gilberto Guevara Niebla, of the CNH

Workers don't know the first thing about anything. All they do is work from dawn till dark. They read *Esto*, if they read anything at all, never anything about politics. How could they be expected to be interested in the petition?

Carlota López de Léon, normal-school teacher

The fact is, workers are very reactionary.

Rebeca Navarro Mendiola, student at the Faculty of Philosophy and Letters, UNAM

Why beat around the bush? Why not say straight out that we failed with the workers?

Heberto Portilla Posada, student at the Faculty of Political Sciences, UNAM

They're so thick between the ears! What a laugh—politicizing workers!

Raquel Núñez Ochoa, student, Iberoamerican University

Government control of factories and labor unions cannot be broken.

Florencio López Osuna, CNH delegate from the School of Economics at IPN; prisoner in Lecumberri

Workers have set hours, definite shifts. How can they attend meetings? And how about peasants? How can they get to the city? Do you think the PRI is going to provide them transportation so they can go to the Zócalo with the students to hoot at the president?

María Salazar de Obregón, mother of a family

I'm a worker. I used to package candy in the Sanborn chocolate factory. My name is Félix Sánchez Hernández, and I'm twenty-nine years old. I was in favor of the Movement from the very beginning—or at any rate interested in it. I knew Cabeza de Vaca and several others and they urged me to go to the demonstrations, so I went to most of them. I also helped hand out leaflets, both in the chocolate factory and in the streets. The workers went to some of the demonstrations, but on an individual basis—on their own, so to speak. There were around five hundred of us who attended. We went to the Silent Demonstration and to the one before that, on the twenty-seventh; we went from Tacubaya—because the factory is at Benjamín Hill—to Chapultepec, and from there we marched in a group all the way down the Reforma to the Zócalo. In the demonstration on the twenty-seventh, I happened by chance to be with the group of electricians; there were about six hundred of us, plus the friends that joined us along the line of march. Many workers sympathized with the Movement but lots of them didn't dare show it for fear of reprisals, or because they were lazy or indifferent, since all of us were very tired when we got off work, but it was mostly because they were afraid of losing their jobs. We have a company union at the Sanborn chocolate factory. Movement propaganda was delivered to the factory and the workers themselves would pass the handbills out.

I don't know what I'm going to do when I get out of jail. I can't go back to the factory. They fired my sister-in-law because they said the three of us—my wife, my sister-in-law, and I—were in cahoots, agitating for better wages and making trouble for the management. I was earning thirty-two pesos a day—I arrived at work at five-thirty in the morning and got out at two in the afternoon.

I don't know why they put me in Lecumberri. I'm a worker, so the only connection I had with the Student Movement was the fact that I'd shown my support by attending public student functions as a spectator, the demonstration on August 27, and the Silent Demonstration on September 13. Or maybe they threw me in jail because I visited a pal of mine who's from the state of Oaxaca, the same as me, a prisoner in cell block N of Lecumberri Prison, Señor Justino Juárez. When I read in the paper that he was in prison, I went to see him because he's a friend of mine. I found out later that the prison authorities gave a copy of the lists of names of people who visited political prisoners to the judicial and federal security police, who have been using these lists to threaten the families of prisoners, and as happened in my case, to arbitrarily arrest people and accuse them of some sort of crime.

On the first of October, 1968, I came to work, the same as any other day. At twelve-forty-five that day four men dressed in civvies entered the factory with pistols in their hands and immediately started roughing me up. Then they grabbed me and hauled me out of the building. I asked them who they were and where they were taking me, and the only answer I got was more punches while one of them held my hands behind my back. They shoved me into a car, and once they got me inside they blindfolded me with a rag and gagged me with another one. This outrage was witnessed by my pals at work—several of them are willing to testify. At the head-quarters of the Federal Judicial Police I was stripped naked, beaten, given electric shocks, and robbed of all my personal belongings. The police officers accused me of having gone to see Justino Juárez to "get orders from him." They subjected me to all sorts of tortures, and made threats so as to try and get me to sign a confession:

"Listen, you jackass, we've got you right where we want you, so you have to confess, even though you haven't done anything. You have to say you're guilty because everybody we haul in here gets sent to the jug, whether he's done anything or not. Either you sign or we'll kill you."

I don't know what it said in the statement I signed. On October 9, 1968, I was sent to Lecumberri Prison and I've been here ever since.

Félix Sánchez Hernández, worker in the Sanborn
chocolate factory; prisoner in Lecumberri

MEXICO—FREEDOM—MEXICO—FREEDOM—MEX-ICO—FREEDOM—MEXICO—FREEDOM—MEXICO
Chant at demonstrations

Mexico is a country in which ten million people are starving and ten million people are illiterate. A cabal in power forces its truth and its law on us. We are ruled by the law of corrupt labor leaders, the law of bankers, the law of industrialists, the law of politicians who have made fortunes from the Revolution. And to top it all off, we have to put up with their student representatives, associations such as the FNET at Poli and the PEFI and the MURO * at the University! These right-wing front organizations must be done away with.

José Tayde Aburto, agronomist at Chapingo National School of Agriculture; prisoner in Lecumberri

During the month of August, a passenger bus on the Topilejo line turned over on the highway outside that town. A number of people were killed or injured in this accident. As usual, the bus company merely offered to pay an indemnity of five hundred to two thousand pesos to the families of each of the deceased. However, the vast popular movement that had caused disturbances in Mexico City and many other parts of the country had also had its effect even in this remote little town in the Sierra del Ajusco. The indignant townspeople were prepared to fight for their rights, and began to take over buses belonging to the company, demanding that new buses be installed on that route, that the road leading to the town be repaired, and that the indemnity paid to the families of the dead and injured be increased. When the talks with the bus company began, a delegate of the CNC † was present to represent the inhabitants of Topilejo, but since the corrupt officials of this peasants' association are mere lackeys of the government, the delegate soon betrayed the townspeople he was supposedly representing, and acting in collusion with the bus company, managed to delay the settlement of the townspeople's claims. The townspeople then held a public meeting and decided to call upon the students to help them. They went to the National School of Economics of UNAM and explained their problem, and after a brief discussion the students decided to do everything in their power to help the town. They sent University buses out to provide transportation for the peasants, since the bus company had suspended service on that route; students in the schools of nursing, agriculture, social work, and medicine set up a camp, "The Soviet," and began to provide the people with useful information in their special fields of competence. They

---

* Rightist student groups covertly supported by the government. (Translator's note.)
† Confederación Nacional Campesina (National Peasant Union).

gave lectures and talks about the townspeople's legal rights and the services available to them, and the town assembly decided about that time to refuse to accept the CNC delegate as their representative and appoint a new commission, including students, to negotiate with the company. The company was forced to give in to this sort of pressure and promised to pay indemnities of five thousand pesos to each family; but it would not agree to put new buses on the line, which meant that there would be more accidents, and the talks were temporarily suspended. Meanwhile hundreds of brigades came to all the villages in the region to help the peasants, who responded with the heartfelt affection of simple people. Students and peasants, two groups who only a few short weeks before had seemed so far apart, now shared the warmest feelings of brotherhood. They were united by a common cause: fighting against injustices. By thus mingling with the people, the students reaffirmed their faith in the cause they were fighting for and were now prepared to work even more wholeheartedly to win their battle. The CNH had decided to back Topilejo in every way possible, and early in September the bus company was obliged to give in and pay an indemnity of twenty-five thousand pesos to each family and provide new buses. And the highway authorities agreed to repair the road to Topilejo. Thus a very important victory was won. And to seal the pact between the students and the villagers, peasant representatives from Topilejo were present thereafter at student meetings all during the Movement.

Gilberto Guevara Niebla, of the CNH

The only real contact we had with peasants was Topilejo, and Topilejo can't be regarded as exactly a rural zone or "countryside," since it is less than thirty kilometers from the Federal District.

Raúl Reséndiz Medina, student at the Faculty of Political Sciences, UNAM

On one occasion students of the ESIME and other IPN schools learned that two hundred owners of market stalls had been arrested and were being held at police headquarters in Villa Precinct. They went out there to organize a public meeting to demand that they be released. Despite the fact that *granaderos* were stationed all around to try to intimidate them, the students stood their ground and the authorities finally had to give in and release the stall owners. The students thus demonstrated that they are fulfilling, and will continue to fulfill, the obligation they feel toward the people. . . . From this time on, many workers began to sympathize with the students' cause, because they saw that the students were also concerned about their interests and were fighting for them too.

Florencio López Osuna, of the CNH

NOTHING THROUGH FORCE, EVERYTHING THROUGH REASON
Banner at the August 27 demonstration

WORKER, DESTROY YOUR FAKE LABOR UNION
Banner at the August 27 demonstration

It is not true that the students acted alone and that the workers refused to lift a finger to help them. There were workers from the Federal Electricity Commission who publicly demonstrated their support in a manifesto published in *Excélsior* on September 13, 1968; the Group of Independent Labor Unions also backed the epic student struggle, as the September 13, 1968, issue of *El Día* proves. The first name on the list of supporters is that of Othón Salazar, on behalf of the Revolutionary Teachers' Movement; and thirty-seven Mexican clergymen (who described themselves as workers for Christ) also publicly sided with this stirring of the youth of the country, in *El Día*, on September 11, 1968. And what about the Worker's Union at the University of Nuevo León? And the medical aides at General Hospital, Juárez, Women's Hospital, the Isidro Espinosa de los Reyes Maternity Hospital of the Social Security Administration, and the Hospital of the Department of Highways and Public Works? And the residents at many hospitals? And the Revolutionary Union of Workers at the El Ánfora pottery factory, which supported the six-point student petition, thanks to the efforts of its advisor, Attorney Armando Castillejos, who is now in prison? And the Telephone Operators' Organizing Committee . . . All these groups demonstrated their support of the Movement in one way or another, and though the students never managed to reach the great mass of workers, the solidarity of these groups constitutes something of a triumph for the Student Movement in 1968.

*Ernesto Olvera, teacher of mathematics
at Preparatory 1, UNAM*

It seems to me that one of the most exciting chapters in our entire struggle began at Topilejo.

*Esther Fernández, student at the
Faculty of Sciences, UNAM*

In Villa Jiménez, Michoacán, at a meeting attended by the director general of Conasupo,* Francisco Ambriz, a peasant, stated that *ejidatarios*† thoroughly disapprove of student scandals and said that if young people aren't willing to study, farm workers should be given the millions of pesos spent on educating them, which they deliberately waste, since money for public works is badly needed in rural districts. Francisco Ambriz spoke these words at a ceremony in the town of Zacapú giving his *ejido* ownership of the municipal granaries.

*Saturday, August 24, 1968, as recounted
in* Revista de la Universidad,
"Review of Current Events," vol. 23, no. 1

**PEOPLE UNITE—PEOPLE UNITE—PEOPLE UNITE—
PEOPLE UNITE—PEOPLE UNITE—PEOPLE UNITE**
Chant at the August 27 demonstration

One of the factors in the current Movement is the eagerness of young people to remedy injustices. The problem must be attacked not by repressing young people but by guiding and channeling their energies. The Movement is not directed against the govern-

---

* Compañía Nacional de Subsistencias Populares, a government organization for distributing food to the poor at supposedly low prices. (Translator's note.)
† Residents of *ejidos*, farm collectives. (Translator's note.)

ment, but against the actions of a few civil servants who have ex-
ceeded the limits of their office.

> *Ifigenia M. de Navarrete, director of the National*
> *School of Economics, on the television round-table*
> *program Anatomías, organized by Jorge Saldaña*
> *and broadcast Wednesday, August 21, 1968.*
> *Heberto Castillo, Víctor Flores Olea, Francisco*
> *López Cámara, and Inigo Laviada also participated.*

Let's have no more vituperative slogans, no more insults, no more
violence. Don't carry red flags. Don't carry placards of Che or Mao!
From now on we're going to carry placards with the portraits of
Hidalgo, Morelos, Zapata, to shut them up. They're our Heroes.
Viva Zapata! Viva!

> *Orders from the CNH*

"I'll carry the red flag."
   "No, I will. . . ."
   "We'll all carry it."
We are marching along behind a huge red flag. The Paseo de la
Reforma is jammed with cars and buses from one curb to the other.
People on the rooftops are shouting, applauding, laughing, and crying too. At the Angel, people have climbed as high up the slender
column as they can so as to have a good look. "A dense cluster of
humanity," as the newspaper reporters put it. And on the statue of
the Caballito too; the classic image of little kids, newsboys, chew-
ing-gum vendors, lottery-ticket sellers, sitting in the lap of Charles
the Fifth, pulling the horse's tail and ears. A sea of heads in every
direction, hands in the air applauding: we were very happy.

POWER TO THE PEOPLE—POWER TO THE PEOPLE—POWER TO THE PEOPLE

On the Avenida Juárez too hundreds and hundreds of people
watching from the curb; tourists coming out of the hotels had
frightened looks on their faces at first and then began applauding;
there wasn't a single inch of empty space on the sidewalks along
San Juan de Letrán; a number of women, schoolteachers I imagine,
were crying and everybody kept applauding; but the minute we
turned the corner and started down Cinco de Mayo my heart stood
still; every bell in the cathedral was pealing and all the lights in this
beautiful square, this square that is the place in my city that I love

the most, had been turned on. It was like a dream! They kept telling me, "Don't cry, silly!" but tears of joy were streaming down my face.

Elena González Souza, medical student,
UNAM

The previous demonstration had been a very large one, around a quarter of a million, but even so we hadn't managed to fill even half of the huge square; but now the Zócalo was completely full, even though half of the groups hadn't arrived yet, since Philosophy was halfway along the line of march. We went on ahead and finally halted in front of the Palacio Nacional. I turned around and looked down the nearby Calle de Guatemala, and noticed that a big crowd was also heading toward Lecumberri for a demonstration in front of the prison. It was ten p.m.; people had been pouring into the Zócalo for four hours.

Luis González de Alba, of the CNH

We were inside Lecumberri listening. There was a crowd of about five hundred people in front of the main gate chanting FREE THE POLITICAL PRISONERS. They were also shouting UNAM, POLI, CHAPINGO, but they mostly kept chanting FREE THE POLITICAL PRISONERS, FREE THE POLITICAL PRISONERS, FREE THE POLITICAL PRISONERS, FREE THE POLITICAL PRISONERS.

We tried to answer them and shouted slogans too. We were very excited about the Movement. That same day a committee of girls from the Faculty of Sciences had visited the prison authorities and asked for Víctor Rico Galán, who came to talk to them. The girls had sent us their regards. This demonstration calling for the freeing of political prisoners was an organized one, but one other time some of the *acelerados* had gotten the entire CNH to come to the prison and they had stood there outside in the street shouting, COMRADES, WE'RE WITH YOU! COMRADES, WE'RE WITH YOU! At two o'clock in the morning! They blew their car horns and made a hell of a racket. We felt we had lots of support on the outside. From there in our cells we followed everything the Movement did, all its victories, and it made us want desperately to be free—and I'm still waiting just as desperately—in order to participate, to march in the demonstrations. We'd had bad luck, really awful luck! I thought to myself, The Movement's on the upswing! Our messages were read twice in the Zócalo: once on the twenty-seventh of August, and once when Vallejo also sent a letter. . . .

I've been in prison since July 26, 1968. I was arrested after the demonstration in the Juárez Hemiciclo in support of the Cuban Revolution. They didn't nab us right there; they arrested us later, at the Café Viena, on Insurgentes across from the Cine de las Américas—I think it's gone out of business now. . . . They put us in solitary first and then took us to cell block N, in Lecumberri. . . .

Arturo Zama Escalante, Faculty of Law, UNAM;
*leader of the CNED; * prisoner in Lecumberri*

They put me in the jug on July 27 too, the day after the first disturbances. Two very large meetings were held outside Lecumberri, and they really moved us. We couldn't hear the shouts from individual demonstrators very clearly, but we did hear the chants, and they really touched our hearts: FREE THE POLITICAL PRISONERS! FREE THE POLITICAL PRISONERS! That cheered us up a lot. I thought, We're going to get out of here. They're fighting out there like never before.

Back then, both before and after October 2, we had no idea that we would not only remain in prison but that our comrades chanting slogans on the other side of the walls of Lecumberri would eventually be there inside with us. . . . They also arrested many other comrades, of course, during those months, but we were more or less confident that we'd all get out of jail. We *had* to. But after October 2 we lost hope—hope of getting out, that is. We're studying in here now, and even though we have political differences we're not divided. On the contrary: we all study together. There are twelve classes: one in German (on records), another in English that Zama teaches, another in French (on records), Luis González de Alba teaches Spanish literature, Raúl Álvarez Garín, Félix Gamundi, and Pino math, Unzueta political economy, Owl-Eyes geography,

---

* Central Nacional de Estudiantes Democráticos (National Democratic Students' Organization).

Saúl ("Chale") world history, and we're going to start a discussion group on *Das Kapital,* a seminar that Pino is also going to participate in.

Félix Goded Andreu, architecture
student, UNAM; member of the Communist
Youth; prisoner in Lecumberri

They arrested me because I was a fool and didn't listen to my wife. On the twenty-seventh of July Gerardo Unzueta, Arturo Marbán, and I went to take over the offices of the Communist Party (at 186 Mérida), which had been occupied by the police. We thought that if we insisted on our constitutional rights the police would clear out. But we were the ones that got cleared out—and taken straight to Lecumberri. They took us prisoner by force—guns are pretty powerful arguments. From that point on we went the route that so many have traveled before us—cell block H, and then J, the one for sexual delinquents, then here in C, where there are lots of us political prisoners. . . . The others are in M.

Eduardo de la Vega Ávila, member of
the Communist Party; prisoner in Lecumberri

We try not to let our political differences affect our daily life here in prison.

Luis González Sánchez, member of the Communist
Youth; prisoner in Lecumberri

We're not puritans or hypocrites or leftist prudes. We're the sort who like to enjoy life to the fullest. But we've somehow gotten the reputation of being people like the mummies before us; the Communist Party mummies who were born encased in mummy wrappings, sober-sided King Tuts.

Eduardo de la Vega Ávila,
of the Communist Party

The only guy that talks almost as dirty as Pino—and that's saying a lot, because Pino's tops in that department—is de la Vega, of the Communist Party. He even goes to the German classes to learn dirty words in that language, in case he should chance to visit Germany some day!

*Pablo Gómez, student at UNAM and member of
the Communist Youth; prisoner in Lecumberri*

We were interrogated by an American agent and two Mexican ones. The specific questions were:
   "Are you members of the Communist Party?"
   "Are you members of the Communist Youth?"
   "Do you have a United States visa?"
   "Do you have relatives in the United States?"
   "What ties do you have with the CNED?"
The ones who were interrogated were Arturo Zama, Rubén Valdespino, Pedro Castillo, Salvador Pérez Ríos (who was freed immediately, perhaps by sheer happenstance), William Rosado, the Puerto Rican, and I.

Félix Goded Andreu, student and member of the Communist Youth

On the twenty-seventh Sócrates Campos Lemus, one of the leaders of the CNH, asked a guard to stay in the Zócalo. They lit bonfires, and we went to buy sandwiches for the guards. . . . Those left on guard began singing "La Adelita," popular ditties, the song about Cananea—and then the tanks arrived.

Félix Lucio Hernández Gamundi, of the CNH

We have been so tolerant that we have been criticized for our excessive leniency, but there is a limit to everything, and the irremediable violations of law and order that have occurred recently before the very eyes of the entire nation cannot be allowed to continue.

*Gustavo Díaz Ordaz, Fourth Annual Presidential
Message to the National Congress, September 1,
1968*

The morning after the night of August 27—five hundred thousand citizens gathered outside the Palacio Nacional, can you imagine that?—government employees were notified that they must attend a ceremony the government was going to hold to make amends for the insult to the national flag, to the *lábaro patrio*, not to Luis Gon-

zález de Alba, you understand, but to the *lábaro patrio* [Luis González de Alba's nickname is "Lábaro"]. The press had reported that
the kids had turned on all the lights on the cathedral and rung the
bells just as the marchers entered the Zócalo, and that they had run
a red and black flag up the central flagpole. The newspapers had
seized upon these "crimes" to toady to the government, but they
had gotten their comeuppance when their stories were immediately
denied by the archbishop and the CENCOS,* who stated that there
was nothing in canon law that made it a sacrilege to ring the bells
or turn on the lights illuminating the façade of the cathedral. Moreover, the priest on duty, Jesús Pérez, stated that the kids had secured his permission before going up to the tower to ring the bells;
and as for the flag, the one the youngsters ran up the flagpole was
just a small tattered square of cheap red cotton cloth, but the next
day there was a huge brand-new red satin banner flying from the
flagpole. I wonder how that happened! Anyway, the officials organized the ceremony of apology. Government workers were already
quite unhappy about being forced to either attend official ceremonies or lose their jobs, or at the very least a day's salary, but this
time they were really mad about being kicked around like that.
We'd been protesting and marching in demonstrations and being
quite vociferous about such travesties of democratic procedures for
a month, and our efforts had not been wasted. The government employees attended this civic purification ceremony all right, but not
in the spirit the government had expected. They flocked out of the
ministries and public offices shouting, "We're sheep, they're herding us around . . . baaa, baaa, baaa. . . ." "We don't want to
go, they're herding us around, we don't want to go, baaa, baaa,
baaa." They kept bleating like that—imagine!—and shouting from
the backs of the buses, "We're sheep!" You could hear them bleating all through the streets: "Baaaa . . . baaaaaaa!" They got a real
load off their chests. What a neat joke! What a kick in the ass for the
government! "We're sheep!" People the authorities thought would
back the purification ceremony to the hilt.

                                   Gilberto Guevara Niebla, of the CNH

---

* Centro de Comunicación Social (Center for Social Communication), a lay organization associated with the Catholic Church.

The government is convinced there's only one public opinion in Mexico: the one that applauds it, that toadies to it. But there's another public opinion: the one that criticizes, that doesn't believe a word the government says, and yet another one, the one that doesn't give a damn, that turns a deaf ear to any more promises, that hasn't been taken in, that's indifferent, that no one has been able to take advantage of, a public opinion that despite its suspicious attitude and its ignorance is a free opinion.

José Fuente Herrera, engineering student at ESIME, IPN

We're *acelerados*.

Ernesto Hernández Pichardo, student at the National School of Economics, UNAM

> **FREE TUITION FOR GRANADEROS ENROLLING IN LITERACY CLASSES**
>
> *Banner at a demonstration*

"I'm not going to carry Venustiano*—you carry him!"
"Who ordered this placard?"
"The Action Committee, but I'm not going to carry it. . . ."
"Listen, that's no way to . . ."
"I'm not going to carry it, and that's that."
"Hey, you guys! We need another brigadier here to carry Venustiano Carranza!"

Hugo Peniche Avilés, student at the Wilfredo Massieu School

I drew Pancho Villa!

Josefina Ondarza López, student at the National School of Dramatic Art

The School of Physics and Mathematics proposed to the CNH that a big demonstration be held in total silence, to demonstrate our dis-

---

* Venustiano Carranza, President of Mexico, 1914–1920.

cipline and self-control. The delegates from Humanities and Chapingo wanted to try to mobilize the workers, but given the situation
at that time that would have been very difficult. Nonetheless I insisted. I always say exactly what I think. I always insist.

> *Luis Tomás Cervantes Cabeza de Vaca,*
> *agronomist; CNH delegate from the Chapingo*
> *School of Agriculture; prisoner in Lecumberri*

"Listen, I don't understand why Barros Sierra * applauded the
president in the Chamber, if he's on our side and the president
didn't agree to satisfy any of the six demands outlined in our
petition. . . ."

"What did you expect him to do, dummy?—put his two fingers to
his mouth and whistle?"

"No, but I didn't expect him to applaud. . . ."

"What kind of a world do you think we're living in, anyway? All
the television cameras were trained on him. . . . Besides, the president did say that he was going to hold public hearings on Article
145 to decide whether it should be revoked. . . ."

"You'll see how far the hearings get."

"Well, it's something anyway, as the old saying goes."

"Listen, the day that a deputy gets up in the Chamber and says,
'Señor Presidente, I don't agree with what you've just said' . . ."

"There'll only be one thing left for him to do after that—commit
suicide. . . ."

"Listen, why did the rector applaud?"

"I just told you! Can't you get it through your head that in the
Chamber even the benches, even the chairs that the deputies sit in
applaud?"

> *Tape-recorded conversation between two students*
> *at the Wilfredo Massieu School*

NATIONAL AUTONOMOUS UNIVERSITY OF MEXICO
APPEAL TO STUDENTS AND TEACHERS

**The present situation at the University, it need hardly be said, is
extremely delicate. Classes have now been suspended for several
weeks, just as the undergraduate academic year was ending and the**

---

* Regent of UNAM.

second semester of the professional schools was not even half over. This interruption, along with the use of University property and services for purposes that are not strictly connected with the University, has not only been detrimental to students but has also seriously interfered with the life of this institution, since it has turned aside from and to a large extent been prevented from fulfilling the functions which have been assigned it by law and which constitute our obligation to the Mexican people.

Our institutional demands, as outlined in the declaration of the University Council made public last August 18, have been essentially satisfied by the recent annual message by the Citizen President of the Republic. It is quite true that certain important juridical questions having to do with our autonomy still remain to be clarified; this will be accomplished, however, through the most appropriate means and methods possible.

Rector Javier Barros Sierra, "Appeal to Students and Teachers," at University City, September 9, 1968

One day we went to the Zenón lunchroom to hand out leaflets. It was one of the first times I'd passed out leaflets, but my comrades said they were old hands at it and knew how to organize the whole thing: some of them would talk to people, others would hand out leaflets, others would act as lookouts, and another one would wait for us in the car with the motor running, see what I mean?

The brigade leader said to us, "Okay, Cecilia, you go down the street to the lunchroom and keep a sharp lookout, and Ofelia, you sit down at a table and order a bowl of soup to throw them off the track, and Margarita, you stand out on the sidewalk and hand everybody who goes in a leaflet. . . ."

"Okay, let's go. . . ."

I went down the street to the lunchroom and saw two cars full of people parked in front of it. I said to myself, Great. I'll start with them. I stuck my head in the window, flashed them a nice smile—you know what I mean?—and said, "Here, comrades, read this whole thing carefully, because it's the instructions for tomorrow, okay? And don't forget to come!"

Then one of them said to me, "Sure! How about giving me five of them, because there are five of us?"

"Of course. Here you are."

"Listen, why don't you give me the whole bunch?"

When he said that, I thought, I wonder why he wants all of them? He probably wants to help, I decided. But I got scared all of a sudden because when I turned around I saw an antenna on the roof of the car, like the ones on the radio taxis, and I said to myself, Maybe he's a plainclothesman! Damn!

I was suspicious, so I started to run. I whistled to the other girls and we all jumped into my car and drove off, and the other car, a yellow one, started following us, bumper to bumper. My car's a little Datsun, a '67, but the one following us was a big late-model car. . . . I was driving because the friend we'd left at the wheel had thought it would take us a long time to pass out the handbills and the little fool had gone off to buy some chewing gum, so we just left her there. . . . I was driving as fast as my Datsun would go, and all of a sudden a handsome guy in a really neat red car drove by—he was so good-looking I forgot all about the cops the minute I laid eyes on him, you know what I mean? And I said to myself, He looks like a student—even if he's from a dumb school like Lasalle, and I began to motion to him to follow us and all that, and I thought to myself, Maybe he'll not only rescue us from the cops— this might be the beginning of a big romance. I kept motioning to him, like, and the guy kept making signs back asking what was going on, and before I knew it the cops had pulled me over, but the guy had guts and he stopped his car too, right there next to us. I said to myself, He'll get us out of this mess—you know?

He got out of his car then and said to me, "What's happening?"

"Listen, pal, what's happened—those cops over there . . ."

And the cops came over and said to the guy, "Thanks for helping us out, buddy, this young lady refused to pull over!"

And the guy says to me, "Okay, let's see your identification."

"What do you mean, let's see your identification?" I said.

And he turned out to be a plainclothesman too!—how about that! He was so good-looking we'd never have suspected! What a boner! Once he'd helped nab us, he said good-by to his pals and went on his way.

Margarita Isabel, actress

Everybody stopped sticking their heads in the sand like ostriches, forgot about their personal problems, and all of us were very friendly; we acted as though we were all brothers. Since those of us in the "José Carlos Mariátegui" and "Miguel Hernández" groups in the Faculty of Philosophy and Letters were Marxists, the Christian Democrats and the students who weren't active in politics had always considered us a rather peculiar lot, more or less enemies, trouble makers, agitators, destroyers of society. But after the bazooka attack at Preparatory 1, we all saw eye to eye and started working together. I don't mean to say that that was the end of our political differences; it was just that our immediate objectives were the same: fighting for an end of repression and the recognition of democratic freedoms.

Carolina Pérez Cicero, student at the Faculty of Philosophy and Letters, UNAM

"What about your lecture?"

"No, Señor Acevedo Escobedo, I'm going to the Silent Demonstration. . . ."

"But you have to give your lecture. There's an audience out there waiting to hear you. Look—there they are in their seats out there."

"No, sir. I'm going to invite the audience to go to the demonstration . . . that'll be my lecture. The Silent Demonstration—that's what I call really good vibes. . . ."

"But you can't do that! The audience has come to attend a lecture, not a demonstration. . . ."

"Listen, Señor Acevedo Escobedo, you can stay here and tell those who don't want to go a cowboy story. . . . I'm splitting the scene!"

Conversation between José Agustín and Antonio Acevedo Escobedo, Head of the Department of Literature of the INBA, in the Manuel M. Ponce Auditorium, September 13, 1968, during the lecture series "Storytellers Meet the Public"

Wow, I thought everybody in this town was dead, that nobody would ever get us off our butts, and look how many of us have turned out! Those cops on the riot squad have gone too far! Have you noticed all the equipment they've got? You'd think there was a war on! What pigs! I'd sure like to beat the shit out of one of them! DOWN WITH CUETO AND HIS HOUND DOG MENDIOLEA, DOWN WITH CUETO AND HIS HOUND DOG MENDIOLEA, DOWN WITH CUETO AND HIS HOUND DOG MENDIOLEA! Pick up the pace—what's the matter with you anyway? You're not walking straight—and never mind telling us how you got clubbed, we've heard all about it a hundred times.

Eulogio Juárez Méndez, student at ESIQIE,* IPN

DOWN WITH CUETO AND HIS HOUND DOG MENDIOLEA

Placard, Faculty of Sciences

Do you remember the night of the bazooka attack? They thought we were going to run away from the tanks, but we didn't—we threw all sorts of things at them, even our shoes.

Leonardo Ávila Pineda, student at the School of Dentistry, UNAM

POLI AND UNAM UNITED WILL WIN—POLI AND UNAM UNITED WILL WIN—POLI AND UNAM
Chant at the August 27 demonstration

What do you punks think you're doing? Do you really think you're such hot stuff you can overthrow the government? That'll be the day!

Police officer to student, at headquarters of the Federal Security Police

Why is Chuy walking all hunched over like that? He looks like an old man. Oh, no—that's not Chuy—Chuy disappeared when they occupied Preparatory.

Servando Hernández Cueto, engineering student, IPN

---

* Escuela Superior de Ingeniería Química, Industrial, y Electrónica (School of Chemical, Industrial, and Electronic Engineering).

Those little shits from MURO do errands for me.

Gilberto Guevara Niebla, of the CNH

**PEOPLE UNITE, DON'T ABANDON US—PEOPLE
UNITE, DON'T ABANDON US—PEOPLE UNITE**
Chant at the August 27 demonstration

Why is that comrade over there crying? She's nervous, she says.
Listen, anybody who's nervous, go on home—we don't want anybody here who's got a personal hangup. She says it's on account of
her brother. What happened to her brother? Tell her to pull herself
together, nothing's going to happen, we're all here together, tell our
comrade that, tell all the comrades that. . . .

Leonardo Bañuelos Tovar, Luis Enrique Erro School

CNF   **TO THE PEOPLE:**

The National Strike Committee invites all workers, peasants,
teachers, students, and the general public to the

GREAT SILENT MARCH

In support of our six-point petition:

1. Freedom for all political prisoners.
2. Revocation of Article 145 of the Federal Penal Code.
3. Disbandment of the corps of granaderos.
4. Dismissal of police officials Luis Cueto, Raúl Mendiola, and
A. Frías.
5. Payment of indemnities to the families of all those killed and
injured since the beginning of the conflict.
6. Determination of the responsibility of individual government
officials implicated in the bloodshed.

We have called this march to press for the immediate and complete satisfaction of our demands by the Executive Power.

We repeat that our Movement has no connection with the Twentieth Olympic Games to be held in our country or with the national
holidays commemorating our Independence, and that this Committee has no intention of interfering with them in any way. We insist,

once again, that all negotiations aimed at resolving this conflict must be public.

The march will begin today, Friday the thirteenth, at four p.m. at the National Museum of Anthropology and History and will end with a public meeting in the Plaza de la Constitución.

The day has come when our silence will be more eloquent than our words, which yesterday were stilled by bayonets.

Paid announcement in El Día, *September 13, 1968*

The helicopter hovered overhead just above the treetops. Finally, at the appointed hour, four p.m., the march began in absolute silence. This time the authorities could not even claim that we had provoked them by shouting insults. A number of delegates maintained that if the demonstration was a silent one, it would fail to show people how angry we were. Others said that none of the demonstrators would keep their mouths shut. What chance was there of controlling and shutting up several hundred thousand boisterous young people who were in the habit of singing and shouting and chanting at demonstrations? It was an impossible task, and if we failed it would betray the weakness of the CNH! That's why the youngest kids wore adhesive tape over their mouths. They themselves chose to do that: they put tape over each other's lips to make sure they wouldn't make a sound. We told them, "If a single one of you fails, we all fail."

As soon as we left Chapultepec Park, just a few blocks farther on, hundreds of people began to join our ranks. All along the Paseo de la Reforma, the sidewalks, the median strips, the monuments, and even the trees were full of people, and every hundred yards our ranks were doubled. And the only sound from those tens of thousands and then hundreds of thousands of people were their footfalls. Footfalls on the pavement, the sound of thousands of marching feet, the sound of thousands of feet walking on, step by step. The silence was more impressive than the huge crowd. It seemed as though we were trampling all the politicians' torrents of words underfoot, all their speeches that are always the same, all their demagoguery, their empty rhetoric, the flood of words that the facts belie, the heaps of lies; we were sweeping them all away beneath our feet. . . . None of the other demonstrations touched me as deeply as this one. I felt a lump in my throat and clenched my teeth.

With our footsteps we were somehow avenging Jaramillo,* his pregnant wife, both murdered, his dead children; we were avenging years and years of cowardly crimes, crimes that had been carefully covered up, crimes resembling those committed by gangsters. While the shouting, the chanting, the singing during other demonstrations made them seem like a popular fiesta, the solemn silence of this one made me feel as though I were in a cathedral. Since we had resolved not to shout or talk as we had during the other demonstrations, we were able to hear—for the first time—the applause and the shouts of approval from the dense crowds supporting us along the line of march, and thousands of hands were raised in the symbol that soon covered the entire city and was even seen at public functions, on television, at official ceremonies: the V of *Venceremos* ["We shall win"], formed with two fingers by young people marching in demonstrations, and later painted on telephone booths, buses, fences. This symbol of unswerving, incorruptible, indomitable will appeared in the most unexpected places, from that time on till the massacre later. Even after Tlatelolco, the V kept appearing, even at the Olympic ceremonies, in the form of the people's two uplifted fingers.

Luis González de Alba, of the CNH

TO THE PEOPLE OF MEXICO:

You can see that we're not vandals or rebels without a cause—the label that's constantly been pinned on us. Our silence proves it.

Handbill at the September 13 demonstration

You know what? I liked them, they made a good impression on me, because even though they were kids they behaved like men. Many of them had adhesive tape over their mouths, and almost all of them looked like scalded cats in their old sweaters and their tattered shirts, but they also looked very determined. The people watching along the sidewalk felt great affection for them, and many of them not only applauded them but joined their ranks, and when they didn't get leaflets they asked for them, and began passing them on from hand to hand. I've never seen such a huge demonstration,

---

* Rubén Jaramillo, peasant leader in the State of Morelos, who was murdered, together with his pregnant wife and children, by the Army in 1962. (Translator's note.)

such a sincere one, such a beautiful one. Here, I've brought you some leaflets.

Paula Amor de Poniatowski, mother of a family

The day the plans were drawn up for the Silent Demonstration, it was suggested that someone from the Faculty of Law ought to explain why Article 145 was illegal and unconstitutional, and since I was the representative from the Law School who was present that day, they called on me to speak. The committee appointed to study Article 145 was made up of all the CNH representatives from the Law School—me and five other comrades. We were fools enough to believe that the government was willing to have a dialogue with us—I say that because when the *granaderos* hit us over the head with nightsticks and truncheons they kept saying, "Go ahead and have your dialogue, go ahead and have your dialogue!" So we thought we should be prepared to have a discussion about legal technicalities, but what happened was that they gave us an illegal and antidemocratic clubbing over the head and the dialogue turned out to be a monologue in the form of a sixteen-year prison sentence and a fine of 1,987,387 pesos, and the only way I'll ever be able to pay it is if they pay me 100,000 pesos for every pound I weigh, because I weigh 220 pounds, and if they won't let me pay it off that way, do you think they're going to let me go because I've only got one eye and buck teeth? * It'll be like trying to get blood out of a turnip. Well, anyway, about the Silent Demonstration. On September 13, the day of Niños Héroes,† I read a speech in the Zócalo explaining the origins, the development, and the changes in Article 145, and the reasons why it should be revoked. Everybody congratulated me and they had a terrible time lifting me off the platform of the truck where I'd given the speech; one woman gave me a sandwich and another one gave me one of those twenty-five-peso Olympic coins.

Roberta Avendaño Martínez ("Tita"), CNH delegate from the Faculty of Law, UNAM; prisoner in the Women's House of Detention

---

* President Díaz Ordaz had just had an eye operation, and had prominent teeth. (Translator's note.)

† A national holiday celebrating the young Mexican cadets who heroically resisted an attack on the Castle of Chapultepec in the United States' war with Mexico in 1845. (Translator's note.)

I left my car on the Calzada de la Milla, next to the Museum of Anthropology, with my mom inside, and we went to the demonstration, and when I got back there was no car and no mom.

Regina Sánchez Osuna, student at the
Mexican Dance Academy

They destroyed my car; the tires, the windshield, the windows were all smashed to smithereens. I asked a man to get word to Manuel. He came in from University City—I think he must have come in a helicopter because he got there in about three seconds. He was deathly pale. He thought I was inside the car.

Marta Acevedo, mother of a family

Listen, Cabeza, why don't you shut up, like in the Silent Demonstration? You've been harping on the same subject for half an hour.

A delegate, to Luis Tomás Cervantes Cabeza de
Vaca, at a CNH meeting

The Student Movement is not the work of delinquents, nor does it intend to subvert Mexican institutions. The student leaders are ready and willing to initiate a dialogue with the highest authorities in the country.

Heberto Castillo, engineer, at Anatomías, *a*
round-table discussion organized by Jorge
Saldaña, August 21, 1968

"Silence is more powerful."

Editorial cartoon by Abel Quezada, Excélsior,
September 14, 1968

We had left fear, confusion, rumors, and internal conflicts behind. Our teachers delightedly exclaimed that we ought to forget about "strategic retreat." This triumph changed everything. We learned that the government had estimated that the demonstration would not attract more than ten thousand people; the CNH thought there would be a hundred and fifty thousand; and instead a crowd of three hundred thousand marchers turned out, exceeding our most optimistic calculations.

All the thousand little difficulties that each member of the CNH had been having in his particular school disappeared. We didn't even have to ask more students to attend the meetings. They came of their own accord. New perspectives opened up. We began to have debates on the most inflammatory subjects. One step, a single step, had gotten the Movement back on its feet and restructured it, because there was only one thing that had been lacking: regaining our confidence in our own strength and finding a meaning, a goal for our concrete tasks, our common labor. That is what the Silent Demonstration accomplished.

Gilberto Guevara Niebla, of the CNH

We cannot rightly regard this as a conspiracy against the authorities. Young people's ability to organize has been proven; the students have all joined together and shown that their just demands deserve our attention.

Víctor Flores Olea, at Anatomías

LETTER FROM A MOTHER TO HER SON
IN THE RIOT SQUAD

Dear Son:

   I have just read about your latest exploits; I am truly touched to know that you, my dear son, the fruit of my holy womb, have so selflessly devoted your entire life to the service of our country.

   You have no idea how terrified I was when I read the papers; I realized the grave dangers you had been exposed to, all for love of Díaz Ordaz. The big hard heads of those savage students might have damaged your nice rifle. I've heard that some of them are such brutes that they might even go so far as to smash their faces against that billy club of yours that you take such loving care of.

   If your father hadn't been devoured by sharks attempting to escape from Islas Marías,* he would doubtless have hastened to your side to congratulate you. Nonetheless, I am certain that he is observing your excellent conduct from up there in heaven and will personally intercede with all the saints to ensure that they will watch over you in your dangerous profession.

---

* A federal prison.

Hoping that you will continue to kill students and teachers with the same furious passion,

Love,

Mom

"La Poquianchis Mayor," *

Women's House of Detention, Santa Marta Acatitla

*Leaflet collected at the August 27 demonstration
and read in the Manuel M. Ponce Auditorium on
September 6, 1968, during the lecture series
"Storytellers Meet the Public,"
sponsored by the INBA*

During the first meeting we held in Tlatelolco, on Saturday, September 7, a comrade addressed the crowd of twenty-five thousand people—it was the first time she'd ever spoken outside of her school—and quoted a phrase from Díaz Ordaz's annual presidential message on September 1: ". . . I shall be forced to confront people who have many means of spreading propaganda, lies, and corruption." Our comrade replied that she would willingly exchange these many means that Díaz Ordaz mentions for those that the government possesses and uses. "We wouldn't hesitate for a minute to exchange our bullhorns for the national radio and television networks; our school mimeograph machines for the presses of the big daily papers; our tin cans (which people drop coins in so we can buy paper and ink—for those are our weapons: paper and ink) for the economic resources of the State." And she also shouted to the crowd, "How is it possible that a hundred and eighty journalists who wanted to protest the invasion of the University and the insults to the rector allowed their own papers to refuse to publish their protest, even as a paid advertisement? . . ."

Florencio López Osuna, of the CNH

Another proof of the power of our propaganda was the great number of dogs we let loose with signs on their backs reading "Freedom for political prisoners," "Death to Cueto," and others that were even more outspoken.

Félix Lucio Hernández Gamundi, of the CNH

---

* La Poquianchis Mayor was the oldest of three well-known owners of a whorehouse who murdered several prostitutes working for them. (Translator's note.)

We also discovered that we had yet another means to augment the power of our fearful propaganda machine. The students of aeronautical engineering at Poli and Chemical Sciences at UNAM came up with balloons that would automatically release propaganda on reaching a certain altitude, showering thousands of leaflets on the heads of Mexicans and the sidewalks of Mexico City.

Gilberto Guevara Niebla, of the CNH

Our means of propaganda were student slogans painted on fences (which the police would cover over with gray paint the next day), but then we'd come back and write our slogans over *their* paint: "Death to Cueto," or "Free the Political Prisoners"; slogans painted on the sides of city buses and streetcars and even on the roofs of buses (it was harder for the authorities to paint these out because it took them a while longer to discover them), on the sides of trolleys, on walls on every street corner in the city. Even when the Federal District cleanup squads painted the slogans over, they left big blotches, and they too were a sort of protest. Painted slogans, mimeographed handbills, and our lungs were our press.

Ernesto Hernández Pichardo, student at the
School of Economics, UNAM

All of them spout a pack of lies to show off. They're more long-winded than a Lenten sermon.

Carlos González Guerrero,
student, Lasalle University

The students—those from UNAM, from the IPN, from Chapingo, from the College of Mexico, and all the rest of them—have only one watchword: "Support the Rector, protect the Rector, support the Rector." Their solidarity sends shivers up your spine. But who is going to support them in the hour of truth? Haven't people perhaps left them entirely on their own?

Isabel Sperry de Barraza, grade-school teacher

SONG FOR TITA, OUR FAVORITE

Our favorite among the gang of students was Tita,
The woman the UNAM adored.
She was so brave and of such ample proportions

That even the director respected her
And you could hear her fond friends all saying:

If Tita disappeared from the Law School
The law students would go to her, weeping:
"Oh Tita, in God's name I beg you,
Please don't forget the Law School."

And if perchance there's a summons
To come calm us all down with your jokes,
Oh, Tita, in God's name I beg you,
Please don't forget the law students.

And if a cop gives you trouble
And Cueto endeavors to club you
Please remember, my plump one,
The Law School's behind you forever.

With great affection and respect
for Tita the voluminous

This was a song one of the boys wrote me before the Army took over University City. It's sung to the tune of "La Adelita." * Why was I popular in the Movement? Why did they always say, "Who shall we send to the press conference? Tita, Tita, let's send Tita." They would vote on who was going to go, and I was always one of the winners because everybody liked me. We agreed beforehand how we'd conduct the press conference, and decided that each student representative would answer those questions that he or she seemed particularly qualified to answer. I never regarded Marcelino Perelló as our number-one star. I think he attracted the most attention simply because he was so brilliant; people listened to what he had to say because he was so intelligent. I always admired his clear thinking.

There was always a carefree, youthful atmosphere in the CNH—lots of joking and fooling around. Every night some of the kids from Economics would bring me chocolates and candy to "bribe" me to

---

* Adelita was a legendary heroine of the Mexican Revolution, celebrated in a famous popular song dating from that period. (Translator's note.)

vote for their school's proposals; it was their way of kidding around with me.

Roberta Avendaño Martínez (Tita), of the CNH

The students couldn't get anywhere if there weren't people backing them, people giving them money. For example: who's paying for the sound equipment for their meetings? The loudspeakers? . . . Where did the handbills come from in '68? From the University printing office. It was all organized at Ciudad Universitaria— they took over all of the CU: the paper, the typewriters, the classrooms, the stencils, the ink, the paint, everything . . . it all came from CU!

Ángel García Cevallos, father of a family

Don't hand me that stuff! The government may have had dirty hands, but there were some on the other side too: the students and the adults who were behind them, all of them playing the hero, and at the same time feeding the hopes of the gullible, egging on young people. . . . A criminal sense or irresponsibility still holds sway in Mexico. I'm a mother of a family and I was simply dumfounded by the attitude of the University professors. . . . They were as bad as the kids: they seemed to delight in stirring up trouble. . . .

María Fernanda Vértiz de Lafragua, mother of a
family and a grade-school teacher

I joined the Popular Student Movement in 1968 largely because the students' goals and values had become my own. Or as one teacher put it very succinctly, speaking to one of his students at the beginning of the Movement, "I have learned so much about being a man from you that the best way to repay you is to support your struggle, which is ours, and see it through to the end."

Dr. Fausto Trejo, Professor of Psychology at the Faculty of
Philosophy and Letters, UNAM; member of
the Teachers' Coalition; prisoner in Lecumberri

To criticize Caesar is not to criticize Rome. To criticize a government is not to criticize a country.

Carlos Fuentes, to Excélsior *reporter Guillermo*
Ochoa, March 4, 1969

The CNH was terribly boring; lots of absurd things were discussed endlessly, but every once in a while there were fantastically funny moments. For example, the 210 or 240 delegates and the rank-and-file members spent hours and hours and hours arguing as to whether the Student Movement was revolutionary or not—discussions provoked by Trotskyists and vague leftists. One time, for example, Romeo proposed a one-hour nationwide work strike, or at any rate a strike in the Federal District, to take place between one and two p.m., and when he was told that nobody ever worked between those hours anyway because it was lunchtime, he said it didn't matter, that in fact that would ensure the success of the strike. . . . The meetings dragged on so long that every once in a while the delegates would take time out to shout and whistle at the audience to wake them up. There were 210 to 240 delegates, so that no one political faction would predominate. Ten per cent of them were political militants and ninety per cent were independents, and this latter contingent was the one responsible for the popular nature of the Committee, its originality, its strength. . . . The political policy of the Committee was shaped not by people's words but by their attitudes. I have no faith at all in words. The PRI's speak a revolutionary language, they use quite radical terms, yet a peasant, who has no command of words, of language, is more revolutionary than all the rest of us put together, simply on account of his attitude.

Raúl Álvarez Garín, of the CNH

Despite the fact that the CNH was made up of untried young people with very little political experience, despite the endless, repetitious meetings, the National Strike Committee came to be the one representative of all the students. I think this was a very important experience for all the students because the CNH shattered all the old molds, all the patterns of organization that had existed previously—the FNET * for example—and others as well, and broke not only with corrupt organizations, but with others so old they were decrepit—the "mummies," the alumni associations, and so on. This entire vertical hierarchy above them that weighed so heav-

---

* Federación Nacional de Estudiantes Técnicos (National Federation of Students of Technology), one of the rightist groups covertly supported by the government. (Translator's note.)

ily on the students—the famous pyramid so often talked about in the field of economics—was transformed into a new form of organization in which the students could actively participate. . . . The pyramid was torn down. . . . The CNH was all the students. They said so themselves, We are the CNH! We are the CNH!

Pablo Gómez, student and member of the Communist Youth

The four leaders of the Movement were Raúl Álvarez Garín of the School of Theoretical Physics of the IPN, Sócrates Campos Lemus of the School of Economics of the IPN, Marcelino Perelló of the Faculty of Sciences of UNAM, and Gilberto Guevara Niebla, also from the Faculty of Sciences of UNAM. Of the four, the most accessible were Sócrates and Marcelino. The other two, whom I also had some contact with, were arrogant and rude and aloof. They kept their distance, and Raúl in particular had a very sharp tongue. That was how they seemed, anyway. But it's a truism that appearances are deceptive. Which of them has gone the whole way with us? Who were the real leaders at the crucial moment? Raúl and Gilberto. . . . The other two let us down. Marcelino was the big star, and Sócrates . . . well, everybody knows what he turned out to be.

Luis González de Alba, of the CNH

In the CNH, when it eventually came your turn to speak—after waiting two hours—and you finally got the floor, you'd almost forgotten what you wanted to say.

Félix Lucio Hernández Gamundi, of the CNH

During the entire Student Movement there was never a more representative organization, never one that the students felt belonged to them as much as this one did. The kids didn't just sit back and applaud one or two big shots; they felt they were really participating; they were not objects but subjects. They were the ones who decided and they were very much aware of this, because the most important decisions were all left to them. When the Army occupied University City, for example, the students from UNAM were scattered. Nonetheless the brigades that had been active in the CU continued working outside the University. They got out handbills and manifestos that established a clear-cut policy, and the rank and file went on fighting.

Pablo Gómez, student and member of the Communist Youth

On September 18, the Army unexpectedly invaded University City. When the tanks and trucks transporting the paratroopers started rolling south, the telephone kept ringing: "Thank you very much, *señora*, don't worry. . . ." "Yes, *señor*, we're going to get the students out. . . ." "Yes, thank you, *señora*, we'll take cover. . . ." "We're very touched that you're worried about us, *señorita*. . . ." "Thank you, comrade. . . ." "Much obliged, comrade. . . ." To make a long story short, all the Schools and Faculties were warned that the Army was heading toward CU, but nobody thought to alert the CNH, which had opened the meeting they were holding by making a number of very cutting remarks about delegates who were absent or tardy. Just as the first tanks arrived at the gates of UNAM, one kid ran to the auditorium at the School of Medicine, elbowed his way past the student guards wanting to see his delegate's pass, burst into the meeting room, and blurted out the news of what had happened. The entire Committee was indignant: "It's not enough that we have to begin tonight's meeting with a whole bunch of delegates missing—they won't even let us work in peace without people interrupting!" The messenger left with his mouth hanging open in amazement. The delegates went on discussing a thousand and one things.

Ten minutes later another comrade entered the room and calmly informed them, "Tanks and paratrooper transports have just pulled up in the faculty parking lot. If you want to get out, you'd better hurry. . . . I'm clearing out this minute."

Luis González de Alba, of the CNH

A girl student had locked herself inside one of the lavatories at University City and stayed in there during the entire two weeks that the Army occupied CU. Alcira her name was. She was scared stiff. She couldn't—or wouldn't—make a run for it. The minute she saw the soldiers, the first thought that crossed her mind was to lock herself in. It was awful. One of the cleaning men found her lying half dead on the tile floor. Two weeks later! It must have been terrible staying in there hour after hour, with nothing but water from the faucet in the washroom. She was trapped there in the lavatory—she slept on the bare tile floor between the toilets and the washbowls—and kept peeking out the little window, watching the soldiers leaning against their tanks yawning or sprawled out in their jeeps taking a nap. . . . She was so terrified she never once left the lavatory!

Carolina Pérez Cicero, student, Faculty of
Philosophy and Letters, UNAM

After the soldiers shot me in the CU on September 19, 1968—I was hit in the femur and the bullet came within a few millimeters of severing my femoral artery—I was in the November 20 hospital for two months, and I never told anybody how I'd gotten hurt, not even other kids who visited me, because there was talk going around that there were "stoolpigeons" and "finks" everywhere; there was fear in the air, an atmosphere of absolute mistrust.

Víctor Villela, writer, member of PEN Club

That first act of repression led to others, absolutely senseless ones that completely polarized national public opinion: on one side the men in power and big property owners; on the other students, professors, intellectuals, and a fair part of the Mexican people.

Ricardo Garibay, in an article entitled
"Getting Out of the Hole, the Zero Hour,"
Excélsior, *September 27, 1968*

I detest passivity and indifference, because I identify them with complicity and irresponsibility. We followed the example set by the young people and modeled our Coalition of Secondary and College Teachers for Democratic Freedoms on their National Strike Committee. I will always remember the question my son put to me a few moments before one of the mass demonstrations of the Student Movement was about to begin: "Aren't you going to go to the demonstration with your students?"

Dr. Fausto Trejo, of the Teachers' Coalition;
prisoner in Lecumberri

They nabbed Armando and me at University City when we went there to pick up our daughter. A soldier recognized my husband, called out his name—"Armando Castillejos!"—and took him aside. They separated the two of us. That is to say, they separated all the men from the women, and Armando and I were both accused of being leaders of the Student Movement, though we had nothing at all to do with it, except for the manifesto published by the union at El Ánfora announcing that it supported the student petition. My husband is secretary of the union. What we're really connected with is the Workers' Movement; we've worked directly with laborers for twenty-six years now, and we have gotten a very good idea of how badly they're exploited and manipulated by corrupt labor leaders and how difficult it is for them to stand up for themselves. Armando and I have spent all our lives explaining workers' rights to them—their rights within the law, that is—because if they don't know what their rights are, how are they ever going to be able to defend them? That's why the two of us have been charged with thirteen felonies in the federal courts and six misdemeanors; we've been put on trial two different times, and have a longer criminal record than any of the political prisoners. . . . On December 24, 1968, the papers published the list of prisoners who were going to be released that day, despite the fact that the day before Christmas is a holiday for government employees. My name was on the list, but that same day the prison authorities got orders not to free me, and I was the only one on the list who wasn't released. There's been talk that Fidel Velázquez * personally intervened to keep me in prison. . . . I had a job in the Secretariat of Labor, but they fired me—after nineteen years. I had a post with the Federal Arbitration and Conciliation Commission as an aide to Group 13 of the petroleum industry, a position I'd gotten because I had seniority, and I was dismissed because I was married to Armando.

Salomón González Blanco told me to my face: "*Señora*, I admire your husband, but we regard him as an enemy of the government. So if you still want to work in this agency, we'll have to transfer you to Guaymas."

I told him I didn't want to go to Guaymas. I fought for my job all through the lower courts and all the way up. In the Supreme Court I lost my suit to get my job back. It didn't matter that I had a record

---

* Leader of the Confederación de Trabajadores (Workers' Confederation), who was suspected of selling out to the government. (Translator's note.)

of nineteen years' hard work, since in these nineteen years I'd always been on the side of the workers!

After that happened, I went to work in my husband's office in 1962, but we found it harder and harder to help the workers, because Armando was unable to get government recognition for many unions, even ones with sixty or more workers such as the one in the Xalostoc sheet-metal works. The Secretariat of Labor and the Federal District Department are the ones that decide what unions can be legally registered—that way they can keep control of all the workers' organizations. You can fight through every court in the land, but they still won't give you the registration papers! This is one of the bottlenecks the government sets up so as to keep complete control of the Workers' Movement.

Since my husband would never take bribes—and heaven only knows he was offered lots of them!—to "sell out" a strike, they regarded him as a dangerous person. Moreover, Armando waged a bitter campaign against Fidel Velázquez and company unions, and neither the corrupt officials of these fake unions nor the government, whose principal support comes from these leaders, have ever forgiven him. That's the real reason why we're in prison.

> *Adela Salazar Carbajal de Castillejos, labor*
> *attorney; prisoner in the Women's House of*
> *Detention*

They arrested me three times. The first time was on September 18. I was dancing in the UNAM's Ballet Folklórico and had gone to a rehearsal, wearing my ballet slippers, of course. I was on the Action Committee of the Law School, the head in fact of the Finance Committee, but that day I was with some girl friends who had nothing at all to do with the Movement; they weren't even studying at the University. They arrested all of us and kept us there on the esplanade in front of the Rectory till three in the morning. There was a French girl who was pregnant standing next to me; she got very sick. She and her husband were tourists; they'd just come out to the University to have a look around, but they took her to Lecumberri anyway; she was there three days with me. There were also two girls from Tamaulipas who'd gone dancing with their boy friends at the Altillo. They'd come to see what was happening when they saw the tanks and the troops go by. The authorities let the girls and their boy friends go in, but they wouldn't allow them to leave later, and the girls said jokingly, "Our folks are going to make us get married now, because they'll think we ran off with our sweet-hearts." A classical ballet dancer standing next to us said, "We must keep calm; relax, girls, take it easy," and began doing yoga exercises. They arrested anybody they pleased at CU, regardless of who they were. I saw the rector's private secretary, Attorney Nogueron, go by with a soldier with a bayonet at his heels, and I said to Señor Nogueron, "What, you too, sir?" and he replied, "It's all a mistake, Nachita, it'll be cleared up soon." They took forty-three of us women from the esplanade to Lecumberri and put us in the women's prison because the other jails were all full: Military Camp 1, the city jail, Santa Marta Penitentiary, the prison of the Attorney General's office, and all the rest of them. Since there weren't any beds for us they took us to the dining room, and we had to sit there on the concrete tables till the next day—we almost froze to death. One of the women with us, an old old lady, said her brother was a judge, and she couldn't understand why she'd been taken there. We were in good spirits because that was the first time we'd been arrested; our one worry was our men comrades; we didn't want anything to happen to them. We took up a collection among ourselves and bought cans of Nestlé condensed milk and cigarettes to send them. We thought they could hear us, so we sang to them and shouted to them to keep their chins up so they'd realize they weren't alone, never dreaming they couldn't hear us because they were in cell blocks a long way away. . . . We felt very brave, but at one point someone screamed, "A rat!" and all forty-three of us immediately climbed up on top of the concrete tables. How they crammed us all into that room I'll never know, but I remember that we had quite a good time. Those days weren't bad—the bad part came later!

> *Ana Ignacia Rodríguez ("Nacha"), of the Action*
> *Committee of the Faculty of Law, UNAM;*
> *prisoner in the Women's House of Detention*

But we are now entering a new phase; I am the object of a vast campaign of personal attacks, slander, insults, and calumny. I grant that thus far they have come from unimportant people, with no moral authority; but all of us here in Mexico know whose dictates they are obeying.

> *Rector Javier Barros Sierra, text of his*
> *resignation submitted to the Board of Trustees*
> *of UNAM, September 23, 1968*

The courageous patriotic document that the rector's resignation represents leaves no doubt as to the nature of the ominous pressures from outside the University that have caused him to take this step.

> *Declaration of the CNH, September 25, 1968*

The rector's resignation is a patriotic act comparable only to that taken by Octavio Paz when he resigned his post as Mexican Ambassador to India a few weeks later, refusing to represent a government that murders its own people.

> *Luis González de Alba, of the CNH*

The problems of young people can be resolved only through education, never through force, violence, or corruption. This has been my ruling principle of action and the goal to which I have devoted all my time and energies, throughout my rectorate.

> *Rector Javier Barros Sierra, text of his resignation*

All the schools were convinced that the sole path to a solution lay in public dialogue. This was beyond question. The powers that be had not succeeded in corrupting the Committee; the government's maneuvers had been foreseen and sidestepped in time. The president played his very last card when he delivered a speech from the country's highest tribunal threatening total repression, but it did not have the effect that he had hoped for. The authorities were forced to abandon the traditional methods that the Mexican government has so often resorted to; they were confronted with a movement that could not be corrupted or discredited. They also failed to understand that there were no national politicians secretly backing the Movement and pulling the strings behind the scenes. Weren't there hidden motives behind the student petition? Could it possibly be

that all the students wanted was satisfaction of their six demands?
The government couldn't believe it and kept trying to find the non-
existent conspirators and gray eminences behind the Movement.
Since it was a regime accustomed to playing a double game, to ap-
plying pressure behind the scenes rather than negotiating issues
frankly and openly, it was unable to understand the facts that suddenly exploded in its face, nor did it possess the proper instruments
and the political flexibility necessary to answer honestly for its acts
before the eyes of the entire nation, outside the offices of ministers
where so many just struggles have come to a sudden end.

Luis González de Alba, of the CNH

VACCINATE YOUR RIOT POLICEMAN!
*Placard at a demonstration, taken from a Rius
cartoon in an issue of the political comic-book* Los
Agachados, *entitled "Special Issue on
Headbusting. July, August, September, October, and Who
Knows How Long"*

LONG LIVE CUBAN WOMEN!
*Placard at a demonstration, from a cartoon by
Rius in* Los Agachados

Cueto for President!
Mariles for Secretary of (personal) Defense!
Corona del Rosal for Ambassador to North Andorra!
Mendiolea Cerecero for the INBA!
In other words: sheer heaven!
Rius, in the "Special Issue on Headbusting" of
Los Agachados

The government never wanted a public dialogue—it wanted secret
talks. And we refused to compromise: THE DIALOGUE HAD TO BE

PUBLIC. Therefore the government could not suborn the Student Movement in 1968.

Marcia del Río Capistrán, student at
the School of Dentistry, UNAM

The jails were being filled with new prisoners when one of our principal demands was the freedom of political prisoners.

Eduardo Valle Espinoza (Owl-Eyes), of the CNH

At eleven o'clock at night, as the official ceremony of the *grito** was ending in the Zócalo, and being repeated in each town and hamlet, we gave the *grito* of independence in the CU and at Poli amid wild jubilation. Heberto gave it at CU. . . . There were stands on the esplanade selling doughnuts, fruit drinks, confetti, *serpentíns;* it was like a carnival, they were selling flowers and paper hats, and "wedding ceremonies" were being held. The Avenida Insurgentes was a riot of color, with banners and spotlights and boisterous merrymaking, a picnic, a popular fair. . . . Later the Attorney General's office was to trot out our "marriage certificates," typical of any fiesta, as evidence against us, proving that we had set ourselves up as authorities empowered to perform civil marriages, thus committing yet another crime and yet another sacrilegious infringement of our constitution. . . . It was only by sheer accident that I hadn't "gotten married!"

Gilberto Guevara Niebla, of the CNH

They were fake wedding ceremonies! I sure wish they'd been real ones!

Cuca Barron de Narváez, student
at the Faculty of Medicine, UNAM

At the meeting held on September 21 in the Tlatelolco housing unit, the authorities kept calling in more and more *granaderos,* but students kept pouring in nonetheless from the many nearby technical schools of the Santo Tomás campus. You could hear the tear-gas explosions and the shooting from the campus. Hundreds of people

---

* The ceremony held each year on September 15, repeating the "shout" (*grito*) given at Dolores in 1810 by Father Hidalgo as a rallying cry at the beginning of Mexico's struggle for independence from Spain. (Translator's note.)

were tear-gassed and many received bullet wounds, but the students and the tenants of the housing unit refused to give up. All night long housewives kept boiling water on their stoves and hunting up soda bottles to fill with any inflammable liquid and throw at the police, together with stones, jars, cans, pieces of wood, paving blocks, and garbage.

A captain of the transit guards sent the men in his charge—all of whom were dressed in civilian clothes—to cordon off the inquisitive bystanders who had gathered, as they always do when a fight starts. The students from the Santo Tomás campus broke through the cordon to help their fellow students from Vocational 7; many of the numerous vehicles used by the police to cordon off the zone were blown up with Molotov cocktails. More and more people entered the fray on both sides. Even the little kids from the housing unit were up on the rooftops throwing stones and trying to get into the fight too!

Félix Lucio Hernández Gamundi, of the CNH

The student body of Vocational 7 is made up mostly of youngsters from the Tlatelolco housing unit and Tepito and Lagunilla. All of them, or most of them, supported the Movement. Before going out to pass out leaflets on the buses, in the markets and schools and elsewhere, the kids would drop by our houses every day to leave handbills and keep us informed as to how things were going. There was also an organization of parents and tenants that openly supported the kids. The *granaderos* knew this. They were very much aware that the Tlatelolco tenants and the mothers of all these kids were prepared to defend them. Twice before the students and the people of Tlatelolco had spied police dressed in civvies and forced them to leave.

Mercedes Olivera de Vázquez,
anthropologist, resident in the Chihuahua building,
Nonoalco-Tlatelolco housing project

We fought the *granaderos* Aztec style: we threw stones. No firearms were involved, because the *granaderos* were armed only with nightsticks and things like that. They had tried to enter places like Zacatenco by themselves and had been unable to. . . . The Army had to

come to their aid. So after September 23, they began arming the
granaderos with M-1 rifles.

Raúl Álvarez Garín, of the CNH

The Poli buses were a great help to the Movement. You felt at home
in a Poli bus.

Félix Lucio Hernández Gamundi, of the CNH

In my day you didn't call a bunch of bums and degenerates
students.

Pablo Lara Vértiz, tailor

I'm from a peasant family in the country. I'm twenty-five years old
and I've seen friends my age die the same way they were born:
fucked by the system. My family moved to the Federal District
because they were starving to death. At first we stayed with some
aunts of ours out near Atzcapotzalco. My father was a bricklayer.
When I was still in grade school, I began working in an oxygen-
bottling factory; later I made up my mind I'd go to secondary
school. I wanted very much to get into Poli, but since I had no inside contacts and no money, how could I? I didn't know anybody.
When you're an outsider, that's the way it is: you hardly ever even
talk to anyone. I was the sort of person who had no interest in political discussions. What I wanted most was to get ahead so my family
wouldn't have to suffer any more, to endure things I'll never forget:
the way they treated my mother in houses where she worked as a
laundress and all that. There were places where instead of paying
her money they'd say, "Here, take this food home with you"—and I
could plainly see that it was table scraps. When you're starving you
have to put up with things like that, but it made me mad. I finally
got into Poli. I worked nights and studied in the afternoon; that's
how I got into engineering school. I didn't join any organizations at
Poli, and I looked down on anybody who started any sort of organization. I slaved like a robot at my job in the factory and at school I
was a grind; nothing interested me but my work. I hadn't been
back to the part of the country I came from for a long time, and
when I finally did go back I saw that my relatives' living conditions
hadn't changed at all, and I was very discouraged. I'd been discouraged, in fact, ever since I was twelve, when I began working in the

oxygen factory. The representative of the do-nothing, government-approved union, the CTM,* dropped around every once in a while to collect dues and all he ever said was, "Everything's going fine, men." Any worker who pressed for his rights was kicked out. All this got me to thinking, and when I saw that the Student Movement was really making headway, I said to myself, This time I'm going to take part. I felt very grown up, and said to myself, I hope we get somewhere. The Movement didn't seem political to me; it was something more than that. First of all, all of the members were young, they were all pissed off, and ready to fight for what they wanted. . . . And secondly, their ideas were different: they were making concrete demands, and it seemed to me they weren't pulling the wool over anybody's eyes. . . . I never felt that I was being lied to or that it was all play-acting, the way the relations between the CTM and the workers had been in the factory!

Daniel Esparza Lepe, student at ESIME, IPN

The IPN buses played a very important role in the struggle. We all felt more secure, more confident in them: they were *our* buses, really, and we took better care of them than of anything else. What's more, the size of the crowds they attracted was simply incredible: the minute one of the red-and-white Poli buses drove up in a certain neighborhood, hundreds of people immediately gathered round. We visited working-class neighborhoods in them: San Bartolo Naucalpan, La Presa, Santa Clara, Nelzahualcóyotl, and others of that sort. And they were great meetings. When a bus from Poli and one from UNAM met in the center of town or someplace else in the city to hold a meeting, people would climb up on top of the buses and use them as an impromptu speakers' platform. They would say what they didn't like about the Movement or tell why they supported it: they considered it *their* movement, *their* fight too. Once three buses from Poli drew up in the Plaza Garibaldi to hold a meeting, with a big loudspeaker mounted on the baggage rack or whatever it is you call that metal grille on top, and the minute we entered with the buses and started our locomotive cheer, the *maria-*

* The Confederación de Trabajadores Mexicanos (Confederation of Mexican Workers).

chi singers shut up, climbed up on our bus-top platform, and talked about their problems and their reasons for supporting the Movement. We drew a big crowd, and the meeting lasted more than an hour. At another meeting, in the Vallejo industrial district, the police cornered a brigade of about two hundred comrades who'd come there in the Poli buses. Some of the Movement people managed to get away, but the cops arrested some 120 others, and took them and all the buses off to the Attorney General's office. They let the Movement kids out two or three days later—those were the first arrests the police had made since July 26. They let the kids go, but they kept the buses—and we really missed them.

Félix Lucio Hernández Gamundi, of the CNH

On September 23, before the mounted police occupied it, there was a busful of *granaderos* in front of Vocational 7, and a comrade who'd just gotten out of jail came over to their bus with a collection box and some handbills. Since we thought they might arrest him, we all surrounded the bus, and we couldn't believe our eyes when we saw that the *granaderos* were being friendly and accepting the leaflets. We went over and talked to them, and one comrade interviewed a corporal in the riot squad, using a battery-powered loudspeaker so everyone could hear, and the *granadero* said that the authorities gave the men in the riot squad thirty pesos for every student they clubbed and hauled off to jail. He also said he had a son who was a student at Preparatory 5; that he didn't approve of the measures taken by Cueto, Mendiolea, and Diaz Ordaz; that he did as he was told only because he had to earn a living for himself and his family, and that if we would give him work and pay him the same salary he earned in the riot squad, he'd leave the *granaderos*. He also said that they'd been offered that special bonus for every student they hauled in because the *granaderos* had threatened to quit en masse, so the authorities had had to offer them more dough to get them to stay on the job. Then a number of other *granaderos* joined in the conversation, all talking at once. They told the crowd that the authorities had offered the riot police a special bonus for every member of the CNH they nabbed. These particular *granaderos* were from the Victoria barracks, down at the headquarters of the Sixth Division, between Victoria and Revillagigedo. . . . The *granadero* who was interviewed first seemed to be quite a sensible person; he didn't have the hard look in his eye that most all of the *granaderos* usually have.

Antonio Careaga, clothing vendor

In every other country in the world, adolescence is a temporary stage youngsters go through—it only lasts a few years. But here in Mexico, you're a callow youth and a "student" just as long as you please. There's no end to the privileges students have. Espiridión or Esperón or Espantón or Aspirin, or whatever the name of that med student was who headed the revolt against Dr. Chávez (who among other things is *my* cardiologist), had been enrolled as a student at UNAM for fifteen years and still hadn't gotten his diploma. Do you call that being a student?

Clemencia Zaldívar de Iglesias, mother of a family

I hate students because *I* hated being one. . . . I dropped out of the University because I wasn't learning one single thing. The profs didn't come to class, we were as crowded as sardines in the lecture halls, a kid who sat next to me taking notes made so many spelling mistakes I felt like socking him one. "Clear the hell out of here!" I felt like telling him. "What the devil do you think you're doing here anyway?"

Antonio Mereles Zamorano,
former medical student

The attack on the Santo Tomás campus on Tuesday, September 24, didn't catch us completely unprepared, as the students at UNAM had been, because we had long since taken certain precautions. We'd stored up Molotov cocktails, zip guns, sticks and stones, fire-crackers, skyrockets—we really had a big supply of Molotov cock-tails on hand, and we shot the skyrockets off through a kind of blowpipe, a hollow reed or a long tube—like a sort of bazooka, do you know what I mean? They didn't hurt anybody—they were quite harmless—but they *did* explode with a loud bang and really disconcerted the *granaderos;* for several hours these "bazookas" scared the hell out of them. We were able to make them keep their distance—till the Army arrived anyway. The confrontation with the *granaderos* began around six p.m. and lasted till nightfall, when the

Army troops appeared on the scene. The mounted police arrived, equipped with firearms, and shortly afterward we heard them shooting at the buildings. They threw tear-gas grenades at the buildings of the housing unit nearby, and men, women, and children began pouring out of them, scared half to death. What possible harm had those people done?—they were mere innocent victims. The most dramatic thing that happened, and the thing that shocked us the most, was when the *granaderos* occupied the medical school, shortly after we'd brought our wounded there. "Things are really hot around here tonight!" a kid shouted to me as he ran by.

Félix Lucio Hernández Gamundi, of the CNH

Students aren't worth a damn. When the government represses them, they retaliate by yelling and throwing stones. They do lots of shouting every time, but that's all. What's needed are firearms.

Cleofas Magdaleno Pantojo Segura,
peasant from Míxquic

The students are right, but they make it hard for us when they burn buses, because then we have to walk to work.

Guillermo Puga Quiroz, worker at the
Ayotla Textile Factory

Setting buses on fire has long been a tradition during student rebellions. It's a way of defying the government, a way of screwing it.

Ernesto Ramírez Rubio, student at ESIME, IPN

We take over the buses because they're the only thing handy. . . . What's more, buses don't belong to the people; they belong to the bus companies.

Eduardo Razo Velázquez, student, Vocational 9

On September 25, after the mounted police had occupied Vocational 7, a peasant dressed in country clothes appeared with four slingshots and handed them out to some of us students there along Manuel González. Then he stood there in the street, showing a bunch of us how to make more slingshots and how to use them, and the kids all began practicing shooting them. That same day, the twenty-fifth, we planned a demonstration for that afternoon, a march from the Peralvillo traffic circle to the Zócalo. Once we'd organized it, we began marching and were attacked by the *grana-deros* before we'd gone a hundred yards. Then the students with slingshots fell back and started using them for the first time. The peasant was the best shot. We saw four *granaderos* who had nabbed a girl student and were holding her prisoner up on top of one of their buses. The peasant started shooting at them with his sling-shot, and hit all four of them, one after the other. One of the kids from Preparatory 3 got hit with a tear-gas grenade that broke his jaw. When we saw what had happened to him, we began fighting hand to hand with the *granaderos,* because we had them outnum-bered five to one, but when we went for them, they fought back with truncheons, so we fell back, and the tenants in the Tlatelolco housing unit nearby started throwing things at the cops from the windows of one of the buildings: water, burning rags, garbage, and what have you. We ran to Vocational 7, but since the mounted police had occupied it by that time, we had to take refuge on the bridge next to Vocational 7.

Fernando Obregón Elizondo,
student at ESIQIE, IPN

I didn't get any kind of a formal education because my folks couldn't afford to send me to school. But if education nowadays is the sort that produces students like that, I'm glad I didn't go to school. I've never in my life seen such disrespectful, vulgar, foul-tongued people.

José Álvarez Castaneda, peso-a-ride
jitney driver along the Diana-Reforma route

Being a student nowadays is a synonym for stirring up trouble.

Trini, dressmaker

I always give them a "fat contribution" when they ask me for money. I like seeing their fresh young faces at my car window. I give them a peso, three pesos, any loose change I have. . . . Stu-dents at least are better-looking, more friendly and outgoing than those guys pestering you for a tip to watch your car.

Marta Zamudio, beauty operator

One night when we were standing guard duty at Vocational 7, we heard some cars screeching to a stop and stuck our heads out the window to see what was going on. Five cars in all drew up, and out climbed a bunch of kids about nineteen or twenty years old, armed with submachine guns. Then they started spraying the whole building with bullets—the outside walls, the auditorium, the classroom windows. We have a hunch those kids were from MURO.

Mario Méndez López, student at ESIME, IPN

It's a great life, kid.

*Salvador Martínez de la Roca (Pino),
of the Action Committee, UNAM*

A policeman climbed up on the platform to speak at a meeting in Atzcapotzalco; he said he was a decent person, took his uniform off, and stamped on it, and then asked us for money to go back to the part of the country he came from. He was so angry that tears were streaming down his face.

*Julián Acevedo Maldonado, student
at the Faculty of Law, UNAM*

On September 23, three people arrived during the night in a car with no license plates; two of them spoke no Spanish. They introduced themselves as news cameramen from the French national television network and asked permission to film the state that Vocational 7 had been left in. We talked with them, and the Action Committee told them to go ahead. They shot footage of the wreckage in the school workshops, the smashed lathes, the broken windows, the damage done, the bullet holes in the walls, the bloodstains. They filmed everything, and gave us a thousand pesos for the Movement.

Alejandro Macedo Ortiz, student at ESIME, IPN

I never walk directly past a vocational school; I go four blocks out of my way so I don't have to. I'm fifty years old; I've been a librarian for thirty years. One night, just for the fun of it, a gang of boys attacked me and ripped off half my clothes. Students are savages! They think they own the entire city; they've gotten it into their

heads that they can do whatever they please, without fear of
punishment.

Margarita Mondada Lara, librarian

We knew that the police got gangs of roughnecks and bullies to
commit outrages against the people, pretending they were members
of the Movement and shouting "Hurray for students!" In Coyoacán,
a notorious gang of good-for-nothings, "Los Conchos," burned
buses and manhandled the passengers and drivers. They wrecked
stores and molested people on the streets, supposedly in the name
of the Movement, but they hardly fooled anybody. . . . Why? Because that wasn't the first time the police had resorted to such tactics, and people realized what they were up to. What's more, even
people who thought it was students who were responsible for such
outrages regarded these incidents as more or less justifiable excesses: the vile language and the intrigues against the University in
the Chamber of Deputies were bound at that point to be met with a
certain amount of violence on the part of students. In general, however, people could easily tell the difference between acts by more or
less rebellious students and the outright provocations and the attempts to blacken the Movement's name plotted by the police.

Gilberto Guevara Niebla, of the CNH

HEY, PEOPLE, OPEN YOUR EYES!
Sign posted in the Faculty of Sciences, UNAM

They stoned my window and shattered it to bits, but I'm not certain
to this day whether it was students or policemen disguised as
students.

Marcelo Salcedo Peña, shopkeeper

University students are the future solid middle class of the Mexican
Republic. So what reason do they have to be doing all this?

Pedro Magaña Acuña, owner of a restaurant

The violence spread throughout the entire city. The repressive measures that were taken created a backlash against those responsible

for them: the police. The government had caught fire, and the
flames were spreading.

Luis González de Alba, of the CNH

JUÁREZ, WHAT SHOULD WE DO NOW?
Signed posted in the Faculty of Sciences, UNAM

WE MUST HATE, WITH REVOLUTIONARY LOVE
Che Guevara, as quoted on a sign posted in the
Faculty of Political Sciences, UNAM

LIVERTAD FOR POLITICAL PRISONERS
Misspelled slogan, daubed on a wall on the
Avenida Capilco

We were having to shut up shop earlier and earlier every day, and
it was the students who were to blame.

Everardo López Sánchez, grocer

Who did those kids think they were, anyway? The first thing I'd ask
them would be to show their semester grades.

Yolanda Carreño Santillán, cashier,
El Fénix Pharmacy

It's the mini-skirt that's to blame.

Leopoldo García Trejo, postal clerk

The students—particularly certain groups of kids from the University high schools and the vocational schools—often scandalized
people, both by their rowdiness on public buses and by their un-
justifiably bad behavior toward people on the streets around their
schools. Many people in Mexico City were only too well aware of
the touchy, disrespectful, and in many cases downright aggressive
behavior of certain groups of students. These youngsters were

warned on several occasions in the newspapers that the police could not be expected to tolerate indefinitely disturbances and attacks on citizens on the streets and aboard public conveyances. We must keep in mind, for example, the fact that there were a number of confrontations between different high schools in Tacubaya that had resulted in fisticuffs and stone-throwing. If the police failed to intervene in these fights, they were criticized by the public; if they did intervene, they were criticized by the students. Aside from the question of whether the police should or should not be condemned for intervening in fights among students that took place in the Ciudadela district, it was inevitable that sooner or later these battles among groups of students would result in such unfortunate incidents as those that took place in the last two weeks of July 1968. All this in no way means that I condone what happened at Tlatelolco on October 2. . . . A child or a teen-ager who badly misbehaves rightly deserves to be reprimanded, and even punished severely, but even so you shouldn't bash in your ten-year-old son's head with a chair or beat him to death simply because the kid has given you a kick in the pants in a fit of anger or hysteria.

Marcos Valadez Capistrán, civil engineer and
teacher at José Vasconcelos Preparatory School

Marili had just given me a nice big poster of Che Guevara as a present—you dig? But she must have really been plastered when she gave it to me, because she'd been offered two hundred dollars for it, I discovered later—it was a fantastic photo, and a neat present. . . .

So I hung it up on the wall of my room above my bed, and later my mom comes home and says, "Listen, Macarela, please go to the supermarket with me—I've got lots of things to buy and I need you to help me"—you dig?

And I said to her, "No, Mom, I can't, because I haven't said my prayers to Che yet. . . ."

"What in the world are you talking about?" she said.

I was just kidding, of course, you know, just pulling her leg a little. Besides, I was already undressed and in my pajamas. . . .

Then she comes in my room and spies the picture of Che there on the wall: "Oh," she says, "that's really disgusting! You've hung a picture of that filthy man where there ought to be a saint's picture!

Darling, please, please, I beg you—take it down and hang a nice saint's picture there!"

"Listen, Mom," I said to her, "I've never asked you to take down the saints' pictures you have over *your* bed—you know, those guys who look as though they never heard of marijuana and were real pansies. *Your* saints have awful faces, Mama—but I haven't said one word about them, and all I'm asking you is to respect *my* nice little saint. . . ."

"Oh, I couldn't possibly!" she says. "He'll bring you bad luck—I'm certain of it. *Please* take him down—he turns my stomach, he's really ugly-looking! And I'm quite sure he's got lice in that beard of his. . . ."

So you see? My mom's really far gone. She's not a monster at all really—she's just absolutely typical of most middle-class moms, unfortunately. She's dead set against communism. When I talked with her about the Student Movement and the whole student bit, she must have imagined all kinds of things, because she said to me, "Why don't they send the whole lot of them to Moscow to worship the Devil himself?" Simple, uneducated people don't have the least idea what communism stands for, or even that a place like Moscow even exists. My mom's typically middle-class though. When she found out that I'd been there at Tlatelolco, for instance, she said to me, "Yes, I know you through and through: I wouldn't put it past you to get yourself killed just to make me so mad I'd go to my grave. . . ." She's terribly set in her ways—you know what I mean? And when my sister talked to me about the Movement, she said to me, "Listen, Margarita, I want to talk to you about all that business—I know you're involved in the Movement and all that. Tell me about it, *please*. It seems to me it's a leftist movement, is that right?" But that's how it is—they think they know everything, that they've caught me red-handed—you know? The way my mom and my sis think is typical of the way almost everybody thinks.

Margarita Isabel, actress

In general, most people—or at any rate the people I have any contact with—approved of the students' six demands. But I must confess that we were surprised that the students never talked about academic problems, about their families' reaction when they saw the bad grades their kids were getting in school, about the total lack of self-criticism on the part of students, their lack of discipline and their failure to really buckle down and study, which in my opinion have been typical of students for many years now.

Manuel Lozano Heredia, teacher, Preparatory 2

Several students collecting money for the Student Movement beat up Antonio de la Concha Valdez, a twenty-year-old office boy, who suffered serious injuries. As the victim explained it, they beat him up because he gave them only one peso, even though he had more money in his wallet. The Red Cross picked him up as he lay in the street on San Idelfonso, in front of the Hotel Coloso.

Saturday, August 24, 1968, as recounted
in Revista de la Universidad

MURO, a Fascist group influenced by the CIA, specializes in armed attacks. . . . Several thousand students belong to it; they commit crimes without fear of punishment, and hide behind the name of UNAM.

Gilberto Guevara Niebla, of the CNH

At a "lightning meeting" once, one of the girl students, María Elena Andrade, began to tell the crowd that had gathered about the continual repression by the government and mentioned how the soldiers were killing students, because this was after the attack on the Santo Tomás campus. A woman carrying a grocery sack in her arm and holding a little boy by the hand, who had been standing there listening with a pained expression on her face, suddenly got very angry and interrupted María Elena.

"The Army was called up and I haven't seen my husband for two whole weeks, all on account of you students. . . . The soldiers have had to leave their families and are living in Army barracks, all because of you. And I can assure you, *señorita*, that my husband isn't a murderer. He's a soldier, but he's not a murderer. God forbid! He loves his own children dearly, so he'd never kill other youngsters."

This woman was pregnant. She tugged at María Elena's arm and said, "You can say what you please, but my husband wouldn't hurt a soul. I'm certain of that—I've known him a long long time and he's a decent man. . . . We may be poor, but we're decent people.

And now you're going to stand here in the market and scream out just the opposite of what you said before; you're going to say that soldiers are decent people, that my husband hasn't killed anybody, because I'm his wife and can guarantee that he hasn't. If you want to say that my husband's killed somebody, go right ahead, but I want you to say it right to my face. We'll settle the question once and for all, just between the two of us—and you'd better watch out!"

"Listen, *señora*, I'd like to invite you to come have a bowl of soup. . . ."

"No, I don't want your soup. These ladies here are neighbors of mine, they'll watch my little boy for me, and the two of us will fight it out, right here and now!"

"*Señora*, please—get hold of yourself!"

A fat chance there was of that! María Elena, a psych major no less, had to take to her heels, because the soldier's wife's friends started screaming insults at her and she was scared half out of her wits.

> *María Alicia Martínez Medrano,*
> *nursery-school director*

The PRI doesn't go in for dialogues, just monologues.

> *Jan Poniatowski Amor, student,*
> *Antonio Caso Preparatory School*

As I lay on the floor in the corridor there where I slept at CU, I could hear the sound of the mimeograph machines cranking out handbills all night long.

> *Luis González de Alba, of the CNH*

Lots of the kids didn't really dig what the Movement was all about and used it as a way of airing their own personal problems. They were a bunch of crappy kindergarten revolutionaries. . . . They thought the Movement meant revolution, but in fact it was petty-bourgeois from the very start.

> *Salvador Martínez de la Roca (Pino), of the*
> *Action Committee, UNAM*

In the Tlatelolco housing unit, a sort of popular movement sprang up among the fathers and mothers and teen-agers, and even little kids six, seven, eight, nine years old, who began playing a new game—marching around with wooden rifles or broomsticks over their shoulders, and parading past the *granaderos* and the soldiers on duty there in the unit in case there was trouble, even before October 2. After the battles between the students and the police, they kept very close watch on us. The kids would go up on the roofs of the buildings or shout down from their windows, "You stupid cops!" and the grownups would chime in and yell, "Murderers!" Many of the kids took an active part in the first meetings.

Lorenza González Soto, tenant,
Tlatelolco housing unit

We've already seen kids ten, eleven, twelve years old who know very well what fighting for the people's freedom means. I remember very well, for instance, the Carlos Marx mini-brigade at the National School of Economics, consisting of one young girl and four teen-age girl students from the College of Madrid, all of them incredible kids: exuberant, brave, determined—some of the finest kids in their school.

I think the Movement made such a deep impression on young kids that if there's any hope at all for this country's future, it's because there is such an immense number of young people here in Mexico. The possibilities of a real revolution lie with the kids of various ages who stood on the sidewalks watching the demonstrations, seeing their older brothers and sisters march by, holding their parents' hands at Movement meetings, those who have heard stories of the days of terror, or somehow felt them in their very bones. The government of this country ought to be wary of kids who were ten or twelve or fifteen in 1968. However much they're brainwashed, however they're drugged, deep down they'll remember for the rest of their lives the clubbings and the murders their older brothers and sisters were the victims of. . . . Despite the government's every effort to make them forget, they will remember that as kids they witnessed the ignominy of clubbings, tear-gas grenades, and bullets.

Eduardo Valle Espinoza (Owl-Eyes),
of the CNH

At about three in the afternoon on September 3, six buses full of *granaderos*—three hundred of them—pulled up at Vocational 7 to occupy the school. All the brigades out working in Tlatelolco rushed back to Vocational to defend it. The women in the housing unit brought us stockings to make slingshots with. The *granaderos* started throwing tear-gas grenades, and my brigade, plus about fifty other kids, left Vocational by another exit, sneaked around the back of the school and attacked the *granaderos* from behind. Then we ran down the street to the corner of Manuel González, just as four buses full of students from Vocational 9, including the entire football team, drove by. The *granaderos* at that point were equipped only with truncheons, razors, shields, riot helmets, nightsticks, and tear-gas launchers. When the kids on the buses saw that we were having a run-in with the police, they scrambled out to give us a hand, and the football team, still in uniform, started tackling the cops. We gave all the *granaderos* a really rough time. Every time we lit into one of them, he'd say apologetically, "We're not the ones to blame! We have to obey orders if we want to keep our jobs!" We took their weapons away from them and commandeered all their equipment. We stripped ten of them down to their undershorts. They looked real cute! Nine of the kids who joined in the fight got clubbed very badly. . . . We let the *granaderos* go and went back to Vocational 7. We weren't able to steal the riot-squad buses because they'd already taken them away. A whole bunch of women from the housing unit made supper for all of us in the cafeteria kitchen at Vocational 7.

Antonio Careaga, clothing vendor

Just think what would have happened if the Tlatelolco housing unit had become a well-organized revolutionary nucleus, a sort of center of urban guerrilla activities! We didn't have the means available to organize one, but perhaps the government thought we did and decided to put a stop to it. The authorities were well aware that the people had started taking active part in the Movement—not just a group of students who had been in the same class or worked together, such as the ones at UNAM or Poli for instance, but working-class people in Mexico City who had banded together to support a student movement. I maintain that it was for that very reason that the authorities chose Tlatelolco as the place to stamp out the

Movement once and for all. It was stupid of us to fall into that very clever trap of theirs, because after October 2, what with the apprehension on the part of students, the terror, and the repression, the Movement naturally lost ground and the brigades completely lost touch with each other. The rank-and-file members of the Student Movement have never again fought as hard as they did before Tlatelolco.

Mercedes Olivera de Vázquez, anthropologist

The most shameful thing about the Tlatelolco massacre is that young people are scared now.

Elvira B. de Concheiro, mother of a family

After a number of very encouraging experiences, after people began feeling that it was possible to have some influence politically, to discuss the measures to be taken, to participate in the decision-making process, to realize that they could actually shape events rather than just passively accepting them as though they were thunderbolts from the blue, October 2 came as a cruel blow, and there was a tremendous feeling of helplessness, of defeat. But in the final analysis, even with all the deaths and the savagery and the terror, the Movement must be entered on the credit side of the ledger, for people have begun to face the fact that *everything* is political, and even though circumstances at present do not permit any overt political activity, there are still many people working to change things.

Carolina Pérez Cicero, student at the
Faculty of Philosophy and Letters, UNAM

Women were responsible for much of the Movement's fighting spirit. I remember lots of the girl comrades: Mirta, from the Wilfredo Massieu School; Tita and Nacha from Law; Bertha from Medicine; Mari Carmen, Evelia, and Betty from Sciences; Consuelito, Maravilia, and Adriana from Preparatory; Marcia, of course—and thousands of others, literally thousands more, and as groups the marvelous girls from the School of Nursing at Poli, the ones from Biological Sciences, from the med school at UNAM, and so on.

The girl comrades from the School of Nursing were real heroines during the attack on the Santo Tomás campus. They did the whole

Adelita bit spontaneously, straight from the heart. They willingly risked their lives to care for our wounded, help get them off the campus, and attend to their every need. Because of their courage and their loyalty to the cause all our women comrades came to play a very important role in the Movement.

The girl students once phoned us that right-wing student groups had taken over a University high school. We immediately rounded up a whole bunch of students to go see what was happening. I saw four girls from my school get on the bus from Economics. "You girls get out of there this minute. We men are the only ones who are going this time," I told them.

They were highly indignant, and immediately replied that Che [Guevara] allowed women to fight in *his* brigade, and the hell with me. I insisted, and thought they'd finally agreed to get off the bus. I went back inside for a moment and then climbed back on the bus, and we started off. Some three hundred of us men students arrived at the high school—plus the four girl students sitting way at the back of the bus from Economics, where I wasn't likely to spot them. Luckily nothing happened there at the high school, and we all got back safe and sound to CU.

In the last speech of the day at the Silent Demonstration, I said something I really regret now. It was a bad mistake, and what's more, entirely unfair of me, to have said at one point in my speech, "Let us not shed tears like women for what we were unable to defend like men." The day after the demonstration, when I got back to my school, I found two brigades of girls waiting there for me. I spent several hours trying to explain, amid angry shouts and quite justifiable protests on their part, that what I had said had merely been a figure of speech. They finally were kind enough to accept my apology, and two days later they brought me a delicious cake, which those of us in the brigade on guard and other comrades devoured on the spot.

> *Eduardo Valle Espinoza*
> *(Owl-Eyes), of the CNH*

At one demonstration where we were surrounded by a huge bunch of *granaderos* and Army troops, the kids were beside themselves—you know?—because there were twenty of them for every one of us, or almost that many anyway. What's more, the riot squad

hadn't appeared on the scene in their usual dark-blue buses—
they'd come in ordinary city buses. As I remember, the meeting
was supposed to be in the auditorium of the Cultural Unit in Chapultepec Park. When the kids saw that they weren't going to be
able to hold their meeting because there were cops and troops all
over the place, they passed the word along: "Let's all go out to CU.
. . . All of you head out to CU and we'll have a meeting out there.
. . . Hitch rides out to CU, everybody." I had my car, and only one
passenger, Marili, with me, so naturally the kids asked us for a ride
out there.

"Listen, take us out to CU and then come back for another load,
okay?"

"Sure, hop in!" I said.

As I was picking up my fourth load of kids, as I remember, back
at the park, they said to us, "Step on it, will you? We've just heard
that Army troops are heading for CU."

"Not again!"

"That's the rumor that's going around."

So I said, "Control tower! Clear for immediate emergency take-
off!" I was barreling down Insurgentes Norte—we were already almost to San Ángel—and a bus in front of me was blocking the street
and refused to let me by. I honked and honked—you know what I
mean?—but the bus driver wouldn't move over and let me past. I
was so furious at being boxed in that way that I really leaned on the
horn. And all the passengers on the bus poked their heads out the
window to see what all that racket was about—and it turned out to
be a bus full of *granaderos*, can you imagine! We were so scared we
made a sharp U-turn right in the middle of the street, I swear, but
then we couldn't decide whether to turn off to the right or to the
left. Everybody was screaming at me at once, all telling me different
ways to go, and to make a long story short, I turned down a narrow
little street by the Club France and eventually ended up at the University. That was the last trip I made out there though, because I'd
had such a scare I almost had heart failure. We stayed out there at
CU then and went to the Philosophy meeting. Oh, listen, I almost
forgot to tell you one part—on one trip from Chapultepec out to CU,
the second one as I remember, I run out of gas and the kids I've
picked up say to me, "Don't worry, *señorita*, we'll solve your little
problem in a jiffy."

They get out and stop a big fancy car passing by and say to the driver, a terribly distinguished-looking gentleman in his fifties, with gray hair, "Hey, buddy! Park over there for a minute." (I think the guy might have been Agustín Legorreta.*)

"Oh, no, please! You've no reason to pick on me. I haven't done anything to you kids! I'm all for you students, a hundred per cent!" (Or maybe it was Juan Sánchez Navarro.*)

"No, no, you've got us all wrong—we aren't going to do a thing to you . . . just park over there for a minute," the kids answer. The kids come up with a siphon—heaven only knows where they found one—and drain every last drop of gas out of the man's tank into mine, leaving the poor guy stranded there.

Oh, those kids were so *beautiful!*

Margarita Isabel, actress

What kind of jobs do students get once they have their diplomas? Where do those kids from UNAM, from Poli, end up after they've graduated? In private companies or in the government. Isn't that what happens to most of them? So why were those students making all those demands and holding all those demonstrations? What were they doing all that for anyway? What's the point if sooner or later they're going to be part of the Establishment that they're fighting?

Heriberto Alarcón Pimentel, industrialist

No middle-class woman dares defy the smallest social unit of all: her own family. So how can she be expected to challenge great institutions?

Elías Padilla Ruvalcaba, sociologist

I believe that regardless of what happens, sooner or later they're all going to join the PRI anyway. . . . So why are they making all this fuss?

Gonzalo Carranza Rojo, owner of a garage

Most of the girls studying at the Faculty of Philosophy and Letters come from petty-bourgeois families. . . . They're girls who've

---

* Legorreta and Navarro: famous bankers, supposedly two of Mexico's richest men. (Translator's note.)

never had to worry about money, and are studying at the University the way they might take painting lessons or dabble in art history. Culture is simply a nice hobby to them. But during the Movement many of them who live in the fanciest neighborhoods—Pedregal, Las Lomas, Polanco—gave money, took part in demonstrations, passed out handbills on the streets, and lots of the students, both boys and girls, from *nouveau-riche* families enrolled at the Faculty of Philosophy and Letters—because that's one of the most *nouveau-riche* schools at the University—painted slogans on walls and worked just as hard as the others. After August, when the members of the CNH and others decided to stay at CU round the clock, the girls brought them food and clothes, and used their own cars to transport huge quantities of leaflets and big heavy piles of paper for the mimeograph machines. Since there was lots of talk about politics going on, they got a different view of the relations between the haves and the have-nots. The Movement politicized many people. Ibero, which is full of middle-class snobs, also painted slogans, distributed handbills, and attended demonstrations, despite the clubbings. I think the Student Movement did us all lots of good.

Carolina Pérez Cicero, student at the
Faculty of Philosophy and Letters, UNAM

How many of the girls who demonstrated in the streets have fought a revolution in their own minds and hearts? How many of them have said to their parents: "Mom, Dad, I'd like you to meet my lover"? How many, I ask you? What exactly does freedom mean to them? Tell me, why haven't they demonstrated against their own prejudices?

Parménides García Saldaña, "new wave" writer

The political problem had an immediate effect on our personal lives. There were daughters who fought with their fathers; married couples split up, but on the other hand there were also lots of wedding announcements; we weighed all our past lives in the balance and everyone suddenly had an entirely different outlook, a different way of confronting his or her basic problems. In those days I was married to Roberto Escudero, the CNH delegate from the Faculty of Philosophy and Letters; we were expecting a baby, and the Movement changed our whole lives.

Carolina Pérez Cicero, student at the
Faculty of Philosophy and Letters, UNAM

The teachers were the most moderate group in the entire Movement, but in it were men such as Heberto Castillo, who was regarded as one of the best engineers in Mexico and a professor whom the students greatly respected; Dr. Eli de Gortari, author of *La Lógica Dialéctica [Dialectical Logic],* a textbook used in every university in Latin America, and a number of other books which have earned him an international reputation and great prestige among professional philosophers, and also the author of the *Problemas Científicos y Filosóficos [Scientific and Philosophical Problems]* series published by UNAM; José Revueltas, the famous writer, one of the purest souls in all of Mexico, in the words of Octavio Paz; Manuel Marcué Pardiñas, editor of the review *Problemas Agrícolas e Industriales [Agricultural and Industrial Problems]* and founder and editor of *Política [Politics],* a periodical that for a number of years had consistently opposed the government; and Dr. Fausto Trejo, a professor of psychology whom the students were very fond of. Men such as these gave the Movement prestige and moral authority. . . . They supported the students, but they did their best to keep them from acting on impulse, to slow down the *acelerados.*

Ana Márquez de Nava, instructor
at a normal school

During demonstrations, we called out the number of students who had been killed thus far—those at the vocational schools and at Preparatory 3—counting as we marched along: one, two, three, four, five, six . . . and so on, up to twenty-five or thirty, and at the end we yelled, "Who killed them? . . . Díaz Ordaaaaaz!"

Ana Ignacia Rodríguez (Nacha),
of the Action Committee, UNAM

Once around three in the morning I was famished and went out to a sandwich shop three blocks from where I lived, see, and ordered a couple of sandwiches. A woman came in just then and said, "Guess what! I just saw the police haul in a bunch of students. . . . I hope the *granaderos* will put a stop to all this soon, because I worry every

HO-HO-HO-CHI-MINH, DÍAZ ORDAZ, CHIN-CHIN-
CHIN, HO-HO-HO-CHI-MINH, DIAZ ORDAZ, CHIN
Chant at the August 1 demonstration

COME OUT ON THE BALCONY, LOUDMOUTH,
WHERE'S YOUR OUTSTRETCHED HAND?
*Student chant led by the CNH delegates from the
Action Committee of the Faculty of Law, UNAM*

*When every granadero
learns to read and write
Mexico will be a better,
more prosperous, and happier country.*
*Song sung by students during
the August 27 demonstration*

GET YOUR CORONA DEL ROSAL HERE: BOTTLED! *
Student chant

DÍAZ ORDAZ IS A DUMB OX; DÍAZ ORDAZ IS A
DUMB OX; DUMB OX, DUMB OX, DUMB OX!
Chant at the August 27 demonstration

GIVE THE YANKS HELL, FIDEL—GIVE THE YANKS
HELL, FIDEL—GIVE THE YANKS HELL, FIDEL—
Student chant outside American Embassy

* A pun: Corona is a popular brand of Mexican beer, and Corona del Rosal the name of the Regent of Mexico City, whose dismissal the students were demanding. Student songs and chants at demonstrations were often parodies of radio or television commercials. (Translator's note.)

time my girls leave the house, what with all the trouble those awful students are causing, chasing around like that!"

I thought to myself, Yeah, they're sure as hell chasing around all right, but it's not your daughters they're chasing after, if they look anything like you, you old bag. And then I started talking back to her, you dig?—but the woman told me to go to hell, grabbed her sandwiches, and left. But the guy behind the counter didn't like what I'd said at all and stood there defending the woman and the virtue of young virgins. I said to myself, Well then, I guess I ought to convert a counterman or two too! Wouldn't a brigade of sandwich-makers be great though! So I stood there bending his ear about the Movement, and all of a sudden I noticed that two men at a nearby table were listening closely to every word I said, so attentively in fact that I got nervous. So then I said to myself, I'd better pay up and split this scene, but as I was handing the counterman my money, the two of them rushed out in a big hurry, and as I went out the door I spotted them hanging around outside, apparently waiting for me.

I thought to myself, Maybe they think I'm a whore hanging around to make a pickup, and I lit out for home, with the two of them right at my heels. They didn't try to pick me up or anything—they didn't hand me any of that stuff like, "What say we drop up to your place for a while, *señorita?*" or "Hey, you're certainly a hot-looking number," or anything like that. They just kept following me, and when I started running they began running, when I stopped they stopped, and when I walked slowly they walked slowly—you know?—hoping I wouldn't notice, see? When I got to the corner, I ran down the street to my building as fast as my two legs would carry me, dashed up the stairs to my apartment, and locked myself in! About five seconds later, I heard the downstairs door open, but those two dumb bastards never dreamed they'd be confronted with so many apartments inside my building—from outside it looks as though there are only two or three of them, but once you're inside it's a labyrinth, like in an Antonioni film—you know?—a real maze, with forty apartments or so, and you go out of your mind if you don't know your way around. They knocked at the door of one apartment and nobody answered, and then another, and somebody inside threw a shoe at the door because it was two in the morning, see. They knocked at several more doors, and all they got for their trouble was a lot of angry shouts and go-to-bloody-hells, and finally they gave up and went away, you dig? But it was some scare, believe me, in the middle of the night like that! What bad vibes! Things were going to be tough.

Margarita Isabel, actress

The second time they nabbed me was on October 6, in an apartment near the office of the Department of Highways and Public Works—a friend of mine who's a doctor and his wife had offered to let me stay there with them. That's where the cops arrested me, there at their place, without any kind of warrant, and said that the chief of police, Cueto, wanted to talk to me. They took me to the headquarters of the secret police; I was scared stiff, and on the way there the one question I kept asking them was "Where are my friends?" and their only answer was "Shut your trap," plus a hard slap in the face. I was twenty-two at the time; I'd already passed my law-school exams and was writing my thesis. I was also attending a sociology seminar.

When I got to police headquarters, there were my two friends, the doctor and his wife. The minute I arrived, the cops there asked them, "Is that Nacha?"

"Yes, that's her," they replied.

They let the two of them go then, and I saw Cueto and Mendiolea standing there. They took me into Cueto's office, and he said to me, "So you're the famous Nacha, are you?"

"My nickname's Nacha, all right, but I'm not famous," I replied.

I spent seven days in solitary then, the very worst experience I've ever been through in my whole life, because I had no contact with anybody. A comrade in another cell somewhere, a girl I never did lay eyes on, shouted to me, "Don't let them take you anywhere during the night, because those bastards tell you they're coming to release you, but they take you somewhere and rape you!" I was so afraid they'd come for me I couldn't sleep at night. They left me there in solitary for three days, and on the fourth day they began interrogating me.

Ana Ignacia Rodríguez (Nacha), of the
Action Committee, UNAM

It was just past eleven when we got back to the apartment house where we lived. The downstairs door was open, and I remarked to Eli that we ought to complain to the owner about it being open, because our apartment had already been ransacked once. Our two-year-old daughter, Ana, went inside first, then me, then Eli. Ana started up the stairs, and met a man sitting there, and as the two of us came up the stairs after her, the man said to Eli, "Good evening, sir."

"Good evening," Eli answered.

But then the man grabbed Eli by the arm and said, "All right, sir, you're to come with me."

"Whatever for?" I said to the man. "Where are you taking him?"

The man didn't answer one word. He just twisted Eli's arm and pushed him toward the door. (Those people are very well trained; they can nab you before you know what's happening, at any hour of the day or night.) In no time at all he'd shoved Eli downstairs to the door of our apartment house, and at that moment another guy suddenly appeared out of nowhere, and between the two of them they grabbed Eli from behind by the belt and started carrying him away bodily, without his toes even touching the pavement. Since they hadn't shown any sort of badge or said where they were taking him or anything, I began screaming for help. I had an umbrella in my hand, and at that point I was so upset that I hit one of them over the head with it and broke it. The man let go of Eli then, and grabbed me and threw me against the wall. When my little girl saw me lying there on the ground, she ran to her daddy, and the other guy grabbed her and threw her to the pavement. The first thought that crossed my mind was, He's bashed her head in! I started screaming like crazy then, and suddenly a Ford Galaxie that I hadn't noticed before drew up. I thought it was somebody coming to my rescue, but several men got out—three of them as I remember, or perhaps four. They left the car doors open and in no more than a couple of seconds, I swear, they'd dragged Eli into the car and started off. I heard him shout, "Get word to our friends what's hap-pened!" as the driver put his foot to the floor and the car roared off down Ejército Nacional. I ran after it trying to catch up with it—fool that I was!—and I saw people's heads pop out of several windows, but nobody came down to help. A man came out of one of the doors along the street just then and said, "Hey, lady, look what's hap-

pened to your little girl!" I remembered then that I'd left Ana lying
there on the pavement, and went back. . . . The car was miles
away by that time. . . . Some neighbors of ours helped me pick up
Ana, the papers in Eli's briefcase that were scattered all over, and
the clean laundry I'd been carrying. One of the neighbor ladies took
me to her apartment, and since I was weeping uncontrollably, she
gave me a tranquilizer. I remembered to phone friends of ours, a
married couple, and can still remember to this day that all I could
say was, "They've taken him away! They've taken him away!
They've taken him away!"

The husband said to me over the phone, "Stay right there in your
apartment. Don't set your foot out the door. We'll be there right
away."

My neighbor lady helped me carry my little girl and the other
things upstairs to our apartment. I turned all the lights on and
opened all the windows. I went out on the balcony and was suddenly tempted to leap off it. I felt all alone in the world, and had no
idea what had happened, or why. Ana clung to my skirt, in tears,
and I think that was what made me pull myself together: I was two
months pregnant at the time. So I stood out there on the balcony till
our friends arrived: I didn't want to wait inside for them for some
reason. When I heard the bell downstairs ring, I left Ana alone there
in the apartment and went down to let them in. We went upstairs,
and I couldn't get one word out. I was unable to explain what had
happened: all I could say was, "They've taken him away!" over and
over. They made me coffee, and sent word of what had happened to
our older children, who were at the Chapultepec cinema. They
rushed home immediately, came in the door and gave me a big
hug, and all they could say was, "What are we going to do?"

Eli has been in prison since September 18, 1968.

                    Artemisa de Gortari, mother of a family

At that point, none of the members of the various Action Committees had been arrested yet, and of the two hundred CNH delegates,
only two comrades were in jail, because somebody had turned them
in to the police. Around nine o'clock on the night of September 25,
one of the delegates from the School of Economics at Poli, Luis
Jorge Peña, was in an apartment that a friend had offered to share
with him "if he should happen to need a place to stay some time."

Ayax Segura Garrido, whom nobody ever really trusted, was supposed to meet Peña there at six that night, but when there was no sign of him, Peña began to worry. Around seven or so, he decided to clear out of the apartment, but since Peña, like almost all the other members of the CNH, had never gone underground and lived the sort of life that requires absolute secrecy and automatic mistrust of anybody and everybody, he didn't light out of there soon enough. The naïveté of many of us can be explained only by the fact that we had never really believed that the government would make it necessary to take such precautions. We were simply not used to having to be that careful. At nine o'clock, Peña was still there in the apartment, worried to death, with nobody to keep him company but a fifteen-year-old kid, the brother of the guy whose apartment it was. There was a knock at the door finally, but Peña was suspicious and only opened it a crack, but suddenly fifteen men armed with submachine guns forced their way in.

When they saw that the only people there in the apartment were two kids, one fifteen and one twenty-one, they asked them, "Okay, where's Jorge Peña?"

It never entered their heads that either of those two youngsters was Peña. They were searching for a dangerous political agitator, and the only people there in the apartment were a fifteen-year-old kid and another young kid with glasses who looked to be still in his teens. Neither of them could possibly be the dangerous character who was funneling money and weapons to the CNH. The intruders began roughing them up then and emptying boxes of books on the floor. They tore the whole place apart looking for weapons.

"Hands up, you!" they said then, and on searching the two of them and going through their pockets, they discovered Peña's driver's license, and realized they'd nabbed the man they were looking for.

Among the books scattered all over the floor was one by Che [Guevara].

"So you've got books by Che, have you? How come you're reading them?" they asked.

"They're assigned reading at school. I'm a poli sci student at the University."

Apparently the cops didn't know that books by Che—and Marx and Lenin and Trotsky and all the rest—can be bought in any bookstore in the city. One volume with a red cover caught another cop's eye, and he grabbed it up off the floor and waved it triumphantly.

"And what's this, may I ask?" he exclaimed.

"The title's right there on the cover," Peña answered. *"The Monetary System from 1820 to 1920."*

So only the cover was "red," not the contents! The cop flung it down on the floor without a word.

The two youngsters were taken to the federal security detention quarters and put in solitary. The interrogators there were determined to get certain information out of them: the names of the state ministers who were financing the Movement, and the source of the weapons the Movement people had supposedly obtained. Since Peña denied that any of the ministers had backed the Movement, the agents began questioning him about one other particular person, Emilio Martínez Manautou, the president's secretary. What they were after was a statement from Peña implicating Manautou as the source through whom the Movement had gotten money and weapons.

Florencio López Osuna, of the CNH

On Friday, the twentieth, I went to the Attorney General's office, and was told I shouldn't be concerned: Eli was safe and sound. They refused, however, to tell me where he was being held. Then when I read in the paper that those who had been arrested were being held at police headquarters, I went down there. The Plaza de Tlaxcuaque was swarming with *granaderos.*

They stopped Rebeca and me at the entrance and asked, "What is it you want? Where do you think you're going?"

"Let me past!" I replied. "I've got an appointment with General Mendiolea."

I was desperate, and ready to force my way in any way I could. Since the *granadero* refused to let us in, I said in a very stern tone of voice, "If you don't let me in, you'll hear about it from the general!"

I think the guy believed my story because I was so highhanded with him, and he seemed to be having second thoughts about the trouble he might get into if he didn't let me in. He let us through then, and we took the elevator up to the fourth floor, where a whole bunch of policemen stopped us.

"Where do you think you're going? What are you doing in here anyway?"

I told them the same fib: "Let me by, I've got an appointment. . . ."

We elbowed our way to a door standing open, which as good luck would have it turned out to be the reception room just outside the general's private office. Once we went inside, they all stopped pestering us, because I kept saying over and over in a determined tone of voice, "I have an appointment with the general." We stood there hoping he'd see us. Suddenly a short, stocky, baldheaded man came out of the general's office, looking very angry and arguing with a reporter: "You wrote in your paper that I'm a murderer! I'd like to see you prove it!"

"No, General, since you and I have always been good friends—" the reporter started to say.

"Oh, is that so? Since when?" the general broke in.

They kept on arguing back and forth, until finally the general retreated to his private office, with the newspaper reporter right at his heels. When the two of them came out again, I think the general was trying to get rid of the reporter, because he came over to me and said, "How do you do, *señora*. What can I do for you?"

"I'm Eli de Gortari's wife. So you know why I'm here," I answered.

"No, *señora*, I haven't the slightest idea. . . ."

"I want to see my husband, who's being held in custody here. . . ."

"That's absolutely out of the question, *señora*."

"General, you're God himself around here, and if you give the word that I'm to be allowed to see him . . ."

He didn't say another word. He just turned his back on me and disappeared into his office again. I said to Rebeca, "We're staying right here. If they want to get rid of us, they'll have to carry us out bodily."

We waited there another half-hour, and when the general came out of his office again, he came over to me and said, "*Señora*, you can see your husband, but you're not to pass any messages to him."

They took us down to Special Services then; it's like a gangster movie down there, because that's where all the top agents are: men in shirt sleeves fingering arrest records or dominoes or who knows what other things, every last one of them with a face like a hood-lum, like a cold-blooded killer. There was such a thick cloud of ciga-rette smoke down there you could have cut it with a knife. There were mug shots of people wanted for murder posted on the walls, and a bulletin board covered with instructions to different agents. . . . We sat there for three hours or so waiting for them to bring Eli to see us.

I asked to use the phone to call home so the others wouldn't worry about Rebeca and me, and one of the agents said to me, "You two can't leave here, you know. You're in custody here."

I. was really scared then, and I said to him, "Why is that? What possible reason can there be for holding us here?"

His only answer was, "Orders from the general."

I went over to Rebeca and said to her, "Listen, they say they're going to hold us here. What do you think we ought to do? Poor Hira! How can we get word to him what's happened?" (Hira is Eli's oldest son; he was waiting for us outside.)

Later on, I simply had to go to the bathroom. One of the agents went with me to the women's lavatory, and warned me not to try to make a getaway.

"Listen," I said to him. "There's not much chance of that, seeing as how I'm not a mosquito." And then I said to him, "Listen, you're not going to go into the john with me, are you?"

"No, I'll wait right here outside," he replied. "But don't be too long in there, or I'll have to come in and get you."

I went back to the Special Services department, where Rebeca was anxiously waiting for me to come back. Twenty minutes later, an agent called out in a loud voice, "Ten-shun! The general's on his way down here."

All the agents' playing cards disappeared like magic; they imme-diately stubbed out their cigarettes, put their holsters on, lined their chairs up neatly, and fanned the cloud of cigarette smoke away as best they could. The general came in, discussing some-thing or other with the men tagging along after him. He walked right by us, not paying the slightest attention to us, and I thought to myself, He must have seen us waiting here. Has he changed his mind? Well, I'm not budging an inch till I've seen Eli.

The General entered a tiny little office then, exchanged a few words with a prisoner, came out, and said to me, "They're going to bring him down here. But remember, *señora,* you're not to pass any messages on to him, or you'll be held here."

"General, you know how much this means to me. Thank you very much," I replied.

He turned as red as a beet then, and said, "Don't mention it, *señora.*"

They ushered us into the little office the general had come out of just a few moments before, and a captain and several Secret Service agents, doubtless the ones who were in charge down there, told me to sit down again. Five minutes later, they brought Eli down to see us. I was shocked when I saw him: he had a three-day growth of beard and a terribly anxious expression on his face, and his suit was a mass of wrinkles. He was terribly surprised when he saw us, because usually the only reason they ever took prisoners out of their cells was to beat them. Eli had heard the moans of prisoners being tortured, and doubtless thought that that was why they'd come for him. When he saw us, he came over and hugged us as though he hadn't seen us for years and years.

"How did you manage to get in here to see me?" he asked.

The security agents were listening to every word we said. Eli asked how we all were, and what had happened to Ana, for it had preyed on his mind ever since he'd been arrested. I tried my best to reassure him that all of us were all right, that our one concern was how much we missed him, and that this whole nightmare would soon be over. I had brought a clean shirt for him from home, and asked one of the agents if I could give it to my husband. I wanted Eli to have a clean shirt, but I also wanted to see if he'd been beaten. How naïve I was!—I didn't know then that when they beat prisoners, they're usually careful not to leave any marks. I had no idea then that they hadn't given Eli one bite to eat all that time. A lieutenant offered him a drink of mineral water and he eagerly accepted—he was terribly thirsty, because they hadn't given him one drop of water to drink since the eighteenth. . . . They let us talk together there in front of all of them for twenty minutes, and we wasted the time exchanging trivialities because we were so nervous and so surprised to see each other. Then the lieutenant who had brought Eli down to see us said he was sorry but he had to take him back. We said good-by, told each other a thousand times to take care, and I promised him we'd come visit him the next day (hoping desperately that they'd let us in to see him again). But I didn't see him again till Sunday, the twenty-second, just before they transferred him to Lecumberri in a paddy wagon.

Artemisa de Gortari, mother of a family

They nabbed Luis Jorge Peña on the twenty-fifth of September. The next day, the twenty-sixth, the house where the delegate from Chapingo, Luis Tomás Cervantes Cabeza de Vaca, lay sick in bed was surrounded by federal security agents. Luis Tomás wasn't living in the house itself, but in a new wing of it that was still under construction. Only two people knew the address of the house: Jorge Peña and Ayax Segura Garrido. The agents went straight to where they thought Cabeza de Vaca would be—in the new part being added onto the house, but as it happened he was inside the house, eating lunch. The agents arrested Cabeza de Vaca and two other kids, the sons of the friends that had taken him in. The agents were armed with submachine guns and had come through the cornfields surrounding the house, which is located on the outskirts of the city. He was taken away by the security agents, and as soon as they got him to police headquarters, they subjected him to the same tortures as Luis Jorge Peña, though this time the agents were after different information: the person they were trying to get Cabeza de Vaca to denounce was not Martínez Manautou, but that professor from the School of Agriculture, Juan Gil Preciado.

Raúl Álvarez Garín, of the CNH

The tallest one came over to me and put a hood over my head, one made of some sort of thick cloth, like burlap, but so coarsely woven that I could see light through it. The thing covered my entire head and neck, down to my Adam's apple. Then they grabbed my arms and tied my hands behind my back.

At that moment I heard the same hoarse voice as before, rasping in a threatening tone, "Who's your successor on the National Strike Committee?"

"I don't have any idea," I answered.

"Well then, we'll just have to refresh your memory. Either you talk or we'll kill you. . . . You traitor, you bastard, you! What do you sons of bitches want, anyway? Tell me, what's the point of what you're doing?" he asked then.

"We want people to obey the Constitution," I answered.

"Don't kid yourself, you shithead. *We're* the ones who decide what's constitutional and what's unconstitutional. Who supplied you bastards with arms?"

"The Movement doesn't have any arms; it's a democratic movement that respects the law. Our only weapons are the Constitution and the power of reason."

"Don't hand me that crap. You yourself were armed. Ayax, Sócrates, and Osuna all told us you were."

"They were lying then. I've never carried any sort of weapon."

"You'd better tell the truth—it might save your neck."

The offer was tempting, but I'd been telling the truth all along. I was sure I was a goner, no matter what I told them. If they had orders to kill me, they'd do just that.

The guy called somebody over—a sergeant, most likely, because he said to him, "Sergeant, refresh the memory of this motherfucking traitor who's trying to make us all turn Communist, and I'll send for the death squad."

I didn't give a damn: I was prepared to meet my death. I couldn't rat on any of my comrades, or dirty the name of the Movement and betray our cause—our pure and just and noble cause. I couldn't be untrue to myself; I had to fight with my last drop of strength, to the very end. I steeled myself and prepared for the worst.

I heard the sergeant's footsteps echoing as he strode over to me. He gave me a punch in the belly and said, "Who's giving you all that money?"

"The people—they've been putting coins in our collection boxes."

"You're lying, you swine! How much has Gil Preciado given you?"

"Not a cent, I swear!"

"They've threatened your life, that's what. If you tell us who's backing the Movement financially, we'll give you police protection. How much has Madrazo given you?"

"Neither Gil Preciado nor Madrazo nor any other politician has given us one cent. It's the public who's been giving us money."

"You yourself are working hand in glove with Gil Preciado."

"That's not true at all. I'm not working with him—or with any other politician. I can't stand the whole lot of them."

Another hard punch in the belly.

"Who were the people you used as shock troops at Tlatelolco?"

This particular question came as a surprise, because it was the first time I'd heard any mention of what had happened on October 2.

"I haven't the vaguest idea. I've been locked up in here since the twenty-seventh of September," I replied.

More punches then, this time right in the balls. The pain was so intense I doubled up and fell to the floor. They stopped punching me then and instead began kicking me from head to foot as I lay there.

"Do you know Heberto Castillo?" they asked me.

"Only by sight," I replied.

"Where is he now?"

"I don't have the least idea."

More blows then—in the balls, the belly, the legs. I lay there on the floor screaming with pain and helplessness and rage, with tears streaming down my face. They kept firing questions at me, one after the other.

"Do you know Eli de Gortari? Marcué Pardiñas? Fausto Trejo? How much money has Marcué kicked in? What was de Gortari doing on the Strike Committee? What's Trejo's position politically? Did Heberto take you to Havana? Who's giving you orders?"

"I don't know any of those people! Marcué hasn't given us one cent! I've never been to Cuba! I don't know anything about all that!"

More punches, plus electric shocks in my testicles, my rectum, my mouth. And more questions.

"What sort of contacts did you have with Raúl Álvarez?"

"The same as with any other member of the Strike Committee."

"What were you and Guevara plotting together?"

"Nothing at all. He and I spent very little time together."

"What about your contacts with Sócrates?"

"I had very little personal contact with him either. I knew him better than Guevara, but I don't have any idea what he was planning to do next."

More tortures then, more blows, more electric shocks. And they kept cross-questioning me:

"You do know Tayde, right? Haven't you noticed that he always has plenty of money and wears expensive clothes? Haven't you tumbled to the fact that he's double-crossed you, that money from Gil Preciado has ended up in his own pockets?"

I was furious when I heard vicious slander like that, and I said, "Tayde and I are classmates, and in the four years or more that I've known him he's been as honest as they come."

Luis Tomás Cervantes Cabeza
de Vaca, of the CNH

I never had the slightest sympathy for the Student Movement; I thought their demands were absurd. "Fire Cueto," for instance. Whatever for, since somebody just like him would step into the job? Every one of their six demands was naïve. . . . But the vicious repression, the violence toward young people on the part of the authorities, the total disproportion between the acts of the youngsters and the government's violent measures in retaliation made me change my mind. . . . The overreaction on the part of the government has made these youngsters heroes.

Héctor Mendieta Cervantes, neurologist

Jesús Bañuelos Romero, Fernando Palacios, another kid, and I were walking down Gorostiza around midnight or so, on our way home from a graduation ceremony, and suddenly some guys in a small van pointed pistols at us and shouted, "Stop right where you are, you shitheads! Don't try to run for it: we've got orders to shoot to kill!"

That scared us, and we stopped dead in our tracks. They scrambled out of the van, keeping their pistols aimed at us, and asked to see our identification. When they found out that we were students, one of them started kicking us and punching us to force us into the van, and shouting that they were going to kill us "because you're students." The van started up and they threatened us some more. We found out later they were security agents. They kept saying to each other, "These kids are going to disappear; we'll beat 'em to death and throw their bodies down the sewer." Every time we asked them where they were taking us, they punched us and told us they were going to kill us. When we got to the headquarters of the Federal District police, they shoved us out of the van, kicking and punching us some more—both the security agents and some soldiers, because there were a whole bunch of them there. We were taken to Special Services and locked up in a room full of trash and garbage, where we spent all the rest of the night.

We realized what terrible trouble we were in, and the only thing we could think to say to each other was, "Why in the world did they arrest us? We haven't done a thing!"

The next morning, October 4, an agent came into the room, and when we asked him why they'd locked us up, he said there'd been a "raid" the night before and we'd be let out the minute his supervisor arrived. That relieved our minds for a while, but a little after nine a.m. the same agents who'd dragged us into the van, and one other one, came into the room.

"Why have you locked us up? What are the charges against us?" we asked them again.

"That you're filthy bastards—those are the charges. That's why you're here, you swine."

And then they went away again, leaving us locked up in there.

They came back again around eleven or twelve that same morning. When they came in the room, one of them, the head man apparently, asked the other agents which one of us was the leader of our little gang.

One of the agents pointed to me and said, "It might be this guy. He's the biggest anyway."

The chief said, "Bring him to my office." The other agents dragged me there by the hair, roughing me up all the way.

"Who's paying you kids to do all this?" the chief asked me.

I said I had no idea what he was talking about.

"Sure you do, you lying little bastard!"

Then he asked me the same question again, but this time he was even more insistent. "Who's paying you kids to set streetcars on fire like that?" he asked me.

He said he had witnesses who would testify that I'd been involved in burning a streetcar on the Calle de Zaragoza. I didn't even know where the Calle de Zaragoza was—and I still don't to this day—and I told him so.

They took me back to that room again, and then they dragged Jesús Bañuelos to the chief's office. When they brought him back and locked him in with us again, he told me they'd asked him the same questions they'd asked me and beaten him. Then the agents

came in again, ordered us to hand over all our personal belongings—which none of us ever saw again—and went away.

Late that same afternoon—the fourth—they took me to the chief's
office again, and he asked me, "Is your name José Luis Becerra
Guerrero?"

"Yes," I answered.

"Do you live in the Calle de Gorostiza?"

"Yes."

"And your story is that you weren't ever involved in setting
streetcars on fire?"

"That's right," I said.

"Are you the guy they call 'Pepito el Diablo'?"

"No."

"What's your name then?"

"José Luis Becerra Guerrero."

"If that's your name, your nickname's most likely Pepito el
Diablo, right?" *

Every time I refused to confess I was guilty of whatever it was
they were accusing me of, the chief and the four agents punched
me. I asked the chief if the mere fact that my name was José Luis
was automatically proof that my nickname was Pepito el Diablo.
Then they began hitting me over the head and in the stomach with
their truncheons and kicking me in the shins. When the chief saw I
wasn't going to confess to any of the things he'd been accusing me
of, he ordered his men to "work me over" and said they'd see
whether I'd go on denying everything after that. They took me back
to the room and made me take off all my clothes, punching me the
whole time, and then they began giving me electric shocks with an
iron prod on different parts of my body—mostly my testicles, my
belly, and my face—and all the while they kept saying, "So you
don't like cops or *granaderos*, eh? Well, you bastards can go fuck
yourselves!"

I have no idea how long they beat me; all I remember is that they
insisted that I own up to having been involved in burning streetcars, and if I refused, they'd go right on beating me till I confessed,
because it didn't matter at all to them if they killed me, since, as
they put it, "Nobody's going to notice if we do in a couple more of

---

* "Pepito" is a common nickname of people named José. (Translator's note.)

you trouble makers who aren't good for anything but burning
streetcars." They left me lying there on the floor half conscious.

José Luis Becerra Guerrero, student;
prisoner in Lecumberri

You're not like Morelos, a servant of the nation; you're a cat's-paw
for Díaz Ordaz.

Luis González de Alba, of the CNH,
to the judge of the Sixth District Court

That was when they began the electric shocks, the "water treatment," where they stick your head in a bucket of dirty water till
you almost faint, making me stay in positions that gave me terrible
cramps in my muscles, psychological torture, a continuous rain of
blows.

Gilberto Guevara Niebla, of the CNH

Pedro had such a drawn look on his face because of the intense pain
he'd suffered that I almost didn't recognize him.

Francisco Gutiérrez Zamora, father of a family

All the people who were arrested were asked whether they knew
Heberto Castillo. Since he was a well-known public figure, most of
them naturally said they did. So when Castillo was arrested, the Attorney General's office presented as evidence against him the fact
that his name was mentioned in more than two hundred deposi-
tions. In all the cases involving persons who were more or less well
known, such as members of the CNH or the Teachers' Coalition,
the same sort of "evidence" was used against them, since there was
no other concrete proof of the supposed "crimes" they were
charged with.

√ Gilberto Guevara Niebla, of the CNH

Late that same afternoon, October 4, the agents who had beaten me
returned to that room they'd locked us up in. They tortured us
again, and made us clean the room up and scrub the floor. There
was a big pile of refuse, or garbage rather, in one corner, and the
floor was covered with puddles of vomit where we'd thrown up
after being tortured. There were some other kids—also students—

we'd never met before locked up in there with us. The agents handed Jesús Bañuelos, Fernando Palacios, and me a bucket of water and a rag and told us to clean the room up, and when we'd finished they made us tidy up the whole office and mop the floor— not the office really, but the big room outside, where the agents line up for roll call every day—and then they made us clean up all the lockers. As we were doing all this, every time another agent came in, he'd ask, "Who are those guys cleaning up in here?" And the others would say, "They're students."

"Oh, they're students, are they? Shall I see if it's true that the little bastards have got balls these days, that they like kicking up their heels like billy goats?"

And then they'd punch us in the ribs and say, "Look at that, will you? You guys haven't got any balls at all— what a bunch of nanny goats! When there's a whole bunch of you, you think you're cocks of the walk, don't you? But now that we've got you here by your-selves, let's see you jump a little. Take that, you dumb shits."

And that's how it went with every agent that came in. He'd ask what we were doing there, they'd tell him we were students, and they'd start punching us again—in the ribs usually.

Around six that evening, they took me back to the chief's office again, and he said to me; "I think maybe you're going to talk now, after that little working over we've given you, isn't that right, you dirty little punk?"

I answered that I'd already told him I hadn't ever been involved in burning streetcars, and then I said, "The only reason you're try-ing to pin that on me is because I'm a student."

They told me to shut my trap, hit me in the arms and legs with truncheons, boxed my ears, punched me in the stomach, and said, "So you think you're pretty tough, do you? Well, we'll see whether you're as tough as you think you are." They handed me a statement they'd already written up, in which I confessed to having ganged up with Jesús Bañuelos R., Fernando Palacios V., Raymundo Padilla S., and Fernando Borja, and burned a streetcar. Raymundo and Fer-nando are two friends of mine who belong to the same soccer team I do; the agents had found their names in my address book. The streetcar-burning they accused us of had taken place on the corner of Gorostiza and Jesús Carranza on October 2, around six at night, according to the statement they handed me, which was an out-and-out lie. Nonetheless they arrested me the following night, around midnight. I found out later that not one streetcar had been burned on that corner—neither on the second or the third or any other day.

José Luis Becerra Guerrero, student

On October 8—around six at night, I would guess—several men came to my cell, number 18. They opened the peephole and shouted, "Come over here to the door."

I heard a voice say, "Cell 18, Gamundi, a member of the CNH." I recognized the voice: it was Sócrates.

Early the next morning, they dragged me out of the cell and started interrogating me, "Do you know a guy named Sócrates?"

"No."

The soldier's reply to that was, "Don't play dumb. Sócrates said he knew you and identified you there in cell 18."

What could I say? Nothing. The same thing happened to many other comrades. Sócrates walked down the cell block, identifying each of them, one by one. The worst case was that of a girl comrade from the Teachers' College. Sócrates had seen her once or twice when he was visiting her school. They'd taken Sócrates to have a look at the girls who were being held in the Military Camp, and as he walked past this girl, he said, "I recognize this one."

"Where have you seen her before?"

"I saw her at a CNH meeting once."

"Do you know her name?"

"No, I don't remember what her name is; I only saw her once or twice at CNH meetings."

Even the soldier was indignant: "You ass, if you're not sure who she is, how come you spoke up like that? You don't really know her at all. . . ."

And the guy went on down the line. Thanks to that soldier, the girl was let out eight days later.

Félix Lucio Hernández Gamundi, of the CNH

At the same time that huge dossiers are being compiled and monstrous trumped-up charges are being filed against innocent leftist activists and they are being jailed by the hundreds, the ruling class has had no compunction about allowing criminals who have committed more than fifty-one thousand reported murders and almost two hundred thousand robberies to go unpunished in the last forty years of "stability," according to Alfonso Quiroz Cuarón! But under the economic systems that prevail today, "criminal tendencies," like wealth, are usually limited to very small groups.

Comment by Fernando Carmona, economist,
corroborating statements by Dr. Alfonso Quiroz
Cuarón, an expert in the field of criminal law

After Tlatelolco and the second of October, the forces of repression have been rapidly acquiring more sophisticated equipment: the riot squads are now using protective shields, truncheons, masks, and modern chemical weapons; the Army garrisons are also being modernized; the troops' old muskets are being replaced by automatic rifles, and they are starting to manufacture "antiriot" tanks at Ciudad Sahagún.

Fernando Carmona, economist

We all sang in Military Camp 1—everything from the "International" (despite the fact that members of the Communist Party have made it more or less their own private property) to satirical songs criticizing our society. There were two very popular ones, one that said:

El señor Cuauhtémoc estaba muy contento
Le importaba madre todo su tormento.*

and another one to the tune of "El Santo":

En la Calle de Insurgentes
Que chinguen a su madre los agentes.†

The "Marseillaise" was popular too. Once when we were chanting those verses about the Calle de Insurgentes, a lieutenant came up and told us that the military camp wasn't a brothel, and we'd soon find out who was going to fuck who: it was us motherfuckers who'd see what would happen if we went on singing those filthy songs of ours. We shut up for a day or two, but then we

---

* Señor Cuauhtémoc was happy as a lark.
  Being tortured didn't faze him a bit.
  Cuauhtémoc was the famous Aztec chieftain tortured to death by the Spanish conquistadors. (Translator's note.)
† The secret-service agents
  Can go fuck their mothers on the Calle de Insurgentes.

started singing all our songs again—except for the one that had made them so mad. Singing helped keep our spirits up and our minds off our troubles when things got rough.

In the slang meaning of the word "sing," we may pride ourselves on the fact that very very few people "sang" to the cops like that stoolpigeon Sócrates. But what informers like that told the cops wasn't true at all—it was all a pack of lies and false accusations, that whole business about "fifth columns, arms, sorehead politicians plotting against the government." In a word, it was all just muddle-headed personal opinions, coming from people who didn't know the first thing about politics, all merely serving to justify the Tlatelolco massacre and corroborate the government's version of what had happened.

Eduardo Valle Espinoza
(Owl-Eyes), of the CNH

Then the torture started again; it was even worse this time though, and lasted longer. I writhed like a rattlesnake, crying and moaning and screaming and swearing. Then they finally stopped torturing me, and the soldier said to me, "Don't kid yourselves, you Communist swine! If you won't talk, we have *gringos* here who'll take over." I just lay there on the floor, keeping my ears open and moaning. I could hardly bear the pain in my testicles, in my stomach, in my legs; and I could scarcely draw breath. I was shaking from head to foot; my heart was pounding like crazy, and my mouth was dry as a bone.

I heard someone say, "The death squad's all set, chief."

I didn't turn a hair.

Someone said in a sarcastic tone of voice, "Since you're an innocent little white dove that refuses to say one word, you're leaving us no choice—we'll have to carry out the orders we've been given. Take him away!"

Somebody grabbed me under the arms and lifted me up off the floor. I could hardly stand on my feet. Then one of them said, "Do you want to see your pals for the last time? They're all here."

"Yes, please, I want to see them. Take me to them, and please let me take this hood off so I can see their faces."

"No. You're going to do things our way, not your way."

I stumbled along, with one of them holding me under the arms so

I wouldn't collapse; they practically had to carry me. Then they tied me to a post and said to me, "Sócrates is here."

I didn't see Sócrates; I just heard his voice saying, "Answer their questions; tell them the truth."

"What do you want me to tell them? I've already said everything I have to say."

Then I heard another voice pipe up and say to Sócrates, "Tell him how we've treated you."

"I can't complain, Cabeza; they've been very decent to me. Look, there was money from the Biology Department at Poli and the Faculty of Sciences at UNAM. Madrazo gave it to them to pass on to us."

"The only money I know anything about is the collections the brigades took up and the money all the delegates collected from the students in their schools and turned over to the CNH. A daily quota of a hundred pesos per school. . . ."

"No, pal, that money wouldn't have gone very far. The CNH had to put out a lot of dough for paint to write slogans on walls all over town, for posters, for leaflets. . . ."

"I never heard a thing about any other source of money."

"Do you know that Tita is working for the police now? That she sold out to them for fifty thousand pesos and that's why they've let her go?"

"No, Sócrates, I don't know a thing about all that, and if you had inside information, why didn't you tell the Committee instead of going to the police with it? What the hell is the matter with you anyway? Why don't you keep your trap shut?"

Another voice said something I didn't hear, and then Sócrates asked me, "Do you remember the contact you had with Genaro Vázquez?"

When I heard him ask me that, right there in front of the death squad, my heart sank. I haven't the least idea to this day who told him that, or why he asked me that, because I've never had any contact whatsoever with Genaro Vázquez. I did know, however, that Vázquez was a leader the authorities were searching for. I was dumfounded, and answered, "You're lying—I've never been in contact with anybody named Genaro."

"Yes, you have—a little short guy with a mustache, from Veracruz from the looks of him. . . ."

"Don't lie like that, don't try to pin that kind of thing on us—why don't you keep your mouth shut? I don't know anything, I tell you—not one thing."

"They're going to kill us, you know. . . ."

"Yes, I know."

Then the other man's voice broke in again: "Take Sócrates away and shoot this one."

Luis Tomás Cervantes Cabeza
de Vaca, of the CNH

When the brigades went out into the streets with their collection boxes, people donated lots of money. What's more, the only things the schools had to spend money for were paper and ink and food for the brigades on guard duty.

Estrella Sámano, political science student, UNAM

Any kid who had anything at all to do with the Movement knows that out biggest expense was paper, tons of it, and paying for the announcements the Committee occasionally ran in the papers. Let's add up the figures: the money the CNH had to pay out, first of all. What for? It was the different schools that put out the handbills, not the Committee, so the only thing the Committee had to pay money out for was running announcements and manifestoes in the paper. A quarter page in *Excélsior* costs three thousand pesos. Let's say we took out two ads a week, at most: that's six thousand pesos. Where did the money come from? Each school had a daily quota of a hundred pesos (which was a nuisance to collect)—a hundred pesos from each of eighty schools adds up to eight thousand pesos a day, and we needed only six thousand a week. And raising the daily quotas in the schools wasn't all that hard. Did the schools usually make their daily quota? Sure, it was a cinch. A fairly big school such as the Faculty of Philosophy collected much more than that just from its own students and those who attended the daily meetings and so on. There simply weren't any other additional expenses: all we had to buy was paper and ink. We took over the mimeograph machines in the various schools, the University press, the press at Poli, the cafeterias. Food cost us a certain amount of money, of course, but it all came from the cafeterias, which stayed open all along and made a good profit during the time we ran them, though naturally not as big a one as usual because we gave lots of kids free meals, but we made most of the students pay for their eats, unless they were on guard duty at night or belonged to one of the brigades that were busting their asses. If you think about it, there weren't any really big expenses involved at all. If you want to know the truth, we could have collected ten times as much money as we did, but what would we have used it for?

✓ *Luis González de Alba, of the CNH*

On the other hand, as far as the political side of it is concerned, the police tried to discredit the Movement by resorting to an old old trick of theirs: misrepresenting our goals by claiming that "subversive agents" working for "hidden interests" were behind the Movement. They always try to cover up the real causes of social unrest, and at the same time they invent trumped-up causes, or imaginary ones, such as how "clever" agitators are at pulling the wool over the eyes of people who are "easily taken in," students especially, since according to them it's students who cause disturbances and "stir up trouble" on the "slightest pretext." This time, however, the authorities couldn't claim that the whole thing was a "Communist plot," because the Movement was so broadly based that nobody would have believed them, so instead they suddenly came up with a new gimmick: they claimed that the brains behind the Movement were a group of "sorehead politicians" who were trying to "create problems for the administration" out of spite. Ernesto P. Uruchurto, Carlos Madrazo, Humberto Romero, Braulio Maldonado, and other former officials were suddenly very much in the public eye again, because their names had been mentioned in "confessions" that a number of the people arrested had been forced to sign. These former officials were accused of being the brains behind the Movement, the source of its money, and the persons responsible for its "disgraceful aims," namely "organizing a party to overthrow the government in power."

Raúl Álvarez Garín, of the CNH

One time, when they read me the trumped-up "confession" they'd written up beforehand, the chief of Special Services told me that if I didn't sign it my family would be sorry I hadn't, that they knew where my family lived, who my parents were, and where they worked. They'd been beating me all along, and when I heard them threaten my family like that, I decided the only thing I could do was sign the confession. Then they took us down to solitary, along with some ninety other prisoners, and shut us up in a cell meant to hold fifteen people. There was sewage leaking from the pipes and the toilets were overflowing; there was no light and no ventilation, and every two hours the agents wet us down with special hoses. As a result of these conditions in which we found ourselves, a number of the students became seriously ill and had such severe anxiety attacks that they fainted dead away. They kept us locked up in there for a week like that.

José Luis Becerra Guerrero, student

"We're going to shoot two others before we shoot you."

I heard two volleys of rifle fire and two *coups de grâce* with a pistol, and then they led me over to touch two bodies lying there. . . . Then they tied me up again and shot a pistol off just half an inch or so from my ear. Then after that they said, "Let's not bother killing him . . . let's just cut his balls off. . . ." After they'd subjected me to what they called a "warm-up," they injected my testicles with an anesthetic and pretended they were castrating me—cutting my scrotum with a razor or a scalpel—I still have a scar there. All this happened on the night of October 2, 1968, and went on till six the next morning, the third. . . . All because I refused to sign a statement denouncing the Popular Student Movement or incriminating myself—the whole bunch of lies they wanted me to sign my name to would have betrayed the democratic cause of our people, and I refused to sign that "confession." At six on the morning of the third, I was taken to Lecumberri Prison again, where I was held incommunicado, in the worst possible conditions: they wouldn't even let me out of my cell to go to the bathroom, and I had to use a five-gallon bucket that was never cleaned once during the entire twenty-eight days that I was kept there in solitary. I didn't even see the guards. I had neither a blanket nor a mattress. They kept me on a near-starvation diet—the only food they gave me was one glass of corn gruel in the morning and another in the evening, pushed through a hole in the door of my cell. . . . All that, as you know, is a violation of the universal rights of man and the Mexican Constitution.

Luis Tomás Cervantes Cabeza
de Vaca, of the CNH

The first time I saw Cabeza, when they transferred him from cell block H to cell block M, I was terribly shocked. It was as though *I* could feel *his* pain—like when you see that someone has been in agony, even though he doesn't say a word. It wasn't just that he was worn to a frazzle; he was a total wreck, pain itself stumbling down the corridor.

Artemisa de Gortari, mother of a family

As I lay there on the cot in my cell in Military Camp 1, I could see a patch of grass, two or three square yards of alfalfa, and the wall around the camp, with lookout posts. On the right, there was a bend in the wall where they'd planted corn; some big black birds, ravens perhaps, had alighted on the dry stalks. I lay there facing the window; I could see a bit of sky through it, and remembered what Oscar Wilde had written: The small blue patch that is the prisoner's sky. For the first time in many days, I burst into tears. After that I always lay with my head facing away from the window.

Luis González de Alba, of the CNH

One day in the military camp, I was awakened about ten o'clock in the morning by the creaking of cell doors opening, a sound that was quite familiar to me by that time. There was someone going from cell to cell peering at the prisoners inside through the little openings in each of the doors—I think they're called judases. Since I was filthy dirty and my hair had gotten very long and I'd lost a lot of weight and wasn't wearing glasses, I'd gotten through all these inspections without ever being recognized. They hadn't questioned my fake identification papers and hadn't bothered me at all after the first night. Only somebody who knew me quite well could have recognized me. They came to my cell and opened the peephole; they ordered me to stand up, and I got to my feet. A few seconds later somebody behind the door ordered me to step back a few paces; a few seconds later I was ordered to walk over and stand against the wall. Someone outside the door said in a whisper, "A CNH member in cell thirteen," in a voice I thought I recognized, and a pair of eyes that I was sure I'd seen before stared at me through the peephole, though I couldn't really tell who it was without my glasses. I couldn't quite remember whose voice it was, or whose eyes it was I'd glimpsed through the peephole.

I sat down on the metal cot again, and then I heard somebody whispering my name over and over: "Valle, Valle, Valle." It was my comrade in the cell across the way. I got to my feet and said to him through the closed peephole, "What's up?" He told me to push the little piece of sheet metal covering the peephole aside with my finger since it wasn't locked. I pushed the cover aside with my finger, and whispered across to him through *his* open peephole, asking him what it was he wanted.

"Do you know who it was who identified you?" he asked me.

"No," I answered.

My comrade's answer was just one word: "Sócrates."

That was all he needed to say, and the two of us closed our peepholes then.

The first day I arrived in Lecumberri, I saw Sócrates Campos Lemus at chowtime that evening. The minute I laid eyes on him I was so mad I went for him. Guevara held me back and persuaded me to keep my temper: this was no time to give the government more weapons against us by getting into fights among ourselves. There'd be plenty of time to get to the bottom of the whole business. I realized that he was right. But I still think that Sócrates should be made to pay for his crimes some day, and the ones who'll see that he does are the students he betrayed after October 2, 1968.

Eduardo Valle Espinoza
(Owl-Eyes), of the CNH

There's been a story going round that when the cops questioned one student we all called "The Pirate"—a shy, diffident little kid—about Sócrates and what he'd done, he'd replied shamefacedly, "I don't know what he did exactly; I've always gotten bad grades in history."

Salvador Martínez de la Roca (Pino), of the
Action Committee, UNAM

I'm from Zacualtipán, in the Sierra de Hidalgo. My father's a
schoolteacher; his first name is Homero. My grandfathers and my
uncles all had Greek names. That's how I came to be named
Sócrates.

Sócrates Amado Campos Lemus,
CNH delegate from the School of Economics at
IPN; prisoner in Lecumberri

Nothing matters to me any more, to hell with the whole thing.

Jesús Valle Baquiero, student
at the School of Dentistry, UNAM

So I'm an Iago, am I? A Judas? A CIA agent? A government spy? An
informer? A traitor? The real truth of the matter is that there are a
whole bunch of people who aren't sufficiently aware of the facts of
the situation to blame the real guilty party—the government, the
system—so even the students have started looking around for a
scapegoat. It's much easier to single out one person to blame—to
start in on the whole bit about "it wasn't me, it was you . . . no, it
was him . . . somebody else finked to the cops . . . I wasn't there
myself, but that's what I've heard, he made a deal with them . . . X
or Y cracked, he didn't hold out even three minutes, it wasn't me, it
was so-and-so," and all that sort of childishness, than it is to really
analyze what our Movement stood for, where we were headed,
what our weak points were. Instead everybody started breaking up
into ridiculous little splinter groups that are never going to get anywhere, and there were all sorts of fights between the Commies, the
Maoists, the Trotskyites, the Spartacists, all hating each other's
guts. . . . Did you know that there in cell block M each little group
kept to itself and had its own little private mess at mealtimes and
never spoke to the others except to run them down or trade insults
back and forth? Even in the slums people stick together better than
that. . . . Those people say I informed on them, that I fingered
them in Military Camp 1, that I was working hand in glove with the
authorities. . . . Listen, when the Student Movement first started,
I'd been a militant for many years and had a great deal of prestige
among the students. I was one of the most active leaders of the

CNH. I spoke at almost all the demonstrations. When the first started at Tlatelolco, I was the one who tried to ke￼ under control: I grabbed the microphone and shouted, "￼ where you are, everybody; keep calm!" There are hundreds of people who'll testify to that. They put me in handcuffs immediately: "You're Sócrates," they said. And right after that the rumor started going the rounds that I'd gone all around Military Camp 1 identifying my comrades who'd been at Tlatelolco.

But what really happened was that the agents kept shoving me from one comrade to the next and asking me,

"Who's this one?"

"I have no idea," I kept saying.

Federico Emery can testify to that. When I spotted him, I told the agents, "I have no idea who this guy is. No, he's not the one you're looking for—the one you're after had a mustache and was much shorter."

I couldn't just keep my mouth shut and not say a word—you can also give your buddies away by saying nothing; you had to play cat-and-mouse with the agents, stall for time. I did my very best to throw them off the track: "I really can't say; I don't remember . . . he wore glasses . . . he had a beard . . . he had blond hair . . ." and so on. There were more than seventy members of the CNH in Military Camp 1. If I'd fingered them, all seventy of them would have stayed there. I didn't finger a one of them. Why did the agents take me there and try to get me to identify Movement people? Because as one of the best-known leaders of the CNH, I obviously knew all of the others who were very active in the Movement. Are you aware of the fact that I was the very first CNH leader arrested?

I had more than 250 names and addresses of kids on me when they occupied CU, because we thought that if they occupied Poli we'd have to keep in touch with the others so as to be able to go on working. If I'd turned their names over to the cops, all the members of the CNH would have been picked up, rather than innocent people, and by innocent people I mean rank-and-file members of the Movement—kids who just distributed leaflets and so on, not people like us members of the CNH who really organized the Movement and were responsible for its political policy.

Sócrates Amado Campos Lemus, of the CNH

I would never venture to pass judgment on a youngster who's been tortured.

Roberta Avendaño Martínez (Tita),
CNH delegate from UNAM

I really don't know what I would have done if I'd been in his shoes . . . I can't imagine. I can't stand physical pain.

Clementina Díaz Solórzano, student at the Faculty
of Philosophy and Letters, UNAM

I'm fed up with this whole rotten business!

Alfredo Valdés Macías, student at ESIME, IPN

Let's talk about this whole business of informing on people. Maybe you think there were very few who "sang"? Do you think that a kid who's never been in a situation like that, who's scared to death on account of all the terrible things he's seen, who's overcome with uncontrollable anxiety, under constant tension, subjected to torture, to threats not only to himself but to his whole family—do you think a kid like that won't "sing"? Do you consider him a yellow-bellied coward, a shit, a traitor? Man! He's simply a victim of circumstances. If you're not a real hero, you shouldn't go around claiming you're one.

Sócrates Amado Campos Lemus, of the CNH

All they do is sit around swapping stories. "I was there at Antonio's, and suddenly . . ." "They nabbed me in the science building . . ." "I tried to sneak out the door and there the Army was . . ." But nobody has any idea what the whole Movement was all about. Why were they fighting? What did they want? To destroy everything? To thumb their noses at everybody? To rough each other up? To get themselves really fucked good? . . . Well, they've really screwed up everything, that's for sure.

Beatriz Urbina Gómez, student at ESIQIE, IPN

Tlatelolco? I hear it's always been a place where human sacrifices were offered.

Francisca Ávila de Contreras, eighty-year-old
resident of the Calle de Neptuno, near
the Nonoalco-Tlatelolco Bridge

I hear tell that our ancestors, centuries ago, slaughtered lots of people, right there in Tlatelolco: there was lots of bloodshed, and that's
why there's a curse on the place. . . . It was the Aztecs who made
those human sacrifices, I'm told, but I have no idea whether it's
true or not. . . . For many years nobody wanted to live there. . . .

Elisa Pérez López, deaconess,
Medio Día Spiritualist Church

I went to Taxco, Guerrero, to spend Christmas with my mother.
There are seven children in our family; I'm the youngest. My dad
died when I was fourteen. My mom doesn't come to see me because
I've got a sister there at home who's an invalid, and my mother
can't leave her there by herself. Since I've been here in prison, I've
seen my mother only once, last May tenth, when she came to Mexico City.

I came back to Mexico City from Taxco on January first, and on
the second, I went out to UNAM; since they'd let me out of jail, I
didn't think they'd arrest me again. I went to the law school and
looked around for Tita, but I couldn't find her anywhere, and asked
a friend, Antonio Pérez Sánchez, "Che" we call him, who hadn't
been very active in the Movement at all and had never had a warrant out for his arrest, if he'd give me a lift to my apartment, not the
one out by the Department of Public Works, but the one in Coyoacán, where I was living with my friends the doctor and his wife.
. . . We were sitting there looking at a chess set my mother had
given me—she makes things out of silver—when suddenly we
heard someone unlocking the door. I thought it was either Mirna or
Tita, my two girl friends, the only ones who had keys to the apartment. But all at once eight guys burst in, with their pistols aimed at
us: "Hands up, you!" they shouted, and one of them immediately
said to the others, "Search the whole apartment—every last inch of
it!" They thought my friend Che was Escudero. They grabbed
books by Marx, publications put out by Prensas Latinas, newsletters
ters from the U.S.S.R., and everything else they thought was subversive propaganda. They shoved Che and me in a car and blindfolded us. They blindfolded me first, before they blindfolded Che,
and afterward he told me that he'd seen the agents point their pistols at me, and one of them asked me, "Okay, call it—is it heads or
tails?" I don't know why they did that—maybe it's because those

security agents are all sadists. "All right, let's see you make the V for Victory sign," they said to me. "What's the matter with you anyway? How come you're not out fighting with the guerrillas?"

They made us lie there on the floor of the car and drove for more than an hour, and finally we arrived at a house—I don't have any idea where it was, because we were blindfolded all the way. They made us lie down on the floor there in the house, and around three o'clock in the morning they took mug shots of us—full-face, profile, three-quarters profile, and so on. We were absolutely blinded by the flash bulbs. The next day they began interrogating us: they kept asking who was supplying us with money and arms and so on.

"We've found out that Madrazo gave you fifty thousand pesos," they said to me, and showed me a receipt with what they claimed was my signature on it. Oh, I forgot—when they arrested me there at the place where I was staying, they'd found a Mexican Air Force helmet that a friend of mine, a captain in the paratroopers, had given me, because in '63 I'd been a member of a group of girls who were parachutists in a Mountain Rescue team. Then the agents said to me, "That helmet we found at your place belongs to a captain you people murdered," and claimed that since I was from the state of Guerrero, I doubtless had had connections with Genaro Vázquez Rojas—though I've never met him in my life, despite the fact that he comes from my part of the country.

The next day they took Che and me to another house, and there we met Tita, who had also been picked up the night before, January 2, 1969. They kept us locked up there in a room for six days, I think it was, with agents guarding us around the clock. When they let us out to go to the john, they put hoods over our heads so we couldn't see anything. I must admit they fed us very well, though. On the sixth day another prisoner arrived, and we learned later it was Rodolfo Echeverría.

Then they blindfolded us again and took us away in a station wagon. On the way they said to Tita and me, "Listen, girls, we're going to let you go now; don't worry. We're going to drop you off in a nice little park."

And I kept begging them, "Please, please, the only thing I care about is getting word to my mother. Won't you please tell her I've been taken into custody?"

The station wagon stopped finally, and they told Tita and me to take off our blindfolds. We did, and saw that they actually had taken us to a little park—the one in front of Lecumberri Prison. They kept us there in the Women's Ward for four days, and on the fifth day—January 15—they transferred us to the Women's House of Detention. When we got there, they showed us papers committing us to prison for an indefinite period, which is another violation of the Constitution, since by law a person can only be detained for seventy-two hours without a hearing. So there we were in prison where only women who have been sentenced after trial are supposed to be confined, and women prisoners' records are always stamped SENTENCED TO A PRISON TERM AFTER TRIAL when they arrive there.

> Ana Ignacia Rodríguez (Nacha), of the Action
> Committee, UNAM

Was there a "hard line" in the CNH? Yes, a hard line against underhanded compromises, demagoguery, backroom conniving, political wheeling and dealing behind the scenes, Díaz Ordaz's paternalistic lectures, the regime's repressive policies, and everything else like that: a hard line we consistently stuck to. And we were also hard-liners when it came to the need to organize and demonstrate, when it came to the principle of public negotiations, to the list of six demands, just as later we were hard-liners when Marcelino and other leaders fucked things up and double-crossed us. We were hard on all the people who fostered and supported the defeatist policy of the Committee after October 2, on all the people who allowed the talks with Caso and de la Vega to go on when there was no longer any point to them at all and they were obviously just more demagoguery on the part of the government; we were hard on the twenty-one members of the Committee who were willing to meet with the Attorney General and allow him to lecture them and hand them his version of what had happened (what's more, they even thanked him for the very helpful briefing he'd given them!), thereby swallowing the government's lies hook, line, and sinker.

Yes, we were hard on such people, from first to last. If that's what's meant by a hard line, then there definitely was one. But if what's meant by the term is an armed uprising: *there was no such thing.* The Committee had never had any arms, and there were no plans whatsoever for an armed insurrection or rebellion. There were no hard-liners in that sense. When the *agent provocateur* Ayax Segura Garrido proposed that the Committee should start organizing along the lines of a guerrilla force, nobody went along with him, and every single member of the Committee, without exception, immediately mistrusted him. This one little detail will give you something of an idea of the atmosphere that prevailed during private Committee meetings.

Our arms were the Constitution; our ideas; our peaceful, legal demonstrations; our handbills and our newspapers. Were these the arms of hard-liners? Of course they were. Here in our country anything that represents a spontaneous movement on the part of the people and of students, an independent popular organization that forthrightly criticizes the despotic regime that unfortunately rules our lives, is considered dangerously militant. That was the only hard line that the CNH took, and the hard line that we must continue to take.

Eduardo Valle Espinoza (Owl-Eyes), of the CNH

      Listen
to the sound   listen
to the clanking of the chains imprisoning the torrent
      Look, listen
terror is charging us, sheltered behind row upon row of bayonets
     Come to me, my love, don't be afraid, it will all be over soon
They bound us fast with bonds of pain
they robbed us of the language of the stars
     Don't be afraid, it will soon be dawn
The image was overturned in the darkness
they cracked our skulls
and my hair waters the seed
     Lie beside me, the cold will not last much longer
The black roots spread
an emerald-green serpent
carved of shouts of clear crystal:
They forbade us to be silent
and felled us with their voices

It will soon be over, my beloved, don't be afraid

*Eduardo Santos, School of Business
Administration, UNAM, in* Revista de la
Universidad, *vol. 23, no. 1, September, 1968*

We also had problems with Ayax. Three days or so after we'd announced the strike at the engineering school at Poli, he turned up at
a morning meeting we were holding, introduced himself as a
manual-arts teacher or a phys ed instructor at Vocational 7—I
don't remember now exactly who he claimed he was—and told us
he'd had lots of experience organizing strikes and so on, and
that since he was a teacher he'd like to help us out. He suggested
that we form a "shock group" which "would act as a sort of Department of Defense for your Strike Committee."

"You people choose the ones you want to be part of this shock
group and I'll train them," he told us. "The authorities are bound to
try to attack you and beat you all up sooner or later, and you ought
to be prepared. An eye for an eye and a tooth for a tooth—that's
what your policy should be. If they club you, club them back; if
they kill, *you* kill. . . ." That was his advice to us. We threw him
out of the auditorium and told him not to show his face around
there again. I didn't hear any more about him till I was taken to
Military Camp 1, where I was told that Ayax had accused me of trying to organize shock groups.

Félix Lucio Hernández Gamundi, of the CNH

Sometimes when I go to sleep at night, I feel as though my cot is
surrounded by a wall of bayonets.

Florencio López Osuna, of the CNH

I work at the slaughterhouse—or rather, that's where I used to
work. I sold sausage casings and tripe and that sort of thing in a
market stall. I know how to butcher carcasses and the whole
bit. . . . I was curious as to what happened when somebody set a
streetcar on fire, and hung around to watch. . . . And that's why
I'm here in prison, really: that's the only reason. I realize now that
I've paid dearly for my curiosity and for standing around there on
the corner of Estaño and Inguarán watching them burn the street-

car, because it never occurred to me that they'd haul me off to jail
and accuse me of all sorts of crimes just because I was standing
there on the sidewalk watching what was going on. Once they got
me to police headquarters they beat me till their arms got tired.
They even threatened to kill me if I refused to confess that I'd been
active in the Student Movement and had attacked policemen. That
wasn't true at all, but it *is* true that I was held incommunicado for
eight days, that they refused to let me see my family, and that I had
no idea how to get any sort of legal help. I did sign a confession, I
admit—but only because they beat me and threatened to kill me. It
was a statement that had been typed up beforehand, a confession in
which I admitted having committed crimes I had had nothing at all
to do with. When they dragged me out of my cell to sign it, I had no
legal advisor of any sort there with me. . . . I know now what my
legal rights are, because my pals here in the cell block have wised
me up, but at that time I had no idea what a public defender was,
or what formal charges or a court hearing were. *I didn't understand
one word of the formal charges against me when they read them to me,*
because they were all in a legal jargon I'd never heard before. I've
never had any schooling. My friends here in the cell block have
helped me draw up a petition to the court; otherwise I wouldn't
have had any idea how to defend myself. All I know is that they
made me sign a false confession obtained illegally, by force. *There
are fifteen other prisoners like me here,* innocent people who had absolutely nothing to do with the Student Movement: there are fifteen
of us here in cell block C, and two, or perhaps more, in cell block
M; I know for a fact that there are two doughnut vendors in cell
block M, Félix Rodríguez and Alfredo Rodríguez Flores, from a
doughnut factory called the Churrería de México, who were picked
up by the police on September 23 in Zacatenco, the day the Santo
Tomás campus was occupied, simply because they happened to be
selling doughnuts around there. . . . Like me, they've been in here
two whole years now, without a hearing, without a trial, and without having had any connection whatsoever with the Movement.

Manuel Rodríguez Navarro, worker; prisoner in
Lecumberri

We Mexicans are quite indifferent to a state of affairs that any civilized society would consider extremely serious; we even regard it as

nothing out of the ordinary. None of the bar associations, lawyers' unions, or professional groups of attorneys are discussing the situation. Perhaps the members of these associations are bank employees, civil-service employees, or litigants who fear that it would harm them professionally if they were to speak out.

Manuel Moreno Sánchez, in an article entitled
"The Anti-Youth Complex: Fictions, Crimes, and
Errors," Excélsior, May 5, 1969

I'm a lathe operator. On October 2, 1968, I left work at five-thirty with my assistant, and headed home—I live at Estaño 15, Colonia Maza, postal zone 2. I sat down at the table around seven o'clock, and as I was eating supper, I heard a noise that sounded like firecrackers going off (I learned later that it was gunfire), over at the Tlatelolco housing unit.

I went outside and walked down the street to see what was going on, and when I reached the Calzada de la Villa I saw that Army troops had surrounded the entire housing unit. There were soldiers all around, armed with rifles and submachine guns, and tanks drawn up. When I reached the Calle de Manuel González, there were soldiers there stopping all the youngsters coming by, for no reason at all except that they were young kids. They stopped me and asked me, "What are you doing here?" and wanted to see my identification papers. Since I didn't have any with me, they took me over to an officer, who asked me what I did for a living, and I told him I was a lathe operator.

"Don't hand me that. You're a student. Give him the once-over," he said to his men.

They spread-eagled me against the side of a black car, searched me, and beat me up, for no reason whatsoever. I was taken into custody simply because I'd come there to Tlatelolco and the soldiers decided I looked like a student. That was how the whole chain of events that landed me in prison began—and here I am, still in jail.

Once they'd searched me, the soldiers took me and the other kids they'd arrested over to an Army truck and made us take our shoes off. Once we were barefoot, they lined us up, with our hands leaning on the truck and our legs spread, and began karate-chopping us, trampling on our bare feet, and punching us in the groin. And then they cut our hair.

We were badly manhandled by the soldiers, in violation of our constitutional rights. It seems to me they don't treat even the worst criminals that badly. Later on, a panel truck full of *granaderos* drove up, and the soldiers formed two lines and made us go down the middle, with each of them hitting us with their rifle butts as we went past them. One soldier hit me in the ribs with his rifle butt and I got a deep cut on my upper lip from the barrel. They shoved us into the truck and on the way back to town it kept stopping to pick up more prisoners; they kept piling them all in one on top of the other, and there were so many of us inside there we almost smothered to death. When we got to police headquarters they took us down to the basement first, and then upstairs to the second or third floor. A whole bunch of *granaderos* and security agents beat us all the way up the stairs, shouting, "You fucking students, you dirty little bastards, we haven't slept for a week, all on account of you," and kept kicking us and hitting us with their helmets and their truncheons and calling us dirty names.

We made our preliminary statements to the stenographer from the Public Prosecutor's office. I signed mine, but I would like to report that they left a blank space at the bottom of the sheet, and when next I saw it, I noticed that they'd falsified my statement by adding a paragraph in which I confessed to having been at Tlatelolco, to having been in possession of a 38-caliber Llama automatic, and to having fired two cartridge clips of bullets at people attending the meeting in Tlatelolco and thrown the gun away in the Plaza.

Your Honor, I would like to inquire what sort of punishment ought to be meted out to authorities who falsify such important documents as a notarized statement, thereby compromising an innocent person, and what means I have of proving that what they've added to the statement is an outright lie. . . . What's more, they made out police records for all of us there at headquarters, and before there had been any sort of investigation, one of the agents told me that they'd put down "Communist agitator" on mine. They also made all of us take paraffin tests. . . . I've been here in Lecumberri for two years now, and still haven't been given a chance to appear in court to defend myself.

Antonio Morales Romero, lathe
operator; prisoner in Lecumberri

The same thing happened to Servando Dávila Jiménez and Alfonso Saúl Álvarez Mosqueda, whose legal rights were also violated. As Servando Dávila Jiménez put it so well: filling the country's jails with young Mexican citizens, both students and others who were not students, throwing them in prison without any sort of trial, to find themselves vilified and accused of imaginary crimes dreamed up by some second-rate cop, is a serious violation of their constitutional rights and an attack on our country's fundamental institutions, quite independent of the question of the government's responsibility for what happened.

Manuel Rodríguez Navarro,
factory worker; prisoner in Lecumberri

There in that freezing-cold cell in the military prison, I was constantly haunted by the memory of that comrade of mine whose dead body I had seen being dragged down the stairs of the Chihuahua building. Far from striking terror in our hearts, that memory of him, and of all our other comrades who were murdered during the struggle, has given us the courage to go on fighting till we win our battle. The people, and all of us who are part of it, will one day win that victory, as was amply proved during the glorious days of the fight in '68.

Pablo Gómez, student and
member of the Communist Youth

A political prison is a real training school for revolutionaries.
Gilberto Guevara Niebla, of the CNH

What's happening in the outside world? How is everybody doing?
Manuel Marcué Pardiñas,
journalist; prisoner in Lecumberri

I was held incommunicado in the military prison. Sócrates's cell was right across from mine. They would take us out of our cells and interrogate us in a special room. One night I heard Sócrates being taken back to his cell by two officers after being interrogated. One of them was walking down the corridor right alongside Sócrates, and the other one, as far as I could tell just listening to their footsteps, was walking a few steps behind the two of them.

They opened the door of his cell and I heard Sócrates say to the officer alongside him, "Oh, I forgot to tell you: I gave him another submachine gun" (I can't remember now whether Sócrates said he'd given it to Cabeza de Vaca or to Peña), "I forgot to mention that. . . ."

The other officer who was following piped up then and asked, "What was that he just said?"

They locked Sócrates in his cell again and the first officer said to the other, "Okay, let's go on back now."

Pablo Gómez, of the Communist Youth

There's one professor, a first-rate economist, a *brain* and a real guts player when the chips are down: Don Jesús Silva Herzog. On May 9, 1968, a banquet celebrating his fiftieth year as a university professor was held at Los Morales in his honor. A whole bunch of his former students and many university professors and specialists in the field of economics attended it, and lots of government bigwigs as well (Norberto Aguirre Palancas, the famous engineer, was among those present, for example, as a special representative of the President of Mexico, Gustavo Díaz Ordaz). Don Jesús rose from his chair to thank everyone for the homage being paid him on this occasion, and in the course of his brief speech made a special plea for the release of teachers and students who had been thrown into prison.

Manuel Marcué Pardiñas, journalist

We'd been put in cell block N some two months before; the other prisoners regarded us as terrible "squares": we sang a lot, not because our morale was low, and not because we were in high spirits either; we simply sang a lot because we liked to sing—I think it's more or less of a habit among "squares" in prison to sing almost every night if there's somebody in the group who can accompany them on the guitar. Apparently they find the long nights behind bars quite picturesque if they can sing like that. We always felt that we were real *acelerados*, the real vanguard, for quite understandable reasons: there were lots of things cooking in August and September [of 1968] in Mexico, and I had the feeling I was right in the center of

things. We had lots of news of what was going on outside: leaflets smuggled in to us there in prison in people's brassieres and
shoes were passed from hand to hand, producing all sorts of com-
ments from us political prisoners shut up there in cell block N at
that particular time. "We'll give the government real hell," "Let's
send our pals a letter so they won't worry about us," "What a
going-over they're giving Díaz Ordaz out there. . . ."

Cell block N was a political fruit salad, I must say: there were
Maoists, Trotskyites, Guevarists, and the most recent "shipment"
that had arrived consisted of twenty-two Communists and four
prisoners who didn't belong to any party. That was obviously a po-
tentially explosive mixture, but nonetheless the prevailing atmosphere was one of mutual respect and comradeship. We were given
a warm and affectionate welcome by Rico Galán, the "Trotskos,"
and all the other political prisoners who'd been sent to Lecumberri
before those of us from the Movement—and all of us will remember
that warm reception we received for the rest of our lives.

One afternoon they locked all the prisoners who were serving
time for nonpolitical crimes in their cell blocks, and the entire
prison fell dead silent, as though something very unusual were
about to happen. We soon found out what it was, because suddenly
we heard voices in the street that got louder and louder. "They're
holding a demonstration for us!" one comrade shouted, and I could
hear the voices outside then, very clearly: FREE THE POLITICAL PRIS-
ONERS—FREE THE POLITICAL PRISONERS—FREE THE POLITICAL PRIS-
ONERS! they were shouting. I suddenly broke out in goose-pimples
and clenched my fists in sheer desperation. We all began shouting
back: UNAM-UNAM-UNAM,   RAH-RAH-RAH—UNAM-UNAM-UNAM,
RAH-RAH-RAH! I yelled so loud my throat ached, and then we all
fell silent, and we heard them shout back from the street, DOWN
WITH DÍAZ ORDAZ! DOWN WITH DÍAZ ORDAZ! I almost burst into
tears, I was both so happy and so frustrated, but I would have been
ashamed to let my fellow prisoners see me crying like that. I felt a
part of those comrades who were free out there shouting up to us
from the street, and all the desperation I felt at being shut up there
behind those prison walls and prison bars that were separating me
from them came pouring out my throat as I shouted back: they *had*
to hear us, they *had* to know that we were still with them, heart and
soul, even though we were locked up there in prison. I was—and

still am—part of them, separated from them by prison bars, but nonetheless still one of them.

We kept up with events by reading the papers, by listening to the news broadcasts on radio or television, and most important of all, by getting reports of what was happening from our families when they visited us. I remember that a number of my comrades were real experts at news-gathering: they knew exactly what station to tune in to at various hours of the day to pick up a spot news bulletin. So when September 13, 1968, rolled around and we were anxious to have the latest news about our demonstration, we didn't have to sit listening for hours at a time to programs on "Radio AAAAA . . . IIIII . . . tops on your dial, folks. . . ." All we had to do was pop into a cell of one of those comrades who knew all the ins and outs of how to pick up news on the radio, and it was just as though you'd pressed some sort of button, because these one-man news agencies would immediately start giving you the very latest scoop on how the demonstration was going. I bet even Díaz Ordaz himself wasn't in that close touch with what was happening!

Sergeant Mares, a nice old guy who never locked us up in our cells at ten p.m. as he had orders to do from the prison warden, didn't happen to be the guard on duty the night of October 2, 1968, so we were locked in our cells as soon as it was time for lights out. The four of us in cell 3 had already corked off when suddenly I heard a voice say in a furtive whisper, "De la Vega, Señor de la Vega," very quietly, so that none of the others would hear. I sat up, heard the cell door open, and a guard tiptoed in.

"Are you awake, Señor de la Vega?" he asked.

"Yes, what is it?"

"I just wanted to tell you that they're killing a whole bunch of students in Tlatelolco."

"What's that?"

"There's been trouble in Tlatelolco, and they've killed a whole lot of students."

"Where did you hear that?"

"I heard the news just as I was coming on duty to fill in for the regular guard, but don't let on to anybody I came into your cell to tell you, because I'd get booted out on my ear if they found out."

"Don't worry, I won't say a word. And thanks very much," I replied.

I sat there thinking and decided it wasn't worth waking up my cellmates to pass on news that seemed to me to be just another of the many rumors that constantly went the rounds there in Lecumberri. Besides, it just wasn't *possible* that they'd kill kids at a peaceful, orderly meeting: a thing like that *couldn't possibly* happen. So I lay down again and went back to sleep.

On the morning of October 3, I came out of my cell to line up with the others at seven a.m., as we did every morning. But the minute I stepped out of my cell, I was caught up in a whole crowd of comrades milling about in confusion, talking about events that had happened the night before that today are no news to anybody. When they told me the news *they'd* heard, I felt very guilty at not having believed my unexpected informant, for not having shouted then and there: WAKE UP EVERYBODY! SOMETHING TERRIBLE IS HAPPENING!

So that's how I heard what happened in the Plaza de las Tres Culturas on October 2, 1968, at six p.m. I have the feeling I've never been the same since; I couldn't possibly be.

Eduardo de la Vega Ávila,
of the Communist Party

We took off down the freeway, and we caught a glimpse of Chapultepec Park through the back windows. "Look, we're going by Chapultepec!" Then I saw the colored lights on the roller coaster, and the signs just before the first sharp plunge warning riders on the roller coaster not to lean out of their seats, and down below the big signs along the freeway indicating the next exit . . . Palmas, Molino del Rey. . . . "Take a good look at what it's like on the streets. You may not see them again for a long time," Pablo whispered to me. We went through the underpass, where there was heavy traffic at that hour, and then the streets gradually became darker and shabbier. We crossed a bridge and drew up in front of the main gate of Lecumberri Prison.

Luis González de Alba, of the CNH

The walls of my cell are iron plates held together with rivets.

Eli de Gortari, professor of philosophy;
prisoner in Lecumberri

When I was taken prisoner, I had been through a long series of terrible experiences: eight months of being on the run, of hiding out, of living alone, with only my own thoughts for company, of not seeing my friends or my loved ones often enough to even halfway satisfy my need to give and receive affection. I was not willing to leave the country because I felt—and still feel—that my own fight is here in Mexico. I had honorable friends in prison whom I could not abandon without compromising my own honor. And that is why I decided to fight for the liberation of all my comrades in prison, and how I landed in prison myself.

Heberto Castillo, member of the Teachers'
Coalition; prisoner in Lecumberri

On January 3 I went to the House of Detention to visit a prisoner whom I was defending in court, Gerardo Unzueta Lorenzana. At eleven o'clock that morning, I was taken into custody by a squad of guards who had no sort of warrant for my arrest. At one p.m. that same day, I was taken out to the courtyard of the prison and shoved into a car full of men I'd never set eyes on before, who later turned out to be federal security agents. They blindfolded me and took me to a hotel, the name and address of which I don't know to this day.

In that hotel I was threatened, bullied, insulted, and beaten because I refused to sign a confession these agents tried to force out of me. After being held the rest of that day and part of the night in that hotel, they blindfolded me again, threw me onto the floor of a car, and took me to a house outside the city limits somewhere. They held me incommunicado there, under heavy guard around the clock, for four days. On the fourth day they blindfolded me once again, shoved me into a car, and took me to yet another house. On the following day, that is to say on January 8, 1969, they took me from this second house to the Federal District House of Detention. I hardly need mention that I was treated on this trip as I had been on all the others.

On January 10 I was formally booked, along with several other comrades, Antonio Pérez Sánchez, Salvador Ruiz Villegas, Roberta Avendaño Martínez, and Ana Ignacia Rodríguez, all of whom had suffered the same sort of mistreatment when they were caught by agents and kidnapped. We were formally charged with ten felonies, and last November 12 we were given sixteen-year prison sentences.

In a few words, this is one chapter in the story of my life as a
revolutionary.

Rodolfo Echeverría Martínez, member of the
Communist Party; prisoner in Lecumberri

"Would you please allow me to go to the lavatory?" I asked them.

They put what seemed to be a sort of hood over my head (I
realized later that it was just a filthy pillowcase) and led me down
the corridor, stumbling and groping my way along. Once I got inside the john alone, I took the pillowcase off my head and removed
my blindfold. I found myself in a primitive little water closet, filthy
dirty, with no windows or anything that gave me the slightest clue
as to where I was. I looked at myself in the mirror and said to
myself, Well, they've caught you and you're in the soup now, Ti-
tita, that's for sure. The agent outside was pounding on the door, so
I put the blindfold and the pillowcase back on and came out of the
john.

The agent took me back to the room they'd put me in before, and
another agent asked me, "Wouldn't you like to lie down?"

"No, thanks."

"Come on, get some rest—there's a cot over there."

"A cot!" I exclaimed. "It'd collapse under my weight the minute I
sat down on it."

"No it won't, come on, try it."

I felt it, and it seemed pretty rickety, but I sat down on it anyway.
I could hear the agents tearing some sort of packages open, and
then one of them said to me, "Wouldn't you like a cracker?"

"I guess so. . . ." I groped for one and swallowed it there under
the pillowcase.

A few minutes later another agent said to me, "Wouldn't you like
some coffee?"

"No, thank you."

"Come on—have some."

"Well, if you insist."

Then the guy said to me, "Stand up and take your blindfold off."

I got to my feet and took it off, and suddenly, without any warning, before I even had time to strike a nice pose, they took mug
shots of me, full-face and in profile. I saw that there were three men
guarding me, a young one who looked to be about twenty-one or

twenty-two, "Blondie," the son of a police captain; another little plump dark-haired one, who seemed to know what was going on in the University, and the med school in particular, and might have been a football player once; and another middle-aged man, about fifty or so, who turned out to be a great cook, "Capi." I lay down on that cot again, and they gave me a blanket. I fell asleep in no time and the next thing I knew it was nine o'clock the next morning.

Roberta Avendaño Martínez (Tita),
CNH delegate from UNAM

You begin to find out what the word government means, what it stands for, when that government sends tanks into the streets.

Alfonso Salinas Moya, student at the
School of Dentistry, UNAM

"You say the government will help us, is that right, professor? Do you know what the government's like?"

"I told you I know it well."

"Well, as it so happens, we know it too. But what we don't know is who its mother was."

I told them its mother was our country.

Juan Rulfo, "Luvina," in El Ilano
en Llamas [The Plain in Flames], *published*
by El Fondo de Cultura Económica

In prison we've learned the real meaning of the word solidarity: students, teachers, and many other people have continually shown us what it means. Speaking for myself, the attitude of my comrades from the Faculty of Sciences has made me feel very proud and very grateful. We've never felt for a moment that we've been forgotten: they've stuck by us in every way they possibly could. In all these two years, I don't think I've ever felt really "separated" from my comrades.

Gilberto Guevara Niebla, of the CNH

I read a lot. I takes notes. I've read *México: Riqueza y Miseria* [*Mexico: Wealth and Poverty*] by Alonso Aguilar and Fernando Carmona, for instance. I learned some horrifying facts from that book; the statistics quoted in it, by the way, refer to the year 1967. . . . For this one reason alone, our fight for change is justified, for the figures in their study present a heartbreaking picture of our country. Just imagine: more than 1 million people who speak only some Indian dialect; 2 million landless peasants; more than 3 million children between the ages of six and fourteen who receive no education of any sort; 4,600,000 laborers who tried to enter the United States illegally in the years 1948 to 1957; nearly 5 million Mexicans who go barefoot all the time and some 12,700,000 others who rarely wear shoes; more than 5 million families whose monthly income is less than a thousand pesos; some 4,300,000 dwellings, housing 24 million people, that have no running water; more than 8 million Mexicans who never have meat, fish, milk, or eggs to eat, and more than 10 million who never eat bread; 10 million workers who have not been unionized; and nearly 11 million Mexicans who are illiterate. What do we need more data for? These figures are proof enough of how badly off this country is and how hard we must fight.

Ernesto Olvera, teacher of mathematics
at Preparatory 1, UNAM

I am convinced that the future of this country lies in the hands of young people of my generation.

Gilberto Guevara Niebla, of the CNH

Laying all the blame for everything on the Mexican government is perhaps our most natural and our most immediate reaction. Any measures that are carried to violent extremes are always to be condemned. Even if someone is clearly guilty of breaking the law and deserves to be reprimanded or even severely punished, there is no justification whatsoever for making him a martyr. Creating martyrs merely compounds the crime. The accused thereby become accusers, and the judge and the executioner murderers.

Fernando Madero Hernández,
teacher at Preparatory 2, UNAM

What's happened to the twenty-one members of the University Committee who passed a resolution supporting the students' six-point petition, who urged the youngsters on, who backed them largely to enhance their own personal popularity, who more or less forced them to play the role of heroes? Aren't these twenty-one in solid with the regime now, the very same regime that they criticized and helped the students attack? Didn't they come out of the Attorney General's office bowing and scraping and thanking him for having briefed them and helped them understand the true significance of the events of 1968? According to these twenty-one, the Attorney General's sage pronouncements were a great help in channeling the energies of university students in the proper direction.

Nicolás Hernández Toro, student at
the School of Engineering, UNAM

Attorney Carlos Pinera, the assistant director of the Santa Marta Acatitla Penitentiary for the past year and a half, resigned this post yesterday.

Attorney Pinera has been appointed director of the Public Relations Office of UNAM.

News item, Excélsior,
Saturday, November 9, 1968

Is it the intellectuals who are responsible for everything that has happened? Basically, they *are* responsible, just as theorists and intellectuals were responsible for our Independence, for the Reform and the Revolution of 1910. They are the ones who ponder, who study the situation, who teach, who pass on philosophical ideas, knowledge, contemporary thought. It is intellectuals who are leading the fight all over the world against social inequalities, injustice, the rigidity of authoritarian regimes, human alienation.

Fernando Benítez, José Emilio Pacheco,
Carlos Monsiváis, Vicente Rojo, in
an editorial in the literary section
of Siempre!, *no. 350,*
October 30, 1968

I have gone to visit the political prisoners and will continue to visit them as often as I am allowed into the prison. Am I openly opposing the government, did you ask? If anyone says to my face that I'm committing a crime and can prove that I am, I'll be the first to admit I'm guilty, but as far as I know it's not a crime to visit prisoners, men who have been deprived of their freedom, who have been subjected to humiliations and harassment, who have suffered terribly. . . . On October 2 I said a mass in Cuernavaca for those who had lost their lives at Tlatelolco, and wrote a sermon on the injustices being perpetrated throughout our country and the nationwide indifference to the fate of prisoners involved in the events that occurred during the Student Movement last year. I sent copies of this sermon to all the faithful in my diocese, and requested that it be read on December 12, the feast day of the Virgin of Guadalupe.

This matter still has not been resolved, and two days ago ninety prisoners began a hunger strike in protest.

Let us stand as one, as brothers, as Christians, in the face of the suffering and the despair of our fellows: the prisoners, their parents, their families, and their comrades.

Let us be mindful of our common responsibility for the improvement or the decline of the general welfare of each and all. We are all responsible, in fact, and cannot excuse ourselves or remain indifferent to the countless miscarriages of justice in our country, abuses which become even more outrageous when perpetrated against defenseless victims and social, political, or economic outcasts.

Such abuses have caused and will continue to cause a great deal of unrest, particularly among young people.

> *Conversation with Dr. Sergio Méndez Arceo,*
> *Bishop of Cuernavaca, outside Lecumberri*
> *Prison, in December, 1969, published in*
> *Siempre!, no. 863, January 7, 1970*

I wrote to José Revueltas, asking him for a list of the names of political prisoners, so that the people in my diocese might pray for them. This may help, perhaps, to forge a consciousness, a national consciousness.

> *Dr. Sergio Méndez Arceo, Bishop of Cuernavaca*

I can assure you that all my actions have been motivated by the conviction that I cannot abandon my fellow man, my brothers, that I must bear witness to the fact that a true Christian has the obligation to condemn any form of injustice, *particularly the sort of injustice which becomes a veritable institution,* the prevailing order of things. For years now we have tolerated many injustices in the name of law and order, of peace within our country, of our international prestige.

> *Dr. Sergio Méndez Arceo, "Christmas Message,*
> *1969," broadcast by radio from Cuernavaca*

When they arrested me I had been teaching for two months at the Felipe Rivera School—the school on the Avenida Central just around the corner from Vértiz. I was arrested on January 2, 1969, about six o'clock at night, as I was on my way to the school. Just as I came around the corner with one of my students, a man suddenly grabbed me by the arm and threw me inside a dark-blue car with four other quite square-looking young guys inside (young people without ideals are pretty sorry types, aren't they?). One of them had his pistol pointed at me and the other even had the safety off his. I suppose they thought I was going to put up a fight. I told them that that wasn't my intention at all, and asked them to please let my student go—they were trying to drag him into the car too. They let him go, and the car then took off like greased lightning. They blindfolded me, and even though I tried to keep track of where the car was going, I had no idea where they were taking me. After a while the car stopped, and the agent sitting on my left got out and another got in. I said to him, "That's Guerlain you're wearing, isn't it?" because I recognized the scent. He told me not to play dumb, and said that I'd have a much easier time of it if I cooperated with them. The other agents had already said to me, "It was your friend Nacha, you know, who told us where you were."

"Oh, is that so?" I replied. "I find that just a bit hard to believe, since she's been in Taxco all this last month."

The guy insisted that Nacha was the one who'd ratted on me and told them where I was.

"Well, since she told you everything, there's nothing more you need to know now, right?"

"Where's Rojo's car?" they asked me. (Rojo was another CNH delegate.)

"I haven't the vaguest idea."

"Sure you have—you've got the key to it right here."

I did have the key to Rojo's car with me, as a matter of fact, but I hadn't been driving it recently. He had another key to it.

"Where does Rojo live?"

"I'm not really sure—somewhere around UNAM, it seems to me."

"Where's Barragán?" (Barragán was another CNH delegate from the law school.)

"I have no idea."

"How about Celia Soto?"

"I don't have any idea where she is either."

"If you cooperate, we won't give you a hard time."

"It seems to me she's gone to Cuernavaca, but I'm not really sure."

The guy went on like that—not actually hitting me, but screaming at me and cussing me out and calling me names. He went on questioning me for a while, and then he got out of the car and one of the agents in the front seat began to make fun of me: "Come on, give us a V for Victory."

"It's very easy to make fun of people when they can't defend themselves—right?" I answered, and he shut up. A few minutes later another agent got in and the car took off again. I was quite sure they'd parked the car along the street somewhere because I could hear other cars going by, and I remember that I sat up very straight in the seat, in the hopes that somebody might see me and come to my rescue. As the driver put his foot to the floor and the car raced off again, it splashed another car that must have been parked alongside; all the agents thought that was terribly funny and roared with laughter.

At that point I'd begun to realize what terrible trouble I was in, and I felt a slight pain or a little twinge or cramp in the pit of my stomach, doubtless because I was scared silly, but I don't think it showed. I asked for a cigarette and puffed on it slowly, telling myself over and over in my mind, Don't worry, they won't hurt you, and I even asked them in a joking tone of voice if I should use the floor of the car for an ashtray or whether someone would throw the butt out the window for me.

Roberta Avendaño Martínez (Tita), of the CNH

> Tell me, tell me, Gustavo,
> Tell me why you're a coward,
> Tell me why you've no mother,
> Tell me, Gustavo, please tell me.
>
> *Student chant during the August 27*
> *demonstration, a parody of a well-known*
> *radio and television commercial*

It isn't true that we planned to blow up the stands at the Olympic Stadium or sabotage the Olympic Games. First of all, how were we supposedly planning to do it? With Molotov cocktails?

Enrique Hernández Alatriste, student at the
School of Dentistry, UNAM

What's the significance of Tlatelolco? How far did our Movement get us? Are we better or worse off than before? I'll be able to answer questions like that in five years or so.

Alejandro López Ochoa,
engineering student, UNAM

There were a number of us, of course, who claimed that we students had to take advantage of the Olympics, of the huge crowds that would attend them, to attract attention to our problems, and we realized, naturally, that we'd be the sour note, the blot on the image—like when the president visits some little town and among the banners reading WELCOME and MANY THANKS there's one that says OUR TOWN HAS NO WATER AND NO ELECTRIC LIGHTS. We were the one voice that was off-key in the universal hymns of praise, but that's a far cry from wanting to sabotage the whole celebration—not to mention actually succeeding in doing so! What's more, there were a few kids who knew what the score was, but the rest of them were just a bunch of sheep, and the dissension and the lack of awareness of what was really going on got so bad that after October 2 there were lots of kids, lots of Movement people, who either actually attended the Games or at least watched them on television. It was revolting! To think they could watch the Games like that—over the dead bodies of their comrades and the thousands of people who'd suddenly disappeared, people we knew had been thrown in jail but had had no news of since. And there those asses were, applauding Sergeant Pedraza! * Those bastards gave me a pain in the balls.

Vicente Saldaña Flores, engineering student, IPN

How is it possible for the government to regard a small handful of young boys and girls as "a very serious danger"? It's downright ri-

---

* Sergeant Pedraza was a member of the Mexican Olympics Team and winner of a medal in one of the competitive events. (Translator's note.)

diculous—especially when everybody knows that the government has very powerful means of repression at its disposal and more or less completely controls the communications media. What danger, what "very serious danger" possibly exists that the regime in power can't control? The way I see it, the only thing the authorities can't control is their own guilt feelings, because if public officials had right on their side and governed the country the way they should they would have nothing to fear and wouldn't need to resort to violence and injustice as a shield to protect themselves and allow them to remain in power. . . . What's more, a large part of the population is passive and indifferent. So what's gotten into the authorities, anyway? Everything was going their way.

Ernestina Rojo González, law student, UNAM

The one with the real power is always obliged to be the most generous.

José Ignacio Barraza, law student, UNAM

If the one thing the Student Movement has accomplished is to strip the Mexican Revolution bare, to show that it was a filthy, corrupt old whore, that alone is enough to justify it. . . .

Esteban Sánchez Fernández, father of a family.

We had no connection with the Student Movement except for the paid ad that the union at El Ánfora inserted in the newspapers announcing its support of the Movement. Both Armando and I are teachers—not university professors, but high-school teachers—and we both belonged to the National Liberation Movement, as did all the leftist intellectuals in Mexico, from Lázaro Cárdenas to González Pedrero—but my husband and I were always mere rank-and-file members, never leaders. Almost all of them dropped out at the time of OLAS, but we stayed on and worked in it, because it seemed to us that its goals were nationalist and that the line it was taking was the right one. They didn't arrest anybody back then. They waited till 1968 to arrest us. . . .

Adela Salazar Carbajal, attorney
specializing in labor litigation

I've been accused of being an undercover agent for the government. . . . Listen, one time they were being very rough on one of my

comrades, another CNH delegate from the law school, and a
member of the Communist Party as well, because he hadn't voted
the way the other delegates had on a certain issue, and in the
heated argument that followed, the rank-and-file Movement people
at the meeting started criticizing not just this one delegate but all of
them in general. My feelings were hurt, and I interrupted the discussion and told the audience that they shouldn't get the idea into
their heads that it was a real ball being a delegate, or that I was
happy about having to live like a gypsy and not having any money,
and announced that I was resigning, but everybody in the audience
started shouting, "We didn't mean *you*, Tita! We've got nothing
against you, Tita! Please don't resign! Tita, Tita, Tita, Tita!" And
they refused to let me leave. That did my heart good, so I stayed,
but at the same time I was sort of angry. . . . I've been here in
prison two years now, and they've handed me a sixteen-year sentence, but people nonetheless still ask me if I'm an undercover
agent for the government. . . . I've got a question or two I might
ask too: like how they can have the nerve to accuse me of that. . . .
There are lots of prisoners in here with me who can testify to the
abuses they've been subjected to: women whose breasts were
burned with lighted cigarettes during interrogation sessions,
women suffering from cancer of the uterus because of the beatings
they got, others who were raped, after being promised they'd be set
free if they submitted, not to mention still others who've had bad
hemorrhages—and those fucking security agents tried to make people believe I was part of their outfit . . . can you imagine! That's
right, Elena, it was the agents themselves who spread that story,
and the students were taken in by it, or at any rate they didn't do
anything to spike the rumor. . . . One of the reasons was that everybody knew I'd been running around loose till January 2. The
authorities never managed to get their hands on me at CU on September 18, even though I weigh 220 pounds and am always spotted
immediately, and they didn't nab me on September 20 either, the
day they arrested a whole bunch of kids who are locked up in
Lecumberri now, when the cops raided a house that I'd cleared out
of just twenty minutes before they arrived on the scene. But does
that make me an undercover agent for the government?

On Saturday, January 11, 1969, they took me out of the women's
ward at Lecumberri and brought me to the "Consultation Room,"

and there my father was. I felt really awful that day, because my
dad was . . . how can I describe the state he was in?—half scared
and half mad, not knowing whether to console me or give me a lecture. I saw tears in his eyes for the first time, and felt really bad. He
left in just a few minutes, because they only allow one member of
your family in to see you at a time. My mother came in then, in
tears. I'd managed to get one of the matrons in the women's ward
to send her a letter from me telling her not to worry, that I was fine,
but she was naturally upset, knowing that I was there in prison. I
reassured both my mom and my dad as best I could, and the two of
them left. That afternoon they transferred me to the Women's
House of Detention, and I've been here ever since. My mom died
a year ago, on November 24; and now it's just my dad who
comes to see me, on Wednesdays and Sundays. My folks had
always had no interest in politics at all, and they could never understand how I happened to end up in prison. My mom died without
ever realizing what the whole thing was all about, and my dad—
well, he does his best to keep his chin up. . . . I don't think the
sentences we were given were fair, or for that matter being thrown
in prison for any length of time, because despite what the government claims we aren't criminals at all, we're young people who
were fighting for an ideal: fighting so that our laws here in Mexico
would not only be admired and regarded as some of the most revolutionary in the world, but would also be respected to the letter,
without any sort of discrimination; so that government officials
would be less corrupt and not abuse their authority; so that the
Mexican people would have the right to hold public officials responsible for their acts, as provided by law; so that, in a word, we
would have a genuine democracy in this country and justice for all.
As I recall, when the president takes his oath of office, he says
something like "as demanded by the people." It occurs to me that
in the Zócalo something like seven hundred thousand people assembled to make quite legitimate demands, which the president
never answered, or rather answered by ordering the *granaderos* to
attack us. I may have sixteen more years tacked on to my sentence
for saying such a thing, which the government may well take to be
an insult, but it really doesn't matter—I'll be so old when I finish
serving my first sixteen-year sentence that sixteen more won't matter a bit! What's more, if I didn't deserve that first sixteen-year

prison term, because I'd never once said anything that outspoken, I might as well give them a good reason for handing me the next sixteen, even though what I've just said isn't a crime either!

Roberta Avendaño Martínez (Tita), of the CNH

VALLEJO-VALLEJO-VALLEJO-FREEDOM! VALLEJO-FREEDOM-VALLEJO-FREEDOM-VALLEJO-FREEDOM
Chant at the August 13 demonstration

ONE HONEST LEADER MEANS ONE POLITICAL PRISONER
Poster at the Faculty of Political Sciences, UNAM

Since his arrest in 1959 for leading the railway workers' movement aimed at creating independent unions, Vallejo has been suffering both the legal penalties and the public ostracism that befall any opposition leader who refuses to have anything to do with the usual compromises and shady deals. Though Article 143 of the Federal Penal Code provides only the very vaguest definition of the crime of "social dissolution," Vallejo was given the maximum penalty under this law. Moreover, other supposedly legal interpretations of the statutes were invoked by the authorities: any sort of criticism of the government should be equated with treason; any person who dissents, even in the most legitimate, open, and legal way, deserves the harshest sort of punishment. . . . The unconstitutional nature of the reasons officially set forth to justify the prolonged incarceration of Vallejo and Campa is as disturbing as the general apathy, the utter indifference of the majority of people in this country toward the existence of political prisoners.

These two phenomena are interconnected. The notorious political apathy of Mexicans is intimately related to their all too obvious amorality, to their feeling of indifference and helplessness at the mere thought of combatting any form of injustice. To depoliticize a nation is not simply to convince all its citizens of the futility of concerning themselves with public affairs, of the inexorable nature of the decision-making process, since no sort of collective pressure can be brought to bear on it. To depoliticize a nation is not simply to make the administration of the country a magical process resulting from deliberations behind the scene that take place every six years.* It is also to deprive an entire country of the possibility of making moral choices, of the possibility of expressing its indignation. It means destroying morality as a collective concern and reducing it to the status of an individual problem. It means the death of a social morality and the encouragement of a petty-bourgeois morality based on the need to create taboos, whereas any genuine morality is based on the ability to make free choices.

Carlos Monsiváis, in Siempre!, *no. 322, April 17, 1968*

popular leftist journal (handwritten)

. . . I found on the desk in my office one of your letters in which you told me of your visit to Vallejo and Campa. What a shame and what a tragedy! One tends to forget the most painful things, surrounding oneself with a sort of vast silence that suddenly is broken by many sounds. That splendid, selfish silence behind which we protect our egos and lose touch with our true selves. How is it possible for us to each live our own separate lives: so "comfortable," so well sheltered, so indifferent? It pains me greatly to imagine Vallejo, a tiny little figure in his cell that is as neat as a pin, drinking milk like a cat, hoping that some day he will be released and go back to . . . to what exactly? To a street somewhere and little knots of people who will stare at him with a certain curiosity, but also with a fundamental indifference. What is he going to do when he gets out? How is he going to live? Whom is he going to love? How is he going to work? This frightens me even more than the thought of him there in his cell drinking milk.

Guillermo Haro, astronomer, in a letter to Elena Poniatowska from Armenia, July 22, 1970

Two concrete bed slabs in one of the first cells in block C are piled high with squeezed lemons. The smell is very strong—the distinctive odor of the hunger strike that eighty-seven political prisoners have now been on for forty days. Of the eighty-seven prisoners

---

* Mexican presidential candidates are chosen every six years by the PRI. (Translator's note.)

who began the hunger strike, only sixty-five now remain in cell
blocks M, N, and C. . . . Fifteen prisoners have had convulsions,
and many are in the infirmary at present; three days after the hunger strike began, Eli de Gortari was found unconscious in his cell,
and the doctor would not allow him to continue to fast, for Eli is a
diabetic. The worst part, however, was not the hunger strike but
the scandalous attack on the 115 political prisoners in Lecumberri
by other prisoners jailed for criminal offenses. On January 1, 1970,
the sixty-eight prisoners in cell block C (the one where most of the
students were put) were victims of a two-hour attack by these common prisoners, who not only assaulted them with lengths of pipe,
metal rods, bottles, and various sharp-pointed objects, but also
stole all their blankets and every one of their books. The same thing
happened to the fifty political prisoners in cell block M, where the
attack lasted forty-five minutes. Rafael Jacobo García, a political
prisoner who is the father of eight children, tried to close the cell-
block door, and was badly pummeled and beaten and slashed with
a razor through the bars; he received deep cuts on his face, his
arms, and his hands, and both his skull and his jaw were fractured.
Rafael Jacobo is a strong man, a peasant—a member of the CCI.*
Isaías Rojas was there at the door with him, trying to defend him
against the common prisoners who were lashing out at Rafael, and
Rojas also received severe cuts on his face and hands. The defenseless political prisoners, who were very weak since they had been
on their hunger strike (that is to say, taking nothing but water with
a little lemon juice and sugar) since December 10, were brutally
beaten, but eventually managed to take refuge in cell block N. The
common prisoners made away with all the hunger strikers' lemons
and every last grain of sugar, and smashed every single bottle of
purified water they had. What would prisoners want with all those
lemons—unless, of course, the authorities had passed the word to
them that they should put an end to the political prisoners' hunger
strike? The common prisoners sacked the entire cell block: among
the articles stolen were Dr. Eli de Gortari's manuscripts and those of
the famous writer José Revueltas, the books belonging to "the intellectuals in cell block M," their blankets, their clothes, their radios,
their watches, their typewriters, their correspondence, their photos

* Central Campesina Independiente (Independent Peasants' Organization).

of their families, their personal papers, their hotplates, their mattresses, their cots, their pillows, their dishes, their cups; their attackers smashed everything they could find: the chairs and the bookshelves made there in the carpentry shop at Lecumberri that the political prisoners had somehow scraped up enough money to buy in the year and more they had been in jail, plus all the other things people had brought them after they had filled out endless requests; the few possessions each prisoner had had such difficulties accumulating were completely destroyed in less than fifteen minutes. Within the prisoners' individual cells (Dr. de Gortari's, for instance), the common prisoners piled up all the books they found and set them on fire. It was like entering prison all over again, for they would once more have to start from scratch to acquire the meager store of indispensable everyday articles that it had taken so many months to come by: a cot, a mattress, a blanket, a few eating utensils, a hotplate. . . . But even this loss of the prisoners' few precious possessions was not as disturbing as the threat to their lives. What possible assurance can prisoners who have been jailed for their political beliefs, students who are completing their course of study there in Lecumberri, have that tomorrow they will not be the victims of another act of vandalism on the part of common prisoners with the connivance of the authorities? On the night of January 1, 1970, many of the prisoners jailed for criminal offenses wandered all through the cell blocks in groups of twenty or thirty, armed with steel rods, broomsticks, and lengths of pipe; "law and order," "prison security," were in the hands of drug addicts from cell block F, of hoodlums and murderers who took over all the inner corridors and cell blocks and did not leave the *redondel*, the main circular walkway leading to each of the cell blocks opening out onto it, until nine the next night, when those on the "outside," friends and relatives who feared for the lives of their husbands, fathers, and sons brought pressure to bear on the newspapers to print a few lines about what was happening in Lecumberri.

According to eyewitnesses, the person who opened the door of cell block F so that the drug addicts confined there could go attack the political prisoners was the assistant director of Lecumberri Prison: Bernardo Palacios Reyes.

From an article by E.P. in La Garrapata, *no. 40, February 16, 1970*

The only persons actively opposing the government were either being persecuted and hunted down or are already "here in jail." The liberal democracy that we had thirty years ago in this country has been replaced by more and more oppressive forms of government. On arriving in France, Attorney F. Jacoby, a representative of the Hague Court, declared that the civil rights of Mexican citizens were seriously threatened in this country and described our government as "pre-Fascist."

From a statement drawn up by the political prisoners and read by Gilberto Guevara Niebla on Sunday, January 18, 1970, two days before the prisoners ended their thousand-hour hunger strike begun on December 10, 1969

. . . I am enraged, and wonder how it's possible to live without feeling beside yourself with rage. How can anybody enter Mexican politics and keep his temper and not make a fuss and keep a smile on his face and get along with everybody and nail down some nice little government job or some nice fat one? I don't agree with what my friends keep writing in the papers: that scientists ought to enter politics. I know what they mean by that. They think that going into politics means getting yourself some cushy government job, being influential, being successful. That's not politics—that's shit, that's being the worst sort of horse-trader. Why don't they enter *real* politics, opposition politics, the sort where there are no soft jobs, where your life and your freedom are constantly endangered? You can't ask another person to make sacrifices, I admit. But at the same time I can't abide all those people who keep telling us it's our sacred duty and absolutely necessary for us to participate in "our" official one-party politics. There's nothing noble or unselfish or honest about that sort of politics. If you go in for that kind of politics, merely to further your own personal interests, you should keep your mouth shut about it, be a decent sort of bandit, and not try to make other credulous people swallow your philosophy hook, line, and sinker. Our duty as scientists is simply to try to teach others how to be good scientists, to help young people, to train competent leaders, to engage in real political action, even though this may imply—and in fact most often does imply—fighting professional political bosses tooth and nail. Admittedly, it makes things harder for us if we don't toady to the "pols," if we cross swords with them. But that doesn't really matter. . . .

It's not true that you can be a good politician if you're no longer a good doctor. It's not true that it's better to be president of Chalchi-comula than a second-rate gynecologist. If you're not any good at something that you've supposedly been passionately interested in for years and years, you won't be any better at anything else. It's a lie to maintain any differently; it's the clearest possible proof of your own failure deep down as a person, of your fundamental me-diocrity. But everybody has the right, of course, to be as mediocre or as stupid as he wishes to be or turns out to be, no matter how outwardly successful he is or how many honors he reaps.

Guillermo Haro, astronomer, in a letter to Elena
Poniatowska from Armenia, July 28, 1970

I feel as though I'm living a secondhand life now.

Paula Iturbe de Ciolek, mother of
a murdered student

What am I going to do now with all the time I have on my hands for the rest of my life?

Carlota Sánchez de Gonzáles, mother of
the student killed by a policeman for
painting propaganda on a fence on
Saturday, November 16, 1968

All that night and all the next morning, mothers who didn't have any idea what the whole nightmare at Tlatelolco was all about, who were desperate for information, who refused to believe anything they were told, searching for their children like animals who had been badly hurt, kept asking, "Sir, please, where's my boy? Where have they taken the youngsters?" And finally in the most pleading tone of voice: "Sir, we beg you—please give us any news you have as to their whereabouts, some hint of what's happened to them, tell us any little scrap of news you may have about them. . . ."

Isabel Sperry de Barraza, grade-school teacher

One kid became hysterical. A big kid. The minute they shoved him into the panel truck, he started crying, "My mom . . . will anybody notify her what's happened? How will they break the news to her? How will she find out where I am?" A soldier spoke up then and said, "Don't worry. You'll get out. . . ." "No, I won't," the kid replied. "They're going to kill me and it'll be the death of my mother. . . . What'll they tell her, how will she find out what's happened?" The soldier got tired of listening to him and finally said to him, "You're not a little kid any more, but you're still a crybaby. Why did you ever get mixed up in a thing like this if you're such a crybaby?"

Ignacio Galván, student at the San Carlos
Academy and the Ciudadela Ceramics Workshop

The rhythm of our lives has slowed down tremendously. We're living the same sort of endless days as the people in Macondo.* And our space, our world, our cosmos is becoming a microcosm. The entire physical scale of our lives is shrinking. My cell used to seem terribly tiny, but now it's expanding all the time; it's getting bigger and bigger. The little tower above, scarcely ten steps from my bed, is a meeting place, an observatory; from up there you can see houses, and even cars passing by. And then there are our afternoons. We go up to the tower, or some of us go down to the garden that we got permission to walk around in a year ago, a very minor victory, but it seems like a major one. Everything is on an entirely different scale now. When I arrived here, I was told that one of the major victories the prisoners had won was not having to line up for inspection at seven in the morning and eight o'clock at night every day. A real victory, in our little world. Later they removed the guards in the tower, and the circular walkway gave us a horizon of freedom measuring twelve yards or so in diameter.

Being confined in a cell is an overwhelming experience at first. The second morning after I'd been locked up in mine, I woke up with the terrifying feeling that I was smothering to death. The dirty, foul-smelling walls were so close to me that they seemed like part of my skull, like an enormous weight pressing on my brain, as though I were being given to understand that bodily imprisonment

---

* A reference to the fictional town that is the setting of Gabriel García Márquez's novel *A Hundred Years of Solitude*.

necessarily implies mental imprisonment as well. I realized that my only world, my cosmos, lay within myself.

Heberto Castillo, of the Teachers' Coalition

We prisoners wait for the day when we will see our parents, our best friend, our fiancées or our wives, our children: that is part of our fight against the walls that prevent personal communication and the satisfaction of our material and emotional needs. But we also wait for the day when we will have daily papers and periodicals and news of our social and political world: this is how we fight against the walls that they have shut us up behind in order to try to cut us off from the world that was of such concern to us that it landed us here in prison; we also anxiously await our court trial, the sentence that will be handed us; we await the absurd that is in store for each of us, the predictable consequence of a system that is equally absurd. It is our parents who suffer the most from this sort of endless waiting; and the unfair sentences meted out to us, which are our parents' only reward for their unswerving loyalty to us, their efforts in our behalf, their fight to secure their sons' freedom, age them terribly. In all truth, they too are prisoners.

But waiting and thinking are not the only things we do, although that is how we spend a great deal of our time. Little by little each of us comes to realize that we must go on fighting: that what the authorities are attempting to do by throwing us in prison is not only to prevent us from participating in political activities by locking us up but also to *exterminate us*. Sometimes we realize this only in an instinctive sort of way—the instinct of self-preservation at work both in our bodies and our spirits—and once we make up our minds to resist, we fight against the forces that would snub out our lives. Almost all of us engage in sports in order to remain healthy—that is how we fight against physical atrophy; we sing—a number of the prisoners have written very beautiful songs; we paint, we write, we read—that is the way we fight against those who would like to deprive us of the possibility of creating. We all experience fits of depression, understandable crises, changes in our personality. . . . All of us have changed a great deal; we have had to become mature adults amid enormous hardships. I know of some really astonishing cases—people who had nothing to do with the

Student Movement who were very puzzled about many things having to do with politics and the way the country is run and the social order, who learned to read and write in order to understand such things. . . . Those students who were members of an organization not only lacked self-discipline, they also had to confront another problem: seeing through the process of mystification and deification that other people had subjected them to. It requires tremendous impartiality to overcome this particular obstacle in the course of changing one's entire personal life. In short, you might say that it is possible to pursue positive goals once we have resolved questions that we may once have been unwilling to face but have sooner or later come to ask ourselves. . . .

I was a very active youngster on the outside, one of the leaders in my school; when I entered prison I was twenty-one years old and had many self-delusions.

> *Romeo González Medrano, of the Action*
> *Committee of the Faculty of Political and Social*
> *Sciences, UNAM. Arrested on September 18,*
> *1968; prisoner in Lecumberri*

Prison isolates a person in the sense that you lose touch with people on the outside. Many of my friends have gotten married and gone back to their home towns—now that there's nothing left of the Movement; they've made new friends and have new interests, and I feel very far away from all of them now. . . . When they come to visit me, we get to talking about some mutual friend or other, but it isn't the same any more. "I haven't seen him for ages. . . ." "I wonder what's happened to so-and-so. . . ." People have lost contact with each other. What's Enrique up to? What happened to Pedro? And Clemente? And Lisandro? Nobody knows. . . . It just isn't the same. It's as though the whole thing happened years and years ago. . . .

> *Roberta Avendaño Martínez (Tita), of the CNH*

There are certain days when I can see "Cuec" in my mind's eye as plain as day, as the expression goes. (His real name was Leobardo López Arreche, but everybody called him Cuec because those are the initials of the Centro Universitario de Estudios Cinematográficos,* where he worked. I can see him as clear as anything, standing there next to me with his hands leaning against one of the walls of the church of Santiago Tlatelolco. . . . Cuec was a very special person: there was nobody like him in the whole world. He had long hair and a long beard: he shot roll after roll of film documenting the Movement—lots and lots of footage. The Judicial Police, the Federal Security Agency, the Attorney General's office or some other authorities—I don't know exactly who—must have all those films now. . . . He would often become terribly enthusiastic about something all of a sudden—and just as suddenly, he'd get terribly worked up about something. I remember that at one meeting he asked for the floor and said, "Do you know how we're going to go back on the streets, comrades?" (Between the demonstration on August 27 and the one on September 13 there had been many arrests, lots of slanderous attacks on us in the newspapers, tremendous repression, and a great deal of confusion within the CNH itself; what's more, the tone of Díaz Ordaz's annual message and his threats—backed up by tanks and bayonets—were a rather impressive show of force.) "Listen, you guys, I want to tell you how it's going to be when we go back out on the streets. . . . Do you know how we're going to fight back? With flowers, with love and flowers. . . . On September 13 we'll be back on the Reforma again, with flowers, comrades: if they attack us, we'll throw flowers at them, we'll throw flowers at their tanks. Everybody will be watching from the windows of their buildings, from the hoods of their cars, from the roofs of the buses, from the housetops, and we'll have a brand new gimmick. If the soldiers are armed with rifles, we'll be armed with love and bunches of flowers. . . ." Cuec's motion was voted down, of course, but that's how he was, it was just like him, and I only wish I could have brought him flowers, love and flowers, the day he died.

Raúl Álvarez Garín, of the CNH

I really like October—it's my favorite month of the year. The air is so clear then that it's as though the city were lolling in the cradle of mountains around it; you look down the streets and there the vol-

---

* University Center for Film Studies.

canoes are, a dark, velvety blue all of a sudden—it always seems as
though I could reach out and touch them, and my hand would sink
into the soft fleece on their sides, basking in the October sunshine,
still nice and warm. . . . You can't see anything from in here, just
iron bars painted green with spikes pointing toward you, just the
green sheet-metal doors of the cells that are shut up tight. But it
smells of October in the air, it tastes of October now, in the year
1969—and I try to pretend that October this year is just like October
of '68, before we all died—because all of us died a little there in the
Plaza de las Tres Culturas.

                              Ernesto Olivera, teacher of mathematics
                                        at Preparatory 1, UNAM

Sometimes, very early in the morning, when dawn is just breaking,
I try to remember Tlatelolco, to recall those who were killed. I go
over the list of their names in my mind—the ones that were published in the papers anyway—in *Ovaciones*, for instance, which was
the list I saw: eighteen dead bodies at the headquarters of the Third
Police Precinct: Leonardo Pérez Gonzáles, a professor at Poli; Cornelio Caballero Garduño, from Prep 9; Ana María Regina, the very
pretty Olympics hostess; José Ignacio Caballero González, the thir-
teen-year-old boy they dragged from apartment 614 in the Chihuahua building; Gilberto Ortiz Reynoso from ESIQIE at Poli . . .
and so many others, so many other dead bodies lying in the Plaza.
. . . What sort of people were they? What would they be doing
now? What would they be doing today if they were still alive?

                              Ceferino Chávez, member of the Communist
                                        Youth; prisoner in Lecumberri

A regime that vents its fury on young people, that kills then, that
throws them in prison, that robs them of hours, days, years, of
their lives that are absolutely irreplaceable, is a weak and cowardly
regime that cannot last.

                              Isabel Sperry de Barraza, grade-school teacher

Yes, we think about Tlatelolco, but it's very hard for us to talk about
it. I confess that personally I find the memory of Tlatelolco very disturbing. I remember what we saw from the speakers' platform: the
crowd panicking, people running every which way trying desper-

ately to find some way out of the Plaza, the dust clouds on the esplanade; and the rows of bristling bayonets that I myself was too far back up there on the balcony to see. . . . I had no idea what was happening. They were firing at the speakers' stand: I think the troops down below were trying to shoot us, but the bullets were hitting the men in the white gloves. The whole thing was a terrible mess! Afterward, when they surrounded us, I remember the huge bullet holes that suddenly appeared in the roof, the plaster falling on us, the terror and the people dying all over the Plaza. I must confess I really don't like talking about Tlatelolco; in fact, I can't bring myself to talk about it . . . I'm sorry . . . please excuse me . . . I just can't . . . Tlatelolco is just too much for me. . . . Here in Lecumberri we say as little about it as possible, to keep ourselves from going crazy.

Gilberto Guevara Niebla, of the CNH

The only thing about the Olympic Games that made them worth while was the Black Power bit, the black fists in the air, the clenched fists of the black athletes, Tommie Smith, John Carlos, Lee Evans, Harry Edwards. By using the victories they won in the Olympics as a political weapon, the black champions made a great impression on the Mexican spectators, and even though it had only an indirect effect, it helped our Movement.

Samuel Bello Durán, student at the
School of Dentistry, UNAM

"Tibio" Muñoz, the one who won the gold medal, was from the Isaac Ochoterena Preparatory School, the school that had the street battle with Vocational 2 and Vocational 3. How ironic! July 22, when the *granaderos* arrived with tear-gas grenades and truncheons to break up the fight, was probably the day the 1968 Student Movement really began.

Pedro Bolaños, father of a family

"I've brought you some pork and beans. . . ."
   "Oh, Granny, I've been having terrible stomach-aches!"
   (Gilberto Guevara walks into the room, with his wool cap on his head, which Luis and Raúl and Saúl ["Chale"] swear he wears day and night. Raúl's grandmother holds out her arms.)

"Guevara, my boy!"

She clasps him to her bosom for a long time. She's the classic granny of children's storybooks: a round, plump, soft little old lady with white hair, a tender little dumpling.

"Did you say you were having stomach trouble, Raúl?" she asks.

"Oh, Granny, it's like a feast day here all week long: we eat chicken in black *mole* sauce as though it were Sunday every day, fricassee, paella, chiles in walnut sauce, pork-and-bean stew, roast suckling pig! You people at home are going to kill us with all that marvelous food! My digestion's ruined!"

Conversation between Raúl Álvarez Garín, of the
CNH, and his grandmother

As Juan García Ponce, the writer, was leaving the *Excélsior* office on October 4, 1968, after dropping by to give the editors an announcement protesting the Tlatelolco massacre that he wanted run in the paper, he was arrested by the police. They let him go after holding him in custody for four hours and subjecting him to the usual harassment. They may have mistaken him for the CNH leader Marcelino Perelló, because, like Marcelino, Juan has to use a wheelchair to get around. Or perhaps they were trying to intimidate him. Juan García Ponce belongs to the Congress of Intellectuals and Artists, a group which publicly announced its support of the Student Movement on Friday, August 16, 1968; he has written about the Movement and taken an active part in it; he has signed manifestoes; he has publicly expressed his great indignation. He said, "What is most important now is not what happened to me, but freeing the kids—so many of them have been brutally beaten. . . . We cannot tolerate this. . . ." And later on he added, "Never in our entire lives will we again experience days like these."

Conversation with Juan García Ponce, in
Siempre!, *no. 802, November 6, 1968*

Prison is the noisiest place in the world. The courtyards downstairs are always full of people, except on Sunday afternoons at four o'clock when our visitors leave. They all file out, all of us go back to our cells, and the whole prison falls silent. Otherwise it's incredibly noisy: at six-thirty in the morning they strike up the band, and there's a terrible racket all the rest of the day. The bugle blows reveille, then mess call, then "break ranks," and then at nine it blows again, just to let us know that it's nine o'clock and time to consult our lawyers if we wish. It blows again at eleven, and then at one o'clock there's mess call again. At four o'clock, the band starts blaring again, to summon us to the *redondel*—the passageway around the Polígono, the central courtyard—for "assembly" at four. "Assembly" is a sort of roll call, so the prisoners can be counted. Raúl, the leader of cell block C, signs the list of prisoners every day. At eight o'clock the band starts up again—bugle calls and drum rolls—they're awful-sounding instruments that give you goose flesh—or maybe that's an exaggeration—and at ten p. m. they sound "lights out." It's after that that prison is hardest on you, because that's when the night watch begins, with the sentries posted on the walls shouting out "All's well!" every fifteen minutes. . . . At night the shouts you've heard all during the day ring in your ears: *Roll call: 61 prisoners present and accounted for, Roll call, roll call, roll call . . .* the cries of the vendors hawking their wares in one cell block after another, the drum rolls in the *redondel,* metal objects grating against the bars, the sound of your own iron cell door slamming shut, and suddenly prison closes in on you: all its iron bars, its barbed wire, the squeaking of the rusty wheels of the chow carts hauling along kettles full of stew, beans, corn gruel, beans, stew, beans, stew, broth with chunks of meat and bones, green vegetables once in a while, corn gruel, kettle after kettle of chow. . . . It occurs to me that I might easily fit into one of those kettles. . . .

Luis González de Alba, of the CNH

There's a prisoner here named Mario Hernández—we call him "The Kid" because he's the youngest of all of us in cell block C; even though he's sixty-seven years old, he's one of the most beloved and most highly respected men in the entire cell block. He's the anti-mummy par excellence. He's a fantastic guy, and what's more, he's a great cook.

Eduardo de la Vega Ávila, of the Communist Party

The "Consultation Room" is a large room with cement tables and benches.

Arturo Martínez Nateras, Secretary General of CNED; prisoner in Lecumberri

A young person is always an unknown quantity. To murder a young person is to kill the mystery, the possibility of what he might have been, his extraordinary richness, his complexity.

José Soriano Muñoz, teacher at the Wilfredo Massieu School

To murder a youngster is to kill hope.

Cristina Correa de Salas, grade-school teacher

Almost no one here has a watch. Among those of us who fix our meals together, nobody has one. Except me. Some of the others have asked me why I want a watch in prison. There are no hours here. Just morning, afternoon, and nighttime. And time contracts. The prisoners say: "It's one long day from Monday to Saturday, and Sunday's a very short day that's over before you know it."

Heberto Castillo, of the Teachers' Coalition

In October there are still squash flowers, mushrooms, black corn from the rainy season—Eduardo's so fond of all of those things. Purslane, *chilacayotes*, and *quentoniles* begin to appear in the markets. I cook them at home, and I always hope the guard doesn't stir them up too much when the things we've brought to Eduardo are inspected.

María Elena Rodríguez de la Vega

Every human being is lonely—that's a cliché, I know. But hardly anybody realizes how terribly lonely a youngster feels between the ages of fifteen and twenty.

Georgina Rubio de Marcos, grade-school teacher

And finally, I should like to say this: perhaps we aren't in the same class as men such as Ricardo Flores Magón, Filomeno Mata, and Valentín Campa,* who among other things are possessed of a marvelous stoicism, but beyond question we are continually encouraged by their example.

Gilberto Guevara Niebla, of the CNH

Of course I helped my comrades! I'm even quite sure that it was because of an interview I had with Mercedes Padrés—who's a very

---

* Famous political prisoners. (Translator's note.)

nice person—that the Movement people who'd gone into hiding up in the mountains and were almost starving to death came back to the Federal District. "Toto," Sóstenes Torrecillas, was one of them. He weighed over 250 pounds when he left Mexico City, and when he came back he weighed just over 150. He's in terrible shape—a total wreck. He was the CNH delegate from the School of Homeopathic Medicine; he'd hidden out for months in swamplands and up in the mountains, eating roots or going hungry altogether. He has a persecution mania now: he was certain they were going to kill him. Other comrades have told me he couldn't even cross the street by himself; two of them had to grab him under the arms and hold him up. If a tire had a blowout, he practically fainted. The slightest sudden noise drove him almost out of his mind. He and the other kids read that interview where I said that nothing would happen if they came out of hiding, so they did. Toto is feeling better now; he's getting over all the things he went through, and so are other kids who suffered terribly.

Sócrates Amado Campos Lemus, of the CNH

And another thing that's also extremely important. It seems to me that before I couldn't possibly have loved my girl the way I love her now. It's beautiful—I can't explain it, but that's how I feel. The changes in me are marvelous. The changes in me, and in all the others too, of course.

Félix Lucio Hernández Gamundi, of the CNH

What's more, living shut up inside four walls teaches you, as nothing else can, to love freedom passionately, profoundly.

Gilberto Guevara Niebla, of the CNH

After twenty-five months in prison, we are better human beings, and we're convinced that in the last analysis no one, no matter what terrible crimes he may have committed, deserves to be shut up in a cage like an animal.

Artemisa de Gortari, mother of a family

> In the Americas
> a new people has already begun to flower
> a people eager for prose that carries weight

and noble verses
and asking for hard work and honesty
in politics
and in literature

José Martí, the great Cuban poet

First grammar lesson for Latin America:
    Freedom is the subject.
    The verb is *rifles.*
    Death is the object.

Anonymous twentieth-century author

Worms are crawling through the streets and the squares
and the walls are spattered with brains. . . .
The water is red, as though it were dyed,
and when we drink it
it is as though we were drinking water with rock salt in it.

We beat our fists on the adobe walls then
and our inheritance was a line of holes dug in the ground.
They wore shields for protection,
but not even shields can guard them against loneliness.
We have gnawed on the branches of *colorín* trees
we have chewed on dog-grass,
bricks of adobe, lizards,
rats, handfuls of dust, worms. . . .
We had almost no meat to eat
but there was a little bit roasting on the fire.
And when it was cooked
they snatched it off the fire
and ate it right there by the fire.

THE CHORUS:

They have seized Cuauhtémoc!
They are rounding up all the Mexican princes!
The Tenochca people are being besieged!
The Tlatelolca people are being besieged!

SOLOIST:

There is mourning everywhere now: tears are falling in Tlatelolco.
Where can we go now? Oh, friends! Can it be true?
Mexico City has been abandoned:
there is smoke rising; the mist is spreading.
Motelhuihtzin
Tailotlacall Tlacotzin
Tlacatecuhtli Oquihtzin

Weep, my friends,
you have heard the story, and you know now
that we have lost our Mexican homeland.
The water has turned bitter, our food has a bitter taste in our
    mouths!
This is what the Giver of Life has done in Tlatelolco.

These were all things that happened to us.
We saw all this
and could not believe our eyes.
Our grievous, terrible fate
lies heavy on our hearts.

Broken darts lie in the roads,
our hair is disheveled.
There are no roofs on the houses,
their walls are red with blood.

CHORUS:

The Tenochca people are being besieged!
The Tlatelolca people are being besieged!

> *Texts chosen for a recital by students imprisoned
> in cell block C of Lecumberri, from the* Visión de
> los Vencidos. Relaciones Indígenas de la Con-
> quista [Events as Seen by the Vanquished.
> Stories of the Spanish Conquest Told by Na-
> tive Peoples], *Nahuátl texts translated by
> Ángel María Garibay K., Biblioteca del Estudiante
> Universitario, UNAM*

The Night of
Tlatelolco

We must bear witness to our surprise and indignation at the events that night at Tlatelolco, when barbarism, primitive savagery, hatred, and the most vicious impulses held sway.

Francisco Martínez de la Vega, in an article entitled "Where Is Our Country Heading?",
El Día, *October 8, 1968*

IN MEMORY OF TLATELOLCO

Darkness breeds violence
and violence seeks darkness
to carry out its bloody deeds.
That is why on October 2 they waited for nightfall
so that no one would see the hand
that held the gun, only its sudden lightning flash.

And who is there in the last pale light of day?
Who is the killer?
Who are those who writhe in agony, those who are dying?
Those who flee in panic, leaving their shoes behind?
Those who fall into the dark pit of prison?
Those rotting in a hospital?
Those who become forever mute, from sheer terror?

Who are they? How many are there? Not a one.
Not a trace of any of them the next day.
By dawn the following morning the Plaza had been swept clean.
The lead stories in the papers
were about the weather.
And on TV, on the radio, at the movie theaters
the programs went on as scheduled,
no interruptions for an announcement,
not a moment of reverent silence at the festivities.
(Because the celebration went right on, according to plan.)

Don't search for something there are no signs of now:
traces of blood, dead bodies,
because it was all an offering to a goddess,
the Eater of Excrement.

Don't search in the files, because no records have been kept.

But I feel pain when I probe right here: here in my memory
it hurts, so the wound is real. Blood mingling with blood
and if I call it my own blood, I betray one and all.

I remember, we remember.
This is our way of hastening the dawn,
of shedding a ray of light on so many consciences that bear a heavy
        burden,
on angry pronouncements, yawning prison gates,
faces hidden behind masks.
I remember, let us all remember
until justice comes to sit among us.

Rosario Castellanos

(*Right*) It all began with a street battle between two gangs, "The Cuidadelans" and "The Spiders," who came to blows in front of Isaac Ochoterena Preparatory. Later, students of this university prep school and a vocational high school also became involved in the fighting.

(*Below*) Such spontaneous mass demonstrations as this were unprecedented in Mexico. The Golden Age, the high point of the Student Movement, were the months of August and September 1968.

The banner in the foreground reads: "The Army should defend the people, not attack it."

One of the first large-scale demonstrations, the one on August 27, 1968, drew a crowd of three hundred thousand people. The demonstrators carried banners, and the youngsters passed out handbills. We never believed that thousands and thousands of people would turn out to support us. The banner in the photo (*left*) reads: "The hopes of students are based on respect for the Constitution. Down with Article 145. Enormous problems cannot be solved with enormous lies."

(*Above*) The railway workers who protested in 1958 had no support from the general public. But the students in 1968 did.

(*Right*) The workers supported the Student Movement and demanded that their imprisoned leaders be freed—men such as Demetrio Vallejo, who had been in jail for eleven years. The sign in the photo reads: "Freedom for political prisoners!"

¡LIBERTAD A LOS PRESOS POLITICOS!

There was support, too, from women's groups. (*Above and facing, top.*)

(*Facing, right*) There were many girls from staid nouveau-riche families who took an active part in the Movement: wealthy girls from the Iberoamerican University and the Faculty of Philosophy and Letters. When the Riot Police began bashing students' heads in, they were as brave as any of the other students; they willingly lent their comrades a helping hand, carting around leaflets and handbills in their fathers' cars.

(*Facing, left*) Some fifteen thousand demonstrators took part in the marches in Mexico City. But six hundred thousand people, from every walk of life, and young people in particular, gathered to show their support. When have we ever seen anything like that? At the statue of "The Angel of Independence," groups of all sorts gathered to demonstrate.

(*Top right*) We entered the Zócalo, the square that is the symbol of our national life. Two students from the med school went up to the cathedral bell tower to ring the bells, with the permission of Father Jesús Pérez.

(*Below*) "We had to 'deconsecrate' the Zócalo—and we did, three times." For the first time in forty years, an indignant crowd of Mexican citizens aware of their constitutional rights made its voice heard beneath the Presidential Balcony in the Plaza de la Constitución.

(*Above*) "Peace and calm must
be restored in our country. A
hand has been extended: it is
up to Mexican citizens to decide whether to grasp this outstretched hand. . . ." The President of the Mexican Republic,
Gustavo Díaz Ordaz, in a
speech in Guadalajara, August
1, 1968.

(*Left*) "The military occupation
of the University City represents an excessive use of force
that our scholarly institution
has not deserved." Statement
by the Rector of the University,
Javier Barros Sierra, September
19, 1968.

It is an eerie, ominous feeling to see
soldiers, with fixed bayonets, moving
in on you.

The young people from the Polytechnical Institute, mostly from poor and peasant families, were always very brave: the Riot Police were particularly hard on them, and most of those jailed were from Poli.

Our only weapons against the Riot Police were firecrackers and Molotov cocktails. These were the only weapons in our supposedly enormous arsenal.

Mr. President, how can you extend your hand in friendship to every nation on this earth when you refuse to offer it to us here in our own country?

(*Above*) The symbol that soon covered the entire city, even during events filmed by the television networks: the V-for-Victory sign, first formed by young people marching in demonstrations, and later painted on telephone booths, the sides of buses, and fences all over the city.

(*Facing*) At five-thirty p.m. a crowd of approximately five thousand people gathered in the Plaza de las Tres Culturas in Tlatelolco to listen to the speakers from the National Strike Committee.

(*Below*) They made us form a line with our hands up to search us.

"They made us line up with our hands up, and took the ones with long hair aside. They made one kid kneel down and lopped his hair off with a bayonet."

(*Facing*) By the ancient church of Santiago Tlatelolco, an innocent crowd of bystanders gathered. Half an hour later, many would lie bleeding in front of the doors of the Convent, which were never opened to give shelter to children, to men and women panic-stricken by the hail of bullets fired at them.

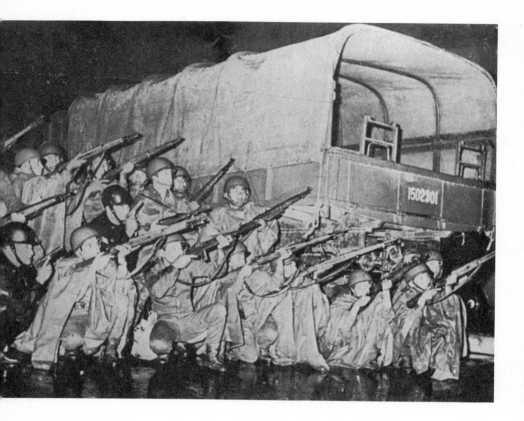

(*Above*) "I'd seen things like that on television, but I never dreamed I'd see them happening in real life."

(*Facing, top and bottom*) " 'Here's a little farewell present for you.' And they started hitting us as though they were breaking *piñatas*."

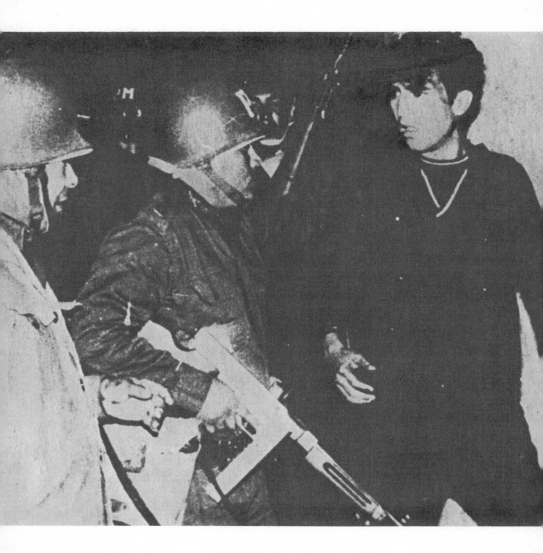

(*Facing, bottom*) "Handle this one carefully, don't jiggle the stretcher—
she's been wounded in the belly!"

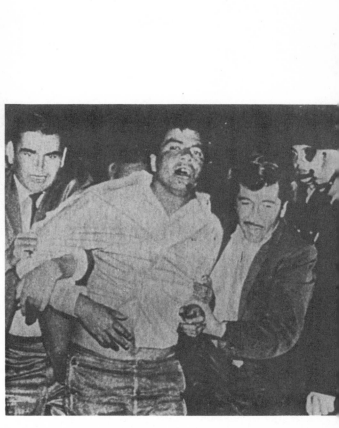

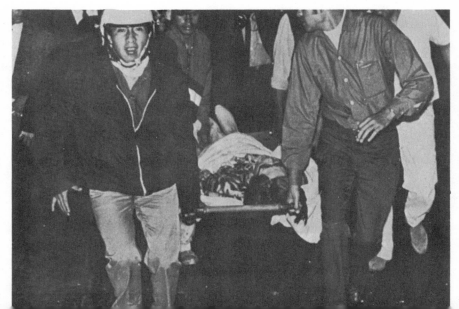

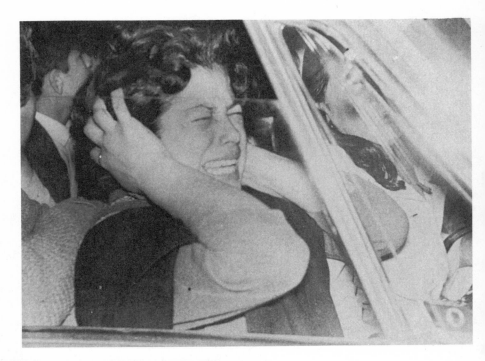

(*Left*) Strewn about on the pavement, among the torn clothing and the plants trampled underfoot, were many shoes, most of them women's.

(*Facing, top and bottom*) After the night of Tlatelolco, people gathered in many places all over the city seeking news of the dead and wounded. In the Third Police Precinct alone, we saw thirty bodies.

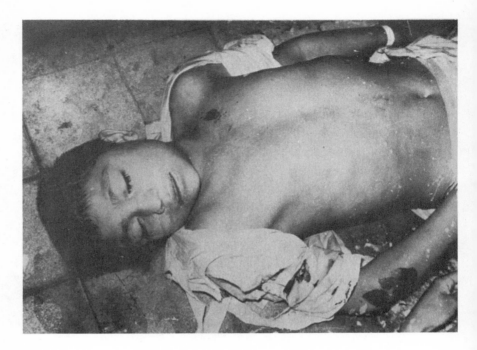

"Who gave orders to do this? Who could possibly have
ordered such a thing?"

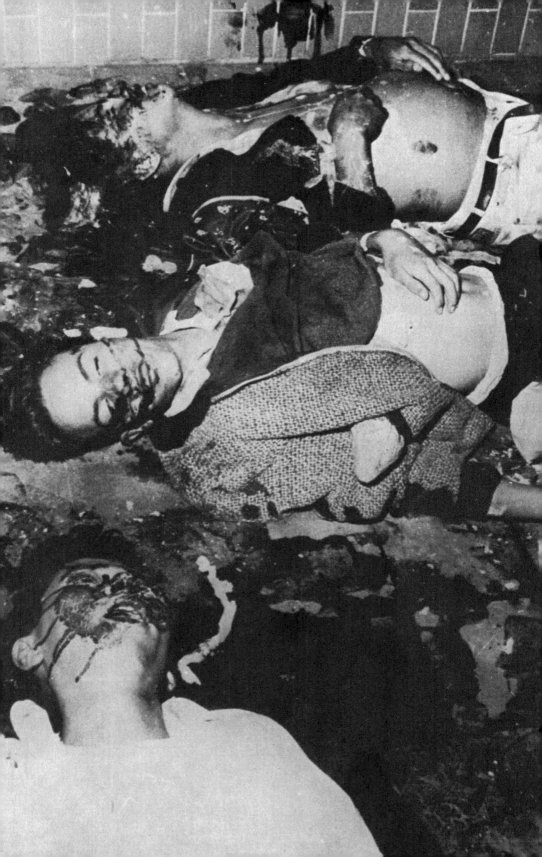

Instead of jailing known criminals, Mexico had imprisoned its young people.

(*Top*) Dr. Eli de Gortari, a university professor (*left*), and Manuel Marcué Pardiñas, former editor-in-chief of *Política*, an opposition periodical (*center*).

(*Bottom*) Ana Ignacia Rodríguez (Nacha), the girl with the long hair; the writer José Revueltas, with his Ho Chi Minh beard; and in the front row, Che (Antonio Rodríguez), Roberta Avendaño Martínez (Tita), Eduardo Valle Espinoza (Buho—Owl-Eyes), at a hearing.

On the second of November, All Souls Day, we placed *cempazúchitl* flowers and candles on the Plaza de las Tres Culturas. There were many Army troops on guard, but suddenly thousands of memorial candles were lighted and hundreds of people popped out from behind the trees and began to pray for their children who had been murdered at Tlatelolco on the second of October.

The majority of the following interviews were recorded in October and November 1968. The students who had been imprisoned offered their testimony during the two years following Tlatelolco. This is their story, woven out of their words, their struggles, their mistakes, their pain, and their bewilderment at the turn events took. Their impatience, their ingenuousness, their confidence also play a part in it. I am especially grateful to mothers who lost their sons and daughters, to brothers and sisters of the dead who were kind enough to allow me to record their words. Grief is a very personal thing. Putting it into words is almost unbearable; hence asking questions, digging for facts, borders on an invasion of people's privacy.

This story is also that of a mother so stunned that for days and days she uttered scarcely a word, and then suddenly, like a wounded animal—an animal whose belly is being ripped apart—she let out a hoarse, heart-rending cry, from the very center of her life, from the very life that had been taken from her. A terrible cry, a cry of terror at the utter evil that can befall a human being; the sort of wild keening that is the end of everything, the wail of ultimate pain from the wound that will never heal, the death of a son.

In these pages there echo the cries of those who died and the cries of those who lived on after them. These pages express their outrage and their protest: the mute cry that stuck in thousands of throats, the blind grief in thousands of horror-stricken eyes on October 2, 1968, the night of Tlatelolco.

E.P.

199

Headlines in the Major Daily Papers in Mexico City on Thursday, October 3, 1968

EXCÉLSIOR:

SERIOUS FIGHTING AS ARMY BREAKS UP MEETING OF STRIKERS.

20 Dead, 75 Wounded, 400 Jailed: Fernando M. Garza, Press Secretary of the President of the Republic

NOVEDADES:

SHOTS EXCHANGED BY SHARPSHOOTERS AND THE ARMY IN CIUDAD TLATELOLCO.

Figures Thus Far: 25 Dead and 87 Wounded: General Hernández Toledo and 12 Other Soldiers Wounded

EL UNIVERSAL:

TLATELOLCO A BATTLEFIELD.

Serious Fighting for Hours Between Terrorists and Soldiers. 29 Dead and More Than 80 Wounded; Casualties on Both Sides; 1000 Arrested

LA PRENSA:

MANY KILLED AND WOUNDED ACCORDING TO GARCÍA BARRAGÁN.

Army and Students Exchange Gunfire

EL DÍA:

CRIMINAL PROVOCATION AT TLATELOLCO MEETING CAUSES TERRIBLE BLOODSHED.

Fight with Army at Tlatelolco Results in Many Dead and Wounded: General Hernández Toledo and 12 Other Soldiers Wounded. One Soldier Dead. Number of Civilians Killed or Wounded Still Not Known

EL HERALDO:

BLOODY ENCOUNTER IN TLATELOLCO.

26 Dead and 71 Wounded; Sharpshooters Fire on Army Troops. General Toledo Wounded

EL SOL DE MÉXICO (a morning paper):

FOREIGN INTERLOPERS ATTEMPT TO DAMAGE MEXICO'S NATIONAL IMAGE.

The Objective: Preventing the Nineteenth Olympic Games from Being Held
Sharpshooters Fire on Army Troops in Tlatelolco.
One General and 11 Soldiers Wounded; 2 Soldiers and More Than 20 Civilians Killed in a Terrible Gun Battle

EL NACIONAL:

ARMY FORCED TO ROUT SHARPSHOOTERS: GARCÍA BARRAGÁN

OVACIONES:

BLOODY GUN BATTLE IN THE
PLAZA DE LAS TRES CULTURAS
**Dozens of Sharpshooters Fire on
Troops. 23 Dead, 52 Wounded, 1000
Arrested, and More Vehicles
Burned**

LA AFICIÓN:

STUDENT MEETING IN
TLATELOLCO RESULTS IN
HEAVY GUNFIRE

All witnesses agree that the sudden appearance of flares in the sky above the Plaza de las Tres Culturas at the Nonoalco-Tlatelolco housing unit was the signal that unleashed the hail of bullets which turned the student meeting of October 2 into the Tlatelolco tragedy.

At five-thirty p.m. on Wednesday, October 2, approximately ten thousand people were gathered on the esplanade of the Plaza de las Tres Culturas to hear the student speakers of the National Strike Committee, who were standing on a balcony on the fourth floor of the Chihuahua building addressing a crowd consisting mainly of students, men, women, children, and oldsters sitting on the ground, street vendors, housewives with babies in their arms, tenants of the housing unit, and spectators who had dropped by to watch out of curiosity, the usual idlers and bystanders who had merely come to "have a look." The mood of the crowd was calm despite the fact that the regular police, the Army, and the *granaderos* were out in full force. Men and women students were passing out handbills, collecting money in boxes labeled CNH, and selling newspapers and posters, and on the fourth floor, in addition to the Mexican reporters covering national events, there were foreign journalists and photographers who had come to Mexico to report on the Olympic Games that were scheduled to begin in ten days.

A number of students addressed the crowd: a young boy introduced the speakers, another student from UNAM announced, "The Movement will continue despite everything," and another from the IPN said, ". . . the consciousness of our Mexican family has been aroused and it has become politically aware"; a girl whom I remember particularly because she was so young spoke of the role the brigades were playing. The speakers criticized the politicians and several newspapers, and proposed a boycott of the daily *El Sol*. The people up there on the fourth-floor balcony spied a group of workers entering the Plaza carrying a banner that read: RAILWAY WORKERS SUPPORT THE MOVEMENT AND REJECT THE ROMERO FLORES– ORDAZ TALKS. This contingent of workers received an enthusiastic round of applause. This group of railway workers then announced a series of escalating strikes, beginning "tomorrow, October 3, in support of the Student Movement."

Just as a student named Vega was announcing that the scheduled march on the Santo Tomás campus of the IPN would not take place because the Army had been called out and there might be violence, flares suddenly appeared in the sky overhead and everyone automatically looked up. The first shots were heard then. The crowd panicked, and despite the fact that the leaders of the CNH up on the fourth-floor balcony of the Chihuahua building kept shouting into the microphone, "Don't run, all of you, don't run, they're just shooting in the air. . . . Stay right where you are, stay where you are, don't panic," the crowd started running in all directions. Everyone was terror-stricken, and many of them fell to the ground there in the Plaza, or leaped down into the pre-Hispanic ruins in front of the church of Santiago Tlatelolco. We could hear heavy rifle fire and the chatter of machine guns. From that moment on, the Plaza de las Tres Culturas was an inferno.

The report on the events at Tlatelolco that appeared in *Excélsior* the following day, October 3, stated, "No one could say precisely where the first shots came from, but the great majority of the demonstrators agreed that the Army troops suddenly began shooting without warning. . . . There were shots from all directions, from the top of a building in the housing unit and from the street, where the military forces fired round after round from the machine guns mounted on their light tanks and armored transports." *Novedades, El Universal, El Día, El Nacional, El Sol de México, El Heraldo, La Prensa, La Afición,* and *Ovaciones* all reported that the Army was forced to return the fire from sharpshooters stationed on the roofs of the buildings. As proof of that statement, they mentioned the fact that General José Hernández Toledo, who was directing the operation, received a bullet wound in the chest and stated to reporters following the operation he subsequently underwent, "It's my opinion that if it was bloodshed they wanted, the blood I've shed is more than sufficient" (*El Día,* October 3, 1968). According to *Excélsior,* "It is estimated that approximately 5000 Army troops, and many police security agents, the majority of whom were dressed in civilian clothes, were involved. All of the latter had white handkerchiefs wrapped around their right hands so that the others could identify them, for in order to protect themselves in case the students attacked, only a very few of them were wearing badges.

"The heavy gunfire lasted for twenty-nine minutes. Then the hail of bullets tapered off, though there were still sporadic bursts of gunfire."

The rifle fire came from many directions and machine-gun bullets whizzed all over the Plaza. As a number of journalists reported, it is quite likely that many of the police and the soldiers killed or wounded each other. "Many soldiers must have shot each other, since as they surrounded the crowd and closed in, bullets were flying in all directions," the journalist Félix Fuentes reports in his story in the October 3 issue of *La Prensa.* The army employed a pincers movement to take over the Plaza de las Tres Culturas, that is to say, the five thousand troops closed in from two directions, firing automatic weapons at the buildings, Fuentes adds. "On the fourth floor of one building, from which three speakers had delivered inflammatory speeches against the government, flashes from firearms were seen. Apparently the federal security agents and the Federal District police had opened fire on the crowd from up there.

"Many people tried to escape by way of the east side of the Plaza de las Tres Culturas, and a large number of them managed to get out, but hundreds of persons came face to face with columns of armed troops pointing their bayonets at them and shooting in all directions. Seeing that escape was impossible in that direction, many people in the crowd fled in terror and sought refuge inside the buildings, but others ran down the narrow little streets in the housing unit and eventually reached the Paseo de la Reforma near the Cuitláhuac Monument.

"This reporter was caught in the crowd near the Secretariat of Foreign Relations. A few steps away a woman fell to the ground—

she had either been wounded or had fainted dead away. A couple of youngsters tried to go to her rescue, but the soldiers stopped them."

General José Hernández Toledo stated later that in order to avoid bloodshed he had given the Army troops orders not to use the heavy-caliber weapons they had been armed with (*El Día*, October 3, 1968). (General Hernández Toledo had previously been in command of Army troops occupying the University of Michoacán, the University of Sonora, and UNAM, and has under his command paratroopers who are considered to be the best-trained assault troops in the country.) Nonetheless Jorge Avilés, a reporter for *El Universal*, wrote in the October 3 issue of that daily, "We have now seen the Army troops in all-out action: using all sorts of armaments, including heavy-caliber machine guns mounted on twenty jeeps or more, they fired on all the areas controlled by the sharpshooters." And *Excélsior* added, "Some three hundred tanks, assault troops, jeeps and troop transports have surrounded the entire area, from Insurgentes to the Reforma, Nonoalco, and Manuel González. No one is being allowed to enter or leave this area, unless he can produce absolute proof of his identity" ("Terrible Gun Battle in Tlatelolco. The Number of Dead Not Yet Determined and Dozens Wounded," *Excélsior*, Thursday, October 3, 1968). Miguel Ángel Martínez Agis reported, "An Army captain was on the telephone, calling the Department of Defense, reporting on what was happening: 'We're fighting back with every weapon we have. . . .' We could see that the troops were armed with .45's and .38's, and 9-mm. pistols" ("Chihuahua Building, 6 p.m.," *Excélsior*, October 3, 1968).

General Marcelino García Barragán, the Secretary of National Defense, stated, "When the Army approached the Plaza de las Tres Culturas it was met with rifle fire from sharpshooters. There was a general exchange of gunfire that lasted approximately one hour. . . .

"There are both Army troops and students dead and wounded: at the moment, I can't say exactly how many there are."

"Who in your opinion is the leader of this movement?"

"I only wish we knew who was behind it."

[This would seem to indicate that General Barragán had no proof that it was students who were to blame.]

"Are there any wounded students in the Central Military Hospital?"

"There are some in the Central Military Hospital, in the Green Cross Hospital, and in the Red Cross Hospital. They've all been placed under arrest and will be available for questioning by the Attorney General's office. We're also holding a number of them in Military Camp 1, where they will be available for questioning by General Cueto, the Chief of Police of the Federal District."

"Who's in charge of the Army operations?"

"I am."

(Jesús M. Lozano, in a story entitled "Freedom Will Continue to Reign," *Excélsior,* October 3, 1968. The secretary of defense then provided an analysis of the situation.)

The Mexico City Chief of Police denied, however, that he had asked the Army to intervene in Tlatelolco, as the secretary of defense had previously reported. In a press conference early that morning, October 3, General Luis Cueto Ramírez made the following statement: "Police officials informed National Defense the moment they received reports that gunfire had been heard in the buildings next to the Secretariat of Foreign Relations and Vocational 7, where troops have been on duty around the clock." He explained that as far as he had thus far been able to determine, no foreign agents had been involved in the student disturbances which had been going on in the city since July. The majority of the arms confiscated by the police were manufactured in Europe and were the same models as are used in the socialist bloc, according to General Cueto. He also declared that he had no evidence that Mexican politicians were involved in the situation in any way, and that he knew of no United States citizens who had been arrested. "Among the prisoners, however, are one Guatemalan, one German, and another foreigner whose nationality I don't recall at the moment," he stated (*El Universal, El Nacional,* October 3, 1968).

No photographs of the dead bodies lying in the Plaza de las Tres

Culturas were taken because the Army troops would not allow it (reported in a story with the heading "Many Killed and Wounded Last Night," *La Prensa,* October 3, 1968). On October 6, in a manifesto addressed "To the Mexican People," published in *El Día,* the CNH declared, "The final list of those killed and wounded in the Tlatelolco massacre has not yet been drawn up. Thus far we know of some 100 dead—those whose bodies were removed from the Plaza. There are thousands of wounded. . . ." That same day, October 6, the CNH announced that it would hold no more demonstrations or meetings, since the attack by the forces of repression "has caused the death of 150 civilians and 40 soldiers." In his book *The Other Mexico* Octavio Paz quotes the figure that the English daily paper *The Guardian* considered most likely, after "careful investigation": 325 dead.

It is quite certain that even today the precise death toll has not yet been determined. On October 3, the figures quoted in the headlines and news reports in the papers varied from twenty to twenty-eight. The number of wounded was much larger, and two thousand people were jailed. The shooting in the Tlatelolco area stopped around midnight. But the buildings in the housing unit were searched from top to bottom, and some thousand prisoners were taken to Military Camp 1. Around a thousand other persons arrested were taken to Santa Marta Acatitla Penitentiary, in Mexico City. The Tlatelolco area continued to be barricaded by Army troops. Many families abandoned their apartments, taking all their belongings with them, after having been subjected to a rigorous search and interrogation by the troops. Platoons of eleven soldiers each entered the buildings in the nearby suburbs to inspect every dwelling. Apparently they had orders to make a house-to-house search.

At present (early in 1971) those still imprisoned in Lecumberri number about 165.

We shall probably never know what motive lay behind the Tlatelolco massacre. Terror? Insecurity? Anger? Fear of losing face? Ill-will toward youngsters who deliberately misbehave in front of visitors? Together with Abel Quezada,* we may ask ourselves, WHY? Despite all the voices that have been raised, despite all the eyewit-

---

* A famous Mexican editorial cartoonist, who after Tlatelolco drew a now celebrated cartoon in *Excélsior* with the caption WHY? (Translator's note.)

ness testimony, the tragic night of Tlatelolco is still incomprehensible. Why? The story of what happened at Tlatelolco is puzzling and full of contradictions. The one fact that is certain is that many died. Not one of the accounts provides an over-all picture of what happened. All the people there in the Plaza—casual bystanders and active participants alike—were forced to take shelter from the gunfire; many fell wounded. In an article entitled "A Meeting That Ended in Tragedy," which appeared in the Mexico City *Diario de la Tarde* on October 5, 1968, reporter José Luis Mejías wrote, "The men in white gloves drew their pistols and began indiscriminately firing at close range on women, children, students, and riot police. . . . And at that same moment a helicopter gave the signal for the Army to close in by setting off a flare. . . . As the first shots were fired, General Hernández Toledo, the commander of the paratroopers, was wounded, and from that moment on, as the troops raked the crowd with a furious hail of bullets and pursued the sharpshooters as they fled inside the buildings, no one present was able to get an over-all picture of what was happening. . . ." But the tragedy of Tlatelolco damaged Mexico much more seriously than is indicated in a news story entitled "Bloody Encounter in Tlatelolco," which appeared in *El Heraldo* on October 3, 1968, lamenting the harm done the country's reputation. "A few minutes after the fighting started in the Nonoalco area, the foreign correspondents and the journalists who had come to our country to cover the Olympic Games began sending out news bulletins informing the entire world of what was happening. Their reports—which in a number of cases were quite exaggerated—contained remarks that seriously endangered Mexico's prestige," the story read.

The wound is still fresh, and Mexicans, though stunned by this cruel blow, are beginning to ask themselves questions in open-mouthed amazement. The blood of hundreds of students, of men, women, children, soldiers, and oldsters tracked all over Tlatelolco has dried now. It has sunk once again into the quiet earth. Later, flowers will bloom among the ruins and the tombs.

E.P.

We ran down one floor after another in the center wing of the Chihuahua building, and on one of them, I don't remember which one it was, I felt something sticky underfoot. I turned around and saw blood, lots of blood, and I said to my husband, "Just look at all this blood, Carlos! They must have killed lots of people here!" Then one of the corporals said to me, "It's obvious, *señora*, that you've never seen very much blood. You're making such a fuss over a few little drops of it!" But there was lots and lots of blood, so much of it that my hands felt sticky. There was also blood all over the walls; it seems to me that the walls of Tlatelolco are drenched with blood. It reeks of blood all over Tlatelolco. Lots of people must have bled to death up there, because there was much too much blood for it to have been that of just one person.

Margarita Nolasco, anthropologist

On October 2, Professor Leonardo Pérez González, a teacher at Vocational 7 and a member of the Coalition of Secondary and College Teachers for Democratic Freedoms, was shot to death in the Plaza de las Tres Culturas.

Abelardo Hurtado, professor at the National
School of Biology, IPN

Yesterday, October 2, I was put in command of two sections of cavalry troops, numbering seventy-five men, all of whom were attached to the 18th and 19th Cavalry Regiment, and given orders to take these two sections to the Tlatelolco housing unit, with my men and myself dressed in civilian clothes but wearing a white glove so that the authorities would be able to identify us, and upon arriving there we were to guard the two entrances to the Chihuahua building in the aforementioned housing unit and mingle with the crowd that had gathered there for unspecified reasons. Immediately upon

209

sighting a flare in the sky, the prearranged signal, we were to seal off the aforementioned two entrances and prevent anyone from entering or leaving.

Ernesto Morales Soto, Captain, First Class, 19th Cavalry Regiment, attached to the Olimpia Battalion, under the command of Colonel Ernesto Gómez Tagle, in an official notarized statement, no. 54832/68, filed in the office of the Public Prosecutor

They're dead bodies, sir. . . .

A soldier, to José Antonio del Campo, reporter for El Día

The dead bodies were lying there on the pavement, waiting to be taken away. I counted lots and lots of them from the window, about seventy-eight in all. They were piling them up there in the rain. . . . I remembered that Carlitos, my son, had been wearing a green corduroy jacket, and I thought I recognized his dead body every time they dragged another one up. . . . I'll never forget one poor youngster, about sixteen or so, who crawled around the corner of the building, stuck his deathly pale face out, and made a V-for-Victory sign with two fingers. He didn't seem to have the least idea what was happening: he may have thought the men shooting were also students. Then the men in the white gloves yelled at him, "Get the hell out of here, you dumb bastard! Can't you see what's happening? Clear out of here!" The kid got to his feet and started walking toward them, as though he didn't have a care in the world. They fired a couple of shots at his feet, but the kid kept right on coming. He obviously didn't have the slightest idea what was going on, and they shot him in the calf of his leg. All I remember is that the blood didn't immediately spurt out; it just started slowly trickling down his leg. Meche and I started screaming at the guys with the white gloves like a couple of madwomen: "Don't kill him! Don't kill him! Don't kill him!" We ran to the door, but the kid had disappeared. I have no idea whether he managed to escape despite his wound, whether they killed him, or what happened to him.

Margarita Nolasco, anthropologist

They started firing from the helicopter, and I began to hear rifle reports overhead. Those idiots were shooting like crazy. That's why the Chihuahua building caught fire, because of the shots from the helicopter.

Estrella Sámano, student

The Plaza de las Tres Culturas is an esplanade quite a bit higher than street level, with several flights of steps leading up to it, and on one side it drops off sharply, giving visitors a good view of the recently restored pre-Hispanic ruins down below. A little church—Santiago de Tlatelolco—was built above these ruins in the sixteenth century. . . .

Luis González de Alba, of the CNH

From the speakers' platform where we were standing, we could see the blue caps of the railway workers below us.

*Graciela Román Olvera, student at the
Faculty of Medicine, UNAM*

I was handing out leaflets and collecting money for the CNH when the three green flares suddenly appeared in the sky behind the church. A lady who was searching in her purse for change to give me started looking for a place to take cover. "Don't panic, they're just trying to scare us a little, don't panic," I said to her. Several people ran past me and I shouted to them, "Don't run, you're in no danger, they're just firing in the air, don't run." Suddenly one of the Movement people ran by and I called to him, "Where are you going? We have to calm the crowd down so they won't panic and start running." But he turned on his heel like a robot and headed for the middle of the Plaza. When I realized after a while that he hadn't come back, I thought to myself, I wonder what the hell's happening; he hasn't come back.

*José Ramiro Muñoz, engineering
student at ESIME, IPN*

When I realized that the helicopter had come down dangerously low, circling right above the heads of the crowd in the Plaza de las Tres Culturas and firing on everybody—we could see the gray streaks of tracer bullets in the sky—I was so dumfounded I said to myself, I can't believe it—it's like in a movie! I've never seen anything like this except in the movies. Those just can't be real bullets! I wandered around in a daze, as though I'd gone out of my mind, until finally somebody grabbed me by the arm and stopped me.

Elvira B. de Concheiro, mother of a family

Ever since then, whenever I see a helicopter, my hands start trembling. For many months after I'd seen that helicopter fire on the crowd like that—as I was sitting there in my car—I couldn't write, my hands trembled so.

Marta Zamora Vértiz, secretary

Two helicopters overhead patrolling the student meeting descended and the crews inside started firing on the sharpshooters stationed on the roofs of the buildings.

It has been reported that the co-pilot of one of the helicopters received a bullet wound in the arm when a sharpshooter fired at him repeatedly from the Chihuahua building. The helicopter then took off immediately in the direction of the International Airport.

News story entitled "Many Killed and Wounded Last Night," La Prensa, *October 3, 1968*

The helicopter had come down so close that I would be able to identify the man who was firing on the crowd from inside it.

Ema Bermejillo de Castellanos, mother of a family

When the shooting began, people immediately headed for the stairs at the front of the Chihuahua building, shouting, "The Committee, the Committee!" Their one thought was to defend their leaders. Then the units of secret agents posted around the building began shooting at the crowd, driving them off with a hail of bullets.

Raúl Álvarez Garín, of the CNH

I couldn't understand why the crowd kept heading back toward where the men in the white gloves were shooting at them. Meche and I hid there behind a pillar watching the crowd coming toward us, shouting and moaning, being fired on, running away in the opposite direction, and then immediately coming back our way again, falling to the ground, running away again, and then coming back and falling to the ground again. The whole thing just didn't make sense: whatever were they doing? A whole great crowd was running first in one direction and then another: they'd run away and then head back our way again, and more of them would fall on the ground. I thought they should all have sense enough to keep away from the men who were shooting at them, but they kept coming back. I found out later that they were also being shot at from the other side of the Plaza.

Margarita Nolasco, anthropologist

The Army units approached from all directions and encircled the crowd in a pincers movement, and in just a few moments all the exits were blocked off. From up there on the fourth floor of the Chihuahua building, where the speakers' platform had been set up, we couldn't see what the Army was up to and we couldn't understand why the crowd was panicking. The two helicopters that had been hovering over the Plaza almost from the very beginning of the meeting·had suddenly started making very hostile maneuvers, flying lower and lower in tighter and tighter circles just above the heads of the crowd, and then they had launched two flares, a green one first and then a red one; when the second one went off the panic started, and we members of the Committee did our best to stop it: none of us there on the speakers' stand could see that the Army troops below us were advancing across the Plaza. When they found themselves confronted by a wall of bayonets, the crowd halted and immediately drew back; then we saw a great wave of people start running toward the other side of the Plaza; but there were Army troops on the other side of the Plaza too; and as we stood watching from up there on the speakers' stand, we saw the whole crowd head in another direction. That was the last thing we saw down below, for at that moment the fourth floor was taken over by the Olimpia Battalion. Even though we had no idea why the crowd had panicked and was running first in one direction and then in the other, those of us who had remained there at the microphone till the very last found ourselves looking down the barrels of machine guns when we turned around. The balcony had been occupied by the Olimpia Battalion and we were ordered to put our hands up and face the wall, and given strict orders not to turn

around in the direction of the Plaza; if we so much as moved a
muscle, they hit us over the head or in the ribs with their rifle
butts. Once the trap they had set snapped shut, the collective
murder began.

Gilberto Guevara Niebla, of the CNH

NOTARIZED DEPOSITION, NO. 54832/68

DEPOSITION BY ONE OF THE WOUNDED.—MEXICO CITY, D.F. *At nine-
thirty p.m. (21:30) on October 3, 1968 (nineteen hundred sixty-eight),
the undersigned, in pursuit of his official duties, legally entered the
Emergency Ward of the Central Military Hospital and recorded the
statement of the patient in Bed 28 (twenty-eight). After being duly informed of his rights, as provided by law, the said patient declared that
his name was* ERNESTO MORALES SOTO, *that he was 35 (thirty-five)
years of age, a widower, a Catholic, with an education, a Captain of
Cavalry, First Class, in the Mexican Army, born in Xicotepec de Juárez
in the State of Puebla, residing in this City in Military Camp Number* ONE. *With regard to the events currently under investigation, the
deponent* DECLARED: *That he holds a commission as a Cavalry Captain,
First Class, in the 19th Regiment, stationed in the City of Múzquiz, in
the State of Coahuila, and at the present time is attached to the Olimpia
Battalion in this City, under the command of Colonel* ERNESTO GÓMEZ
TAGLE, *which has been assigned the special duty of preserving public
order during the Olympic Games; that yesterday he was placed in command of two sections of Cavalry, numbering 65 (sixty-five) men, attached to the 18th and 19th Cavalry Regiments, and ordered to proceed
to the Tlatelolco housing unit with his men, all of whom were to be
dressed in civilian clothes and wear a white glove so that the authorities
would be able to identify them, and upon arriving there they were to
guard the two entrances to the Chihuahua building of the aforementioned housing unit and mingle with the crowd that had gathered there
for unspecified reasons; that immediately upon sighting a flare in the
sky, the prearranged signal, his unit was to station itself at both entrances and prevent anyone from entering or leaving; that after the
aforementioned flare was set off, they began to hear a great many shots
being fired, both from the top of the aforementioned building and from
the windows, aimed at the crowd of people gathered below, who attempted to protect themselves by hugging the walls of the building; that
a number of people in the crowd attempted to enter the building,*

whereupon the unit under the command of the deponent, in accordance with the orders they had received, fired in the air to disperse the crowd, these events having occurred at approximately four-forty p.m. (16:40 hours); that one of the shots from the top of the building wounded the deponent in the right arm, whereupon one of his men notified his superior, who ordered the deponent transferred to the Hospital, where he is at present a patient; that upon being wounded, he lost consciousness and therefore does not know what happened subsequently, and that owing to the fact that he is not familiar with that particular area of the city, he is unable to state precisely what streets the entrances to the Chihuahua building are located on, and does not know who the persons were who fired the shots or how many persons were wounded; that for the present this is the sole testimony that he has to offer. After reading the above deposition, the deponent attested to it by stamping it with his right thumbprint, since the wound in his arm made it impossible for him to sign his name.

STATEMENT ATTESTING TO WOUNDS INCURRED—*The undersigned, in pursuit of his official duties, visited Bed 28 in the Emergency Ward of the Central Military Hospital, where he personally examined the patient occupying said bed, who declared that his name was* ERNESTO MORALES SOTO, *and in witness whereof the undersigned states: that the said* SOTO *has the following wounds: a jagged bullet wound on the anterior surface of his right elbow, measuring one centimeter in diameter, and a second wound where the bullet exited, presenting the same characteristics and measuring two centimeters in diameter, on the posterior surface of the elbow, indicating a probable fracture. —Wounds of such a nature as not to endanger the life of the victim and requiring more than two weeks to heal. —Case covered by* PART TWO *of Article 289 of the Penal Code presently in effect. —Hospitalization not required. —The same wounds attested to and described in the certificate signed by Dr.* ALFREDO NEME DAVID, *the original of which has been examined and annexed to the present statement. . . .* HEREWITH ATTESTED TO:

> GERMÁN VALDEZ MARTÍNEZ, *Attorney*
> *Official Notary, Office of the Public Prosecutor*

> ALBERTO LÓPEZ ISLAS
> LÁZARO RODRÍGUEZ MORALES
> *Witnesses*

A heavier rain of bullets than any of the ones before began then, and went on and on. This was genocide, in the most absolute, the most tragic meaning of that word. Sixty-two minutes of round after round of gunfire, until the soldiers' weapons were so red-hot they could no longer hold them.

Leonardo Femat, in an article "A Tape Recording
That Tells the Whole Story," Siempre!, *no. 79 (The*
Night of Tlatelolco), October 16, 1968

I left the University with a group of comrades. We arrived at the Plaza de las Tres Culturas, and it started to rain. We all assembled in our various groups, and I was carrying a banner that read, THE LAW SCHOOL REPRESENTED HERE TODAY. There were other banners, one for instance that said, "The blood of our brothers will not have been shed in vain." I was sitting on the steps in front of the Chihuahua building when suddenly I saw the flares go off, and a few seconds later I heard what I found out later were machine guns firing on the crowd. Our comrade on the speakers' stand shouted, "Don't move, anybody! Keep calm! Sit down!" So I sat down, holding onto my banner. I had no idea what was happening, or rather, I didn't realize how serious the situation was, so I just sat there clutching my banner till a comrade shouted to me, "Get rid of that thing!" because I was a perfect target sitting there with my banner. I threw it down and started running with Tita. We ran to where the flags were flying, the flagpoles in the Plaza de las Tres Culturas, over to one side of Vocational 7, and Tita and I tried to get under cover. Then I heard a girl begging for help: "Oh, God, please help me!" I also heard voices shouting things like "My purse, my purse, where's my purse?" At one point we leaped over those pre-Hispanic walls there and fell into a sort of ditch. I lay there on the ground, and other people started falling on top of me. We heard shouts and groans and cries of pain, and I realized then that the gunfire was getting heavier and heavier. Tita and I crawled out of there and ran toward the Calle Manuel González, and the soldiers yelled to us, "Get the hell out as fast as you can!" As we ran out of the Plaza, a white Volkswagen full of students drove by, and they shouted to us, "Come on! Climb in!" I can't remember if they called us by name: "Come on, Nacha, Tita, get in!" and one of the funny things about the whole bit is that I don't remember how we managed to pile into that car that was already crammed full of a whole bunch of students. We lit out down the Paseo de la Reforma to the Avenida de la República de Cuba, and then Tita climbed out because everybody knew her by sight and she would have been recognized instantly. We all said as much. "You're so big they'd spot you half a mile away," we told her. I went back in that same car with two Movement people from Theoretical Physics at Poli—I don't know who they were—to see if we could find a couple of comrades we had no idea what had happened to. The boys stopped the car somewhere near the Secretariat of Foreign Relations—I don't know the name of the street because I'm not from Mexico City, I'm from Taxco, in the state of Guerrero. They got out and said to me, "Stay here in the car," and I stayed there in the car waiting for them all by myself, but as the minutes ticked by, I got more and more nervous; the shooting still hadn't stopped, it was worse in fact, and ambulances were drawing up with their sirens screeching, more and more soldiers were going by, tanks and convoys of troops armed to the teeth. An ambulance drew up right in front of me, and the attendants put a student in it: his head was all bloody; he was dripping blood from head to foot. I was sitting there in the car no more than ten or twelve feet away, and seeing that student in that shape turned my stomach. Then a whole bunch of people ran by shouting, "They've set fire to the Chihuahua building!" I looked up and saw smoke. A high-tension wire fell down then, and everyone running past that Volkswagen I was in was screaming. I was suddenly frightened and scrambled out of the car in a panic and started running. I must have run for a much longer time than I realized, because I suddenly found myself at Sanborn's, on Lafragua. An acquaintance of mine stopped me there on the street. "What's the matter?" he asked me. I realized then that I'd been crying and my mascara was running down my cheeks. I felt as though I didn't have one ounce of strength left—I was really in terrible shape. Some kids went into Sanborn's and brought me out some coffee because I was trembling so. "Take it easy, take it easy," they kept saying. Then some more kids came to the door. The only thing I could blurt out was, "They're killing the students!" These same kids then took me to an apartment on the Avenida de Coyoacán, where I was living with Tita and another girl friend.

Ana Ignacia Rodríguez (Nacha),
of the Action Committee, UNAM

It never occurred to us that the government might attack us on October 2, because a few days before there had been a meeting at Tlatelolco and in the morning several members of the CNH—the ones who had the most sense and the most savvy, though I never mention names, you know—went to the Casa del Lago to talk with Caso and de la Vega, and we thought that a sort of tacit truce had been arranged, since it looked as though the government was about to reach an agreement with the students. So we scheduled another meeting, but at the same time we decided to cancel the march on the Santo Tomás campus, which had been occupied by Army troops, so we wouldn't be accused of stirring up more trouble. This was announced from the speakers' stand almost immediately after the meeting began. . . . No, I wasn't on the speakers' stand; I stayed down below on the esplanade with Nacha. . . . But then they started shooting—and got their own asses shot off.

Roberta Avendaño Martínez (Tita), CNH delegate from UNAM

There was lots of blood underfoot, lots of blood smeared on the walls.

Francisco Correa, physicist, and professor at IPN

I put my hands over the back of my neck to protect it, with my cheek and my belly and my legs pressing against the floor of the room. I was one of the ones closest to the door of the apartment, almost right next to it. The reports of all sorts of firearms frightened me, and I asked my comrades there in the room to move over and let me share the minimum shelter offered by the partition dividing off the front part of the apartment where we were.

I heard people outside shouting, "We're from the Olimpia Battalion, don't shoot, we're from the Olimpia Battalion!"

My comrades lying there on the floor moved over and I managed to crawl over to the partition. I lay there for some time—I don't know how long exactly—and I kept thinking, The dirty sons of bitches, the filthy murdering bastards.

None of us said much, except once in a while a couple of swear words of the same sort that had been running through my mind broke the impressive "silence" where all we could hear was bullets whizzing all around us. I'd also lost my glasses.

I heard a sob from time to time from one or another of my men or women comrades, and I remember hearing someone say (or perhaps I only imagined it), "Don't cry, this is no time to cry, to shed tears: this is the time to engrave what's happening in letters of fire in our very heart of hearts so we'll remember it when it comes time to settle the score with the people responsible for this." Maybe I dreamed it.

At one point the shooting died down a little, and we made our way on our hands and knees into two other rooms in the back of the apartment. As I crawled back there, I saw several of my comrades from the CNH: all of them had a very odd expression on their faces. It wasn't terror, or even fear; it was a gleam of intense hatred in their eyes, plus a look of pain at being so completely helpless.

We all crawled into one little bedroom, and a few seconds later there was another heavy burst of gunfire. We lay down on the floor again, but it was covered with a film of water, and our clothes got soaked. It turned cold as night fell. Amid the continuous burst of rifle fire, we suddenly heard even louder rounds of gunfire, and immediately afterward it began to pour. We were even more concerned at that point, because the building had started swaying when this very loud gunfire began. It could all be summed up in two words: "A tank."

Eduardo Valle Espinoza (Owl-Eyes), of the CNH

Am I losing much blood?
Pablo Berlanga, to his mother, Rafaela Cosme de Berlanga

There was nothing we could do but keep running. They were firing at us from all directions. We ran six or eight feet, keeping under cover, and then ten or twelve feet out in the open. Rifle fire sounds very much like a jet taking off. There was nothing to do but keep running. We heard the display windows of the shops on the ground floor of the Chihuahua building shatter, and we suddenly decided we ought to make a run for the stairway. As I stood down there, babbling all sorts of nonsense, I also suddenly remembered all my many friends and comrades at the meeting and got terrible cramps in my stomach. I remembered names, faces. As I reached this stairway that the people from the CNH who were going to speak had been going up and down all during the afternoon, I met Margarita and Meche, who said to me in the most despairing tone of voice, "María Alicia, our children are up there on the fourth floor!"

For the first time I had the feeling I might be able to do something useful amid all this confusion and suffering, despite my sense of utter helplessness, and I said to them, "I'll go up there with you."

The youngster who had saved my life—by leaping on me and throwing me to the floor there on the speakers' stand when they first started shooting at us—went upstairs with us: he was my armor, my cape, my shield. I have no idea who he was. I have a photographic memory, but I can't remember his face at all. . . . The three of us started up the stairs, and on the first landing we met another youngster. I had seen him on the speakers' stand there on the fourth floor of the Chihuahua building, too, talking with various Movement people as though he knew them very well. I remember him particularly because he'd apparently been wounded in the right wrist and had a white handkerchief wrapped around his hand.

"Don't leave, *señora,* it'll all be over soon," he said to me.

I was about to go downstairs again, because I'd spied some girl friends of mine down on the esplanade. But the boy took me by the arm and very solicitously helped me up the stairs. I was touched by this courageous behavior on the part of yet another student hero, and went upstairs with him.

Then Mercedes shouted, *"Señor,* my children are there upstairs!"

Margarita shouted that her children were up there too, and I stopped there on the stairs and looked at the youngster escorting me, thinking that the courage of those kids is really incredible sometimes. Many hours later, I discovered that my escort was one of the assassins guarding the stairway so that none of the CNH people would escape. He took us back downstairs then, and I remember that we were caught up in a whole crowd of people and shoved to the corner of the Chihuahua building, and that meanwhile there was a steady hail of bullets from the buildings.

A girl came by shouting, "You murderers, you murderers!" I took her in my arms and tried to calm her down, but she kept screaming, louder and louder, until finally the youngster behind me grabbed hold of her and started shaking her. I noticed then that her ear had been shot off and her head was bleeding. The people in the crowd kept piling one on top of another, seeking shelter from the rain of bullets; we were all right on each other's necks, and I felt as though I were caught in the middle of a riot or squeezed in a sardine can.

I stood there staring at the tips of the coffee-colored shoes of some woman. Several rounds of machine-gun bullets suddenly raked the spot where we were standing, and I saw one bullet land just a few inches from that woman's shoe. All she said was, "Oh, my goodness!" and another voice answered, "Make a run for it. If you stay here you'll be even worse off; you're sure to get hurt here." We all started running again and just then I spied a red Datsun with a young girl at the wheel. She'd been shot, and I saw her collapse on top of the steering wheel; the horn kept blowing and blowing. . . . The youngster kept saying, "Don't look, don't look." We ran on toward one of the buildings behind Chihuahua. . . .

María Alicia Martínez Medrano, nursery-school director

Then I heard voices shouting things like "We're wearing white gloves, don't shoot, don't shoot!" And then other voices shouting, "We need a walkie-talkie here, don't shoot us, contact us by walkie-talkie!" There were desperate cries, coming either from down below us on the third floor, or from up above on the fifth or sixth floor: "Olimpia Battalion!" And then I heard whistles blowing. . . . "Olimpia Battalion, line up over here! . . ." And then all I heard was "The eighth and the fourteenth . . ." "The eighth . . . are you all here?" "The fourteenth . . . how many are missing in the fourteenth?" Then voices shouted, "Have the ones from the elevator turned up?" and then more whistles blowing: "Olimpia Battalion, Olimpia Battalion, over here, all of you! Olimpia Battalion, answer!" There were desperate shouts from the police for a long time: "Don't shoot! . . . They're wearing white gloves!" This will give you some idea of how absolutely chaotic the whole affair was, on one hand, and also how it took on proportions that the organizers hadn't expected and got completely out of control. I can assure you that the whole thing was obviously planned in advance; the authorities knew exactly what they were up to. They were trying to prevent any sort of demonstration or student disturbance before the Olympics and during the games. The flares were the signal to start shooting, and they began firing from all directions at once. As for the supposed "sharpshooters," I can assure you—because those of us who were there saw it with our own eyes and know it's true beyond the shadow of a doubt—that the sharpshooters were agents playing their part in the government's plan.

Mercedes Olivera de Vázquez, anthropologist

The authorities said, "Stop all this, right now." They hadn't counted on the fact that the *granaderos,* the soldiers, the security agents would act entirely on their own initiative—they've always had a mind of their own.

Roberta Ruiz García, grade-school teacher

One agent got scared stiff and started shooting. That's what started the whole thing.

Luis Argüelles Peralta, geology student at ESIME, IPN

Hundreds of persons on the fourth floor of the Chihuahua building saw that after arresting the people they had found up there, the plainclothesmen wearing white gloves began firing on the crowd attending the meeting and also on the troops that were moving forward. Immediately thereafter, as the soldiers answered their fire, the agents in civilian clothes took cover behind the cement balustrade, their guns still aimed at the prisoners, who continued to stand there with their hands up, directly in the line of fire. The first shots the soldiers fired landed on the roof, but as the troops moved forward across the Plaza they began aiming lower and bits of plaster started falling off the wall. Then the agents ordered the prisoners to lie down, and as a hail of bullets struck the Chihuahua building, the men in the white gloves, a number of whom had shouted that they were from the Olimpia Battalion, began yelling in chorus to make themselves heard over the heavy gunfire: "We're the Olimpia Battalion, don't shoot!" As the rifle fire grew heavier and heavier and the high-power machine guns mounted on the tanks began to chatter, the men in the white gloves started desperately searching about for a walkie-talkie. One of them, apparently the leader of the battalion, ordered the others to stop shooting. Shouts of "Stop shooting, let's get a walkie-talkie!" were heard. Amid all the shooting they had recognized the burst of small bombs being launched from the tanks to clear openings in the walls for the troops to shoot through. The men with a white glove or a white handkerchief on their left hand kept crawling by, very cautiously, on their hands and knees. Apparently they had no way of communicating with the troops that were firing on everyone in the Plaza. We were surprised it was taking them so long to kill all of us.

Félix Lucio Hernández Gamundi, of the CNH

We lost sight of Reyes and I heard a shout from my brother: "Don't let go of my hand." We clutched each other's hand and headed toward the right, trying to reach the park with the ruins. There were lots of people down there, trying to find cover from the terrible hail of bullets coming from all directions. We could hear shells exploding over all the other noise; the ruins were being shattered by the bullets, and bits of stone started raining down on our heads. I was still clutching my brother's hand, despite the fact that there were other people between us, and I tried to pull him closer to me. Some students were lying there on the ground between us, some of them dead and others wounded. There was a girl right next to me who had been hit square in the face with a dum-dum bullet. It was ghastly! The entire left side of her face had been blown away.

The shouts, the cries of pain, the weeping, the prayers and supplications, and the continuous deafening sound of gunfire made the Plaza de las Tres Culturas a scene straight out of Dante's *Inferno*.

Diana Salmerón de Contreras

"A doctor, please, I beg you, in the name of everything you hold most dear, get me a doctor!"

Olga Sánchez Cuevas, mother of a family

They wouldn't even let the Red and Green Cross ambulances through! They pulled up with their sirens screeching. They were told to turn off their sirens and their lights.

Berta Cárdenas de Macías, tenant in the
Tlatelolco housing unit

I warned all of them that the Plaza was a trap—I told them. There's no way out of it, I warned them. But they thought they knew it all. I told them they would have no way of getting out of the Plaza, that we'd be surrounded there, boxed in, like cattle in a corral. I kept telling them that, but they paid no attention.

Mercedes Olivera de Vázquez, anthropologist

I love love.

Hippie button found in the Plaza de las Tres Culturas

I tugged at my brother's arm. "Julio, what's the matter?" I asked him. I tugged at his arm again; his eyes were half closed and there was a very sad look in them. And I heard him murmur the words "I think . . ."

My mind was a total blank. The tremendous crush of people screaming in panic made it hard for me to hear what he was saying. I thought later that if I'd known, if I'd realized that Julio was dying, I would have done something absolutely crazy right then and there.

Later some of the soldiers who had been shooting at the buildings around the Plaza came over to us. The smell of gunpowder was unbearable. Little by little people made room for me so I could kneel down beside Julio.

"Julio, Julio, answer me, little brother," I said to him.

"He must be wounded," one woman said to me. "Loosen his belt."

When I loosened it, I could feel a great big wound. I found out later at the hospital that he had three bullet wounds: one in the stomach, one in the neck, and another in the leg. He was dying.

Diana Salmerón de Contreras

That's enough of this! When are they going to stop all this?

Pedro Díaz Juárez, student

"Hey, little brother, what's the matter? Answer me, little brother . . ."

Diana Salmerón de Contreras

The hail of bullets being fired at the Chihuahua building became so intense that around seven p.m. a large section of the building caught on fire.

The fire burned for a long time. All the floors from the tenth to the thirteenth were enveloped in flames, and many families were forced to leave the unit, amid the heavy gunfire, carrying their children in their arms and risking their lives. We also saw many others struck by bullets fall to the ground.

Jorge Avilés R., in a story entitled "Serious
Fighting for Hours Between Terrorists and Soldiers,"
El Universal, *October 3, 1968*

Little brother, speak to me. . . . Please, somebody get him a stretcher! I'm right here, Julio . . . a stretcher! . . . Soldier, a stretcher for somebody who's been wounded. . . . What's the matter, little brother? . . . Answer me, little brother. . . . A stretcher! . . .

Diana Salmerón de Contreras

A number of dead bodies lying in the Plaza de las Tres Culturas. Dozens of wounded. Hysterical women with their children in their arms. Shattered windows. Burned-out apartments. The outer doors of the buildings destroyed. Water pipes in a number of buildings broken. Water leaking all over many of them. Yet the shooting went on and on.

News story entitled "Terrible Gun Battle in Tlatelolco.
The Number of Dead Not Yet Determined and
Dozens Wounded," Excélsior, *October 3, 1968*

Now that I'd managed to get to Julio and we were together again, I could raise my head and look around. The very first thing I noticed was all the people lying on the ground; the entire Plaza was covered with the bodies of the living and the dead, all lying side by side. The second thing I noticed was that my kid brother had been riddled with bullets.

Diana Salmerón de Contreras

This reporter was caught in the crowd near the Secretariat of Foreign Relations. A few steps away a woman fell to the ground— she had either been wounded or had fainted dead away. A couple of youngsters tried to go to her rescue, but the soldiers stopped them.

> *Félix Fuentes, in a news story entitled "It All Began at 6:30 p.m.,"* La Prensa, *October 3, 1968*

"Soldier, please have somebody bring a stretcher!"

"Shut up and stop pestering me or you'll be needing two of them!" was the only reply I got from this "heroic Johnny," as our president calls the soldiers in the ranks.

Just then a med student hurried over and said to this "heroic Johnny," "That boy there ought to be taken to the hospital right away!"

"Shut your trap, you son of a bitch," the soldier answered.

Everyone standing around watching began shouting in chorus, "A stretcher, a stretcher, a stretcher!"

A couple of people made a makeshift stretcher out of some lengths of pipe and an overcoat. But the med student who helped us was arrested.

> *Diana Salmerón de Contreras*

In a few minutes the whole thing became a scene straight out of hell. The gunfire was deafening. The bullets were shattering the windows of the apartments and shards of glass were flying all over, and the terror-stricken families inside were desperately trying to protect their youngest children.

> *Jorge Avilés R., in "Serious Fighting for Hours Between Terrorists and Soldiers"*

Lucianito is there upstairs!

> *Elvira B. de Concheiro, mother of a family*

"Please let me go with him—I'm his sister!" I begged.

They gave me permission to leave the Plaza with the stretcher-bearers. I climbed into the Army ambulance with my brother.

> *Diana Salmerón de Contreras*

> PEOPLE—UNITE—PEOPLE—UNITE—PEOPLE—UNITE
> *Chant at demonstrations*

Why don't you answer me, *hermanito?*

Diana Salmerón de Contreras

Everything was a blur—I don't know if it was because I was crying or because it had started to rain. I watched the massacre through this curtain of rain, but everything was fuzzy and blurred, like when I develop my negatives and the image begins to appear in the emulsion. . . . I couldn't see a thing. My nose was running, but I just snuffled and went on shooting pictures, though I couldn't see a thing: the lens of my camera was spattered with raindrops, spattered with tears. . . .

Mary McCallen, press photographer

[As they started lining us up against the wall of the church] I saw two of my pals from *Excélsior* there, a reporter and a press photographer. They'd grabbed Jaime González's camera away from him. The reporter was saying, "I'm a journalist," but one of the soldiers answered, "Very pleased to meet you, but I couldn't care less whether you're a journalist or not; just stand over there against the wall." They'd slashed Jaime González's hand with a bayonet to get his camera away from him.

Raúl Hernández, press photographer, in a story
entitled "The Gun Battle as the Press
Photographers Saw It," La Prensa, October 3, 1968

Before I climbed into the Army ambulance, a "student" whom I'd seen at UNAM came up to me and said, "Your handbag, please. . . ."

"What do you want it for?" I asked.

The soldier who was with me was surprised too: "Who are *you?*" he asked him. But then he noticed a white handkerchief or something in the fake student's hand and said to him, "Oh, you're one of *them*, are you?"

The guy was an undercover agent posing as a student. I handed him my purse, and he searched through it and then gave it back to me. I have no idea to this day why he asked me for it.

They took my brother to the hospital then, and I waited there for hours to find out how the operation had gone. A male nurse kept coming in every so often, and one time he asked the women who were there waiting it out, just as I was, "Which one of you was with a boy in a blue suit?"

"He was with me . . . I came here with a boy in a blue suit," I said.

They took me to identify Julio's body and sign the necessary papers.

When we held the wake for Julio, I was deeply touched by his fellow students' loyalty to him and their concern for us. All the boys from Vocational 1 came to the house the minute they heard the tragic news of his death. They had taken up a collection and offered us some five hundred pesos. My sister told them we didn't really need the money, and would prefer that they use it for the Movement. "No," they all said. "The way we see it your brother *is* the Movement. We'd like you to accept the money."

Julio was fifteen years old, a student at Vocational 1, the school out by the Tlatelolco housing unit. That was the second political meeting he'd ever gone to. He had asked me to go with him that day. The first meeting we went to together was the big Silent Demonstration. Julio was my only brother.

Diana Salmerón de Contreras

I'm going to die. I'm badly hurt. I'm certain I'm going to die. I've been sure of it ever since the police put their pistols to my chest and made all of us put our hands up. I think to myself, Well, this is the end. I guess my number's up. . . . I could hear shots and terrible screams down below. The cops kept their pistols trained on us and ordered us to lie face down, and I suddenly regretted that I hadn't accomplished more during my life. I had a few brief thoughts about what I'd done with my life up to that point, and then suddenly I realized that a bullet had struck me. And there I was, in Tlatelolco, on October 2, 1968, at the age of twenty-four. I'm losing lots of blood, I thought to myself. That guy over there is bleeding lots too. He moved a minute or so ago, but he's not stirring now. How come, I wonder? I didn't feel a thing when that bullet struck me, not one thing, but man, it sure hurts now! I even managed to run a few steps and now I've fallen on the ground here. Everybody's running every which way! And I can't even move my leg now. There's not one damned stretcher-bearer anywhere in sight, and nobody can hear a thing with all those machine guns rattling. If I die China * will take up half her column writing about me, or maybe even the whole thing. I gave her the info she needed for her column on Luis H. de la Fuente. It was a good obit, China. Who'll give you the info for mine?

Rodolfo Rojas Zea, reporter for El Día

I saw blood smeared on the wall.

Luz Vértiz de López, mother of a family

I didn't get arrested at Tlatelolco—and it was probably just by luck or fate or some instinct of self-preservation or something that I wasn't nabbed; but we saw that afternoon how a person's life can be snuffed out in just a few moments or a few hours, whether he's lived it well or badly; we saw many lives come to a sudden end in that brutal attack on the Mexican people: Tlatelolco. They eventually arrested me and threw me in prison, but that was later, not at Tlatelolco.

We kept tugging at people's arms, trying to calm them down: "They're trying to stir up trouble, don't run, don't panic, that'll just make it worse, don't try to run for it, take your time and just file out slowly," we told them, but the crowd had had a number of bad experiences earlier and wouldn't obey the Movement people or anybody else. There was a general stampede then, because just after the first shot, all hell broke loose and a hail of bullets started raining down on us from all directions. I saw several comrades fall to the ground, and I tried to make my way over to help them, but the gunfire got heavier and heavier and there was nothing I could do but run for cover. There were several little kids that were either shot to death or trampled to death as the crowd panicked. The soldiers had already blocked off the back of Vocational 7, and I saw that people

---

* "La China" Mendoza, a popular reporter who in 1968 had a column in *El Día*. (Translator's note.)

were leaping down into the pre-Hispanic ruins; it was utter mad-
ness, because they were all landing one on top of the other; everyone was screaming and moaning—women with little babies in their
arms, workers, students, railroad men, little kids. The soldiers were
advancing toward us with fixed bayonets, like in the movies; they
would crouch down and move forward a few yards and then duck
behind the vehicles and fire at the Chihuahua building. I couldn't
believe my ears when I heard a machine gun start chattering. I
remember especially—and this is a very important point—that
when the machine gun started firing, two comrades, a boy and a
girl, raised their hands way up in the air to surrender and I don't
know whether it was because the soldiers had been given drugs, or
what, but they suddenly fired round after round at the two of them.
Other comrades who had also seen that happen screamed in terror;
that was the only thing they really could do, because they had
nothing to defend themselves with. The machine gun was right
there near them, firing directly at the building; the spent cartridges
kept falling all around and we were absolutely desperate, because
there wasn't a single thing any of us could do. . . .

I was able to get under cover almost immediately because one
lady opened her door, or perhaps made the mistake of just opening
it a crack, and we all flung ourselves on it and piled inside: in seconds there were about sixty-five of us there inside that apartment in
the San Luis Potosí building. We heard the machine gun still chattering away, and then a real war of nerves began: one lady fainted,
and the owner of the apartment went all to pieces; the Movement
people fell into a helpless rage at not being able to defend themselves, at not having any way to fight back, and lots of my pals,
comrades I had thought were pretty tough kids, started to cry, and
it was some of the girls who finally calmed them down. By sheer coincidence, I'd spotted my sister in the crowd a few moments before.
I'd dropped everything, dragged her away by the hair, and refused
to let go of her. My sister's much more aggressive, much more of a
hothead than I am—as a militant she's got me beaten all hollow—
and she was so indignant she started cussing a blue streak. . . .

We couldn't leave the apartment—not till the shooting died down
anyway. The lady who lived in the apartment was worried because
her children hadn't come home, and for the moment we were her

children. Her own kids came home two or three hours later and she calmed down then. "All right, you youngsters, the problem now is how to get all of you out of here," she said. We thought, Well, there are several middle-aged ladies here; we can take them along with us. So then we ditched everything we had with us that would identify us as students and left it behind there in the apartment, because at that stage of the game being a student was a worse crime than committing murder. My sister and I left with one of the older ladies about three in the morning.

The lady whose apartment we'd invaded was really great. All the people who lived in the Tlatelolco housing unit were wonderful to us. They had given the students a hand at the meeting on September 21, too. The tenants in many of the buildings in the unit had thrown boiling water down on the *granaderos* from their windows: we were all defending Tlatelolco together. So that's why they were just as heartsick about what happened on October 2 as we were.

Daniel Esparza Lepe, student at ESIME, IPN

We all felt absolutely helpless. On the other side of the street, across the Paseo de la Reforma, I happened to see comrades—kids no more than twelve or thirteen or fourteen—trying to throw stones at the cops and the troops across the boulevard. I think they might have been junior-high-school kids, and they were in tears at what was happening: they were trying their best to help us, and were weeping with helpless rage. I went over to one of them then and said, "Listen, that isn't going to do any good. A bullet's got much more velocity than a stone. You'd better cool it, because they can kill you with their bullets over here, but your stones aren't landing anywhere near them over there on the other side of the street." The kid thought about it for a minute and then said, "You're right," and climbed down off the wall and went away. A man came along shouting, "Murderers! Cowards! Killers!" He wasn't wounded, but they dragged him away, because he was trying to get back to the Plaza. A family—they were Chinese, I think—was walking toward the Plaza de las Tres Culturas, all of them clinging desperately to each other. Nobody could understand a word they were saying, but everyone moved aside to let them by because they were all in tears.

When I got home, a comrade who lives nearby wanted to go back to Tlatelolco to look for her mother, who'd gone to the meeting with my friend's youngest brother.

José Ramiro Muñoz, student at ESIME, IPN

Lucianito's there upstairs!

Elvira B. de Concheiro, mother of a family

A little trickle of blood started running down his cheek, from just below his eyelid.

Blanca Vargas de Ibáñez, mother of a family

By the time I got there, the shooting had already started. Dozens of people ran past me, and I heard one girl shout, "Lots of people have been killed, a whole bunch of them! . . ." I was absolutely beside myself when I heard that, and started screaming. There were troops blocking off the whole Plaza. I thought I might be able to crawl in between them on my hands and knees, but some women stopped me, and a whole crowd of people gathered round.

"Let her through, let her through, she's looking for her son! Her son's in there!" they all shouted.

I was screaming terrible things, and could hardly stand on my feet. People around me were saying, "She's right . . . if her son is in there . . ."

"It's not just *my* son—they're all *your* children too. . . ."

More soldiers arrived. Suddenly one of the women who had been standing there listening to me took an empty milk bottle out from under her coat—I still have it in the cupboard over there—and handed it to me. "Here, take this, maybe it'll be of some use to you," she said to me.

Elvira B. de Concheiro, mother of a family

There were tragic scenes that no one who witnessed them will ever forget. We will always remember the look of terror on people's faces, the moans of the wounded as they were taken away, and the continuous gunfire. The people watching what was happening from several blocks away were livid with rage. They didn't know whether it was the authorities who were to blame for the turn events had taken or who, but they were cursing everything and everybody. People in the city, who naturally had been badly upset at what had happened, were in an ugly mood and tried to march on the area where the shooting was going on: at nine-fifteen p.m. the troops had to drive a crowd on the corner of Allende and Nonoalco back with tear-gas grenades.

Jorge Avilés R., in "Serious Fighting for Hours
Between Terrorists and Soldiers"

My father died shortly after Julio was killed. He had a heart attack as a result of the shock of his death. Julio was his only son, his youngest child. He would often say, "Why did it have to be my son?" My mother has managed to go on living somehow.

Diana Salmerón de Contreras

He had a huge cut over his eye and the blood was streaming down his face. I said to him jokingly, "Have you gone a couple of rounds in a boxing ring?" And he burst into tears, because he was so upset I think, since ordinarily he's a quiet, self-contained youngster.

José Merino Gasca, engineer and father of a family

Who was responsible for this? Who gave orders for this?

Pablo Castillo, student, Iberoamerican University

All that shooting was the very worst yet! The gunfire at Santo Tomás was mere child's play by comparison!

Juan Medina Castro, engineering student at
ESIQIE, IPN

I was in the Aguascalientes building—it's very elegant—the one right next to Vocational 7 in the Nonoalco housing unit. The minute the first shots rang out, as if someone had given them orders, all the tenants of the building lay down on the living-room floor of their apartments. The minute the shooting started—at six-fifteen, I think it was—the supervisor of the building ran and hid in the basement and didn't appear again till four hours later. Up on the eighth floor an engineer, a man of about fifty, was hit in the right shoulder with a bullet which shattered it completely. It was apparently a dum-dum bullet. Someone phoned the Red Cross to come, but two soldiers appeared instead, armed with submachine guns. That was the last we saw of the engineer. There was a look of terror and desperation on the faces of all the tenants of the building. Once the shooting died down, they tried to get in touch with their husbands, their wives, their children, or their relatives who were somewhere else at the time to tell them what had happened to them and warn them not to try to come back to the housing unit, because anybody who tried to enter or leave was immediately taken into custody.

They began talking about all the recent events and making bitter remarks about the national press "which never tells the truth about what's really happening." They mentioned the case of Lieutenant Uriza Barrón in particular, a man who had killed two policemen or two members of the "special riot squad." They said, "All the reporters claimed that the lieutenant had shot them because they'd beaten up his mother, but those of us who live here in Tlatelolco know he shot them because they insulted his sister. The reporters never said a word about that. . . ."

I don't know whether that's true or not—there are so many rumors going around—but they must have done something terrible to Lieutenant Uriza Barrón for him to have pulled out his pistol like that and murdered those two police.

There was no water and very little food available for a time. The tenants all banded together and shared whatever food they had on hand with their neighbors. Those who had the biggest families and bare cupboards were given food by their neighbors, who all stuck by them. The littlest kids were all crying and the bigger ones were staring at their parents with terror-stricken eyes.

Alfredo Corvera Yáñez, student at the School of Commerce and Business Administration, UNAM

Those of us in the CNH have been accused of having piles of money at our disposal. But the real story is that there were many very large brigades (some of them had two hundred students in them, all going out in our buses to visit various neighborhoods in the city); we divided them into groups of ten students, and gave each group a box to collect money for the Movement. Since people always contributed very generously, there were always at least fifty pesos in each of their boxes.

Félix Lucio Hernández Gamundi, of the CNH

They nabbed one kid with one of the boxes used by the Action Committees to collect money from people, and the authorities started looking for the member of the CNH who'd given him orders to do that. They lined us all up in front of him and shone flashlights in our faces, one by one, so he'd be able to recognize us. "Is this the one? . . ." "No." "This one? . . ." "No." He didn't recognize any of us.

The officer got mad and started beating him up. Then he said to him in a very angry tone of voice, "You taught classes in guerrilla warfare, didn't you, you little bastard?"

"No, the only things I taught were algebra and math, which don't really have very much to do with guerrilla warfare."

There was great pride in his voice when he answered back like that. His attitude really warmed the cockles of my heart.

Eduardo Valle Espinoza (Owl-Eyes), of the CNH

When I heard that comrade who'd been taking up collections speak up like that, it struck me that things weren't going all that badly, that we weren't beaten yet by a long shot. Then after a while, long past eleven o'clock, the shooting started again.

Luis González de Alba, of the CNH

The sharpshooters weren't satisfied just to fire a hail of bullets at the women and children and innocent bystanders who had turned up at the meeting; they began to fire on the Army troops and the police who had surrounded the Plaza to prevent the crowd from marching on the Santo Tomás campus.

As the first Army troops and police were hit and fell to the ground, orders were given to return the fire, and one of the most terrible gun battles ever to occur in our city began. Despite the fact that the Army troops and the police immediately responded and fired round after round at them, the sharpshooters continued to shoot at the panic-stricken crowd of women and children and innocent bystanders fleeing for their lives in all directions.

News story entitled "Many Dead and Wounded Last Night," La Prensa, *October 3, 1968*

My daughter's blood was tracked all over the Plaza by the shoes of youngsters running from one end of it to the other.

Dolores Verdugo de Solís, mother of a family

I turned the dead body face up. His eyes were wide open, and his clothes soaking wet. I closed his eyes. But before I did so, I saw that there were tiny little raindrops on the whites of his eyes. . . .

Luisa Herrera Martín del Campo, grade-school teacher

I saw a child eleven or twelve years old who suddenly raised his head a few inches—he was only a little boy, after all—and a bullet went clear through his cheek. His sister was with him. We were all lying on the ground on the esplanade as the soldiers had ordered us to do, but this little boy raised his head up. His sister, who looked to be about sixteen years old, began to scream hysterically, "My little brother's been shot!" but the soldiers and the Movement people told her that if she stood up, they would probably shoot her too. They didn't give the boy any sort of medical attention until the shooting was all over. He had a big gaping wound, and they waited two or three hours before taking care of him! I imagine he died, but I don't know for sure because around eleven p.m. they came and took us around behind the church.

Esther Fernández, student at the
Faculty of Sciences, UNAM

They're shooting very low, terribly low! Crouch way down!

An Army officer

Stop shooting! Stop shooting! Stop shooting!

Voices in the crowd

I can't stand this another minute!

A woman's voice

Stay under cover! Don't move!

A man's voice

Surround them! Over there, over there! Hem them in, I tell you!

A voice

I've been wounded. Get me a doctor. I've been . . .

A voice

It looks like the shooting's almost over. . . .

A voice

The Plaza de las Tres Culturas was a living hell. Every so often we could hear gunfire and the bullets from the machine guns and high-powered rifles were whizzing in every direction.

Miguel Salinas López, student at the School of
Commerce and Business Administration, UNAM

It was also reported that many persons had been wounded by bullets coming in the windows.

Meanwhile, Roberto Legorreta reported to the city desk that a fire had broken out in the Chihuahua building and the flames had reached a number of apartments in this building, the center of most of the action.

Reyes Razo reported that on the thirteenth floor of the Tamaulipas building a man had been killed in one of the corridors. There was also another fatality in the San Luis Potosí building.

At seven-thirty-five p.m., firemen arrived to put out the fires inside the Chihuahua building, which by now was burning on three floors. There were continual reports of more wounded who had been found, among them both Army troops and civilians, including many women.

News story entitled "26 Dead and 71 Wounded;
Sharpshooters Fire on Army Troops..General Toledo
Wounded," El Heraldo, October 3, 1968

I had blood on the edges of my shoes, on the hem of my dress.

Eugenia Leal Lima, medical student, UNAM

The majority of the corpses were lying face down, swelling in the rain, but there were also some lying face up. They looked like trampled flowers, like the mud-spattered, crushed flowers planted around the Chihuahua building.

Pilar Marín de Zepeda, grade-school teacher

They're dead bodies, sir. . . .

A soldier, to José Antonio del Campo,
reporter for El Día

Get down, I tell you! They're going to kill us!

A man's voice

I saw a soldier stretched out on the ground with his rifle, his face dead-white with fear. He didn't dare shoot and asked us not to move, because if they saw the slightest movement, they'd shoot in our direction and he'd be hit too.

Esther Fernández, student
at the Faculty of Sciences, UNAM

Their fingers were on the triggers of their rifles. There were a number of direct hits. They shot immediately at anybody who moved.

Santiago Ruiz Saíz, student at the Faculty of
Sciences, UNAM

Medical Corps! Officer! We've got somebody who's been wounded over here!

Voice in the crowd

Grab that man! Make him let go of that damned thing!

A man's voice

A child no more than five or six years old who was running about crying fell to the ground. Several other children who had been with him fled in terror, but one six-year-old came back and started shaking him: "Juanito, Juanito, come on get up!" He began to pull at him as though that would revive him. "Juanito, what's wrong with you?" he asked him. He obviously had no idea what death was, and was never to find out that his little friend was dead, because his questions suddenly were heard no more, just a moan. The two tiny bodies were left lying on the pavement there, one on top of the other. I saw the whole thing. I wanted to get the littlest one into the ditch where I was hiding. I called to him several times, but bullets were whizzing all over the place and I didn't dare go out there and get him. I just shouted several times, "Come on down here, little boy!" but he was too busy trying to revive his friend to notice. Then the bullet hit him! I know I'm a coward, and I also know now that the instinct to save your own neck is terribly selfish.

Jesús Tovar García, political science student,
UNAM

Gently! Gently! This one's got a chest wound!

A stretcher-bearer

If you make one move, I promise I'll let you have it. . . .

A soldier

And the smell of blood moistened the air,
And the smell of blood stained the air.

José Emilio Pacheco, reciting Nahuátl texts
translated by Father A. M. Garibay

I told you not to go over there! Crawl in under the bus!

A soldier, to Alberto Solís Enríquez,
student at Vocational 1

One of the soldiers stumbled and fell to the ground right there beside us. We lay there on the ground, because one of the Movement people had shouted, "Get down, everybody, lie down on the ground!" We were on the esplanade in front of the Chihuahua building. The soldiers were running back and forth as though the whole thing were a training maneuver.

Then one of them came over to the soldier who'd fallen down and said to him, "Don't shoot at them, man, shoot in the air! They're not criminals—they're just kids. Don't shoot at them, shoot in the air, shoot over their heads, man!"

We were reassured because of the way those two soldiers had acted, so we got to our feet, ran right in front of them, and went into the 2 de Abril building. We stayed there for the next two and a half hours, which seemed like sixty to me. . . .

María Ángeles Ramírez, student at the School of
Anthropology, a division of the SEP *

We all started running and leaped down off a wall about six feet high. All the little kids and the women who had jumped off it had fallen down, and we tried our best not to land on top of them, because there was nobody to help them to their feet or give them a

---

* Secretaría de Educación Pública (Department of Public Education).

hand. It was every man for himself. There were lots and lots of shoes lying around, a whole bunch of women's shoes. . . . I remember one shoe especially, one with a little strap. I kept on running till I came face to face with three or four soldiers. They pushed me and shoved me and my brother and ten or fifteen other people over toward the ground floor of one of the buildings; I don't know the name of it, it's the one opposite the Chihuahua unit. We could see more troops pouring into the Plaza from all directions. We tried to go up to the second floor of this building, one of the biggest ones in the housing unit, but the soldiers gave us strict orders: "You're not to budge an inch. . . ." They were quite polite to us, and I'm quite sure they were trying to protect us, because there was already heavy gunfire at that point, and we could also hear the chatter of machine guns. We asked them if we could leave, and they told us not to, to stay where we were. We thought that if we could disappear from sight, they wouldn't come looking for any of us, and little by little we all sneaked up the stairs to the second floor of the building. The soldiers downstairs had their hands full at that point, and didn't even notice. We knocked at the door of one apartment after the other, but nobody answered at any of them. We sat down on the floor in the hall upstairs there and waited. Around seven o'clock, or seven-fifteen, we heard the sound of hobnailed boots and the thud of the heavy Army shoes of the soldiers downstairs, and two kids went down to ask them if we could leave, and they told them it was okay. The kids yelled to us to come down, and we all left the building. But instead of letting us go home, the Army troops searched us, asked us to show our identification papers, and made us line up down there. The first one they ordered to step forward was my brother.

"All right, you, come over here."

And then they began to beat him.

Carlos Galván, student at the School of Library
Sciences, UNAM

. . . But trivial little remembered details linger in one's mind. Women with their bellies raked with machine-gun bullets; children with their heads smashed in from the impact of large-caliber bullets; innocent bystanders riddled with bullets; street vendors and reporters wounded or killed while going about their everyday jobs;

students, police, and Army troops dead and wounded. . . . Perhaps the most tragic sight of all was the blood-stained shoes scattered all over the Plaza, like mute witnesses of the sudden flight of their owners.

José Luis Mejías, in an article entitled "A Meeting That Ended in Tragedy," Diario de la Tarde, *October 3, 1968*

We knocked on all the doors of the 2 de Abril building, but nobody would let us in. A woman who lived there in the Tlatelolco housing unit and had gone out to buy bread with her little girl became hysterical and started screaming. We tried to help her and pushed a little slip of paper under the door of one apartment that said, "Please let a lady and her little girl take shelter in your apartment." The people inside answered by pushing another piece of paper under the door: "We can't—we're afraid to." That's exactly what their note said. I lost that piece of paper; it never occurred to me that I ought to keep it. I think the only reason people answered at all was to stop us from knocking on the doors like that, because Lina and I were pounding on them like crazy. I don't know where we found the strength to hammer on them like that—I guess it was because we were so scared.

María Ángeles Ramírez, student at the School of Anthropology, SEP

We went up to the third floor and knocked on the door of several apartments, but no one answered. Then we went on up to the next floor, and the next, and the next. We went from one floor to another, in desperation, but nobody would open their door and let us in. We heard the thud of the boot heels of the soldiers coming up after us. I stood outside the door of one apartment then and shouted, "Please let my wife and children in, at least!"

Ramón Oviedo, geologist, IMP *

In the apartment where we were hiding, there were kids chewing up their identification papers and swallowing them.

Gerardo Martínez, student at the School of Economics, UNAM

---

* Instituto Mexicano de Petróleo (Mexican Petroleum Institute).

The soldiers helped me get out with my daughter, who was pregnant, and my four-year-old grandchild.

Matilde Galicia, age seventy

Then he gave me a kiss to give me courage and said to me in a quiet
but very firm voice, "Clear out of here!" He took me by the hand
when he saw that I was paralyzed with fear. "Come on, get a move
on, there's nothing wrong with you!" I couldn't move. "Okay,
crawl then . . . you can't stay here," he said. They were shooting at
us from every direction. He threw himself on the ground beside me
then and started dragging me along, as though I were a big heavy
bundle. . . .

Magdalena Salazar, psychology student, UNAM

I have six children. Pepe, Sergio, a biology student we call "Pichi,"
Miguel Eduardo, whom everybody calls "Buho"—Owl-Eyes—
Chelo, my only daughter, and a pair of twins, Rubén and Rogelio,
who never took any sort of active part in the Movement. Eduardo,
on the other hand, is a member of the CNH. At three o'clock that
afternoon, Chelo and Sergio were getting ready to go to the demonstration. My husband, Cosme Valle Miller, was going to go with
them, but I stayed behind to do some housework. At eight o'clock
my daughter came home again. Her clothes were all torn and her
knees were bloody.

When I opened the door and saw her standing there looking like
that, the first thing I asked her was, "Chelo, what in the world's
happened?"

"They attacked us, Mama, they attacked us," she replied.

She could hardly talk. I'd never heard her voice quaver like that.

"Has anything happened to your brothers?"

We hadn't seen Eduardo for almost three weeks because, like
other members of the CNH, he'd gone into hiding. Chelo burst into
tears and said that Army troops had occupied the Plaza de las Tres
Culturas, that a helicopter had fired on the demonstrators, and that
agents wearing a white glove on one hand had started shooting at
anybody who made the slightest move, no matter who they were.
She'd seen one security agent shoot at three little kids, from four to
six years old, who'd been left behind when their mother ran off,

carrying an even smaller child in her arms. Chelo had been with my husband. He'd said to her, "Lie down, Chelo; if you don't, you're going to get killed." She had lain down and started dragging herself along, and one whole side of her face got scraped raw. "The bullets were raining down like hailstones, Mama," she said to me. She managed to get to a wall with barbed wire on top of it, behind the Chihuahua building. That was the last she'd seen of her dad, who had been trying to help people find some way out of the Plaza. He motioned to her to make a run for it, and that was the last she'd seen of him. She finally got out to the street, and met a soldier there who said to her, "Don't try to go back in there—you'll get killed."

Chelo wanted to go back and look for her father and Sergio and Miguel, but as she was walking down the street she met some men who were driving away with a whole carful of students. The driver handed her ten pesos and told her, "Pay somebody to give you a ride out of here."

She says she saw lots of private cars loaded with students. They were stopping along the street to pick them up, and then taking off with the driver's foot to the floor so the soldiers wouldn't catch them.

Then Chelo went to the factory where Rubén and Rogelio work, and she told Rogelio, "They got us this time, kid."

Rogelio brought her back home, and we sat there waiting for the other kids to turn up. But the only one who showed up was my husband: "They've arrested everybody in the CNH! I saw Eduardo up on the balcony on the fourth floor. . . ."

"What about Sergio?"

"He went back to look for Eduardo. . . ."

I sat there at the window all night waiting—we live in the Loma Hermosa housing development—because I thought they might try to sneak back home if they could dodge the police. I thought to myself, I have to stay awake so I can open the door for them the minute they show up. But there was no sign of them. I waited there at the window all night long, watching for the slightest movement, listening for the least little sound. But I didn't see or hear one thing. How many times I opened the door leading to the corridor outside, thinking I'd heard them coming home!

Celia Espinoza de Valle, grade-school teacher and
mother of a family

We hid the student on the floor of the car under a blanket. I even climbed into the back seat and sat there with my feet on top of the blanket so nobody would notice him. Before that, I'd tried to bathe his wound, but the water had stopped running everywhere in the housing unit. There was no water and no electricity anywhere! My daughter was in the front seat, my husband was driving, and what worried me most during the whole trip getting that boy out of Tlatelolco was that he seemed to have stopped breathing—I couldn't hear him breathing at all. We finally got to his house and dropped him off. . . . Afterward, my husband drove another boy out; he hid this second one in the trunk of the car, but this time my husband didn't take my daughter and me along so the soldiers wouldn't suspect anything. Each time we had gone in or out, the soldiers had stopped the car and asked us to show our identification papers to prove that we lived in Tlatelolco. . . .

Isabel Montaño de la Vega, tenant
in the Tlatelolco housing unit

Who got out safely? Did everybody make it out all right? Is everybody here? Did Marta get out? Has anybody seen Juan? Which of you saw Juan last?

Rosalía Egante Vallejo, biology student, UNAM

Concha's mom says that Concha went to the demonstration with her things for school, her textbooks and her notebooks, under her arm, and that she was wearing a blue sweater. . . .

Ernestina de la Garza, medical student, UNAM

The doors of the elevators had big bullet holes in them. Only high-powered firearms could have penetrated them like that. The bullets had gone right through them, just as they went straight through the bodies of so many defenseless people.

Roberto Sánchez Puig, student at Vocational 1

I looked at the pools on the Plaza, lost in thought as I stared at them: reflecting pools is exactly the right name for them. I thought to myself, Just yesterday morning, children were playing there, splashing around in them! . . . Just yesterday I saw a man selling balloons in the park next to San Marcos! I had gone up to the fourth floor of the Chihuahua building just the day before to see whether the public-address system was going to work all right, because I was scheduled to speak as the representative of the National Union of Mexican Women. Just yesterday there were men sitting there on the benches in the Plaza reading their newspapers! . . . How stupid, how really stupid I am! When I saw the three flares go off behind the church, I thought to myself, That's really neat! These kids are really something. They think up some new gimmick every time they have a demonstration! And this time they've arranged a fireworks display! I thought they'd turned the whole meeting into a fiesta, a real celebration—everybody always associates a fireworks display with some kind of gala occasion. And despite the tension and the presence of Army troops, the students' meetings had always seemed like a fiesta: joyous greetings being exchanged, big hugs and kisses, handshakes, how's it going pal, great to see you, hey don't let your girl friend hook you into marrying her, hi there, fancy meeting you here, what's with you these days, man, live it up a little, have you seen Luis? His old lady's really worried about him. . . . I saw the flares from the stairway, going off just over the church, about fifteen or twenty feet above the cross.

María Alicia Martínez Medrano, nursery-school director

It was just another meeting—one like all the others we'd held before. Reports, briefings, plans for the future and guidelines laid down by the Strike Committee—and laughter, joking, slogans shouted in chorus, hand-clapping, and shouts from the crowd. The announcements from the speakers' platform were warmly received and there was lots of applause from the crowd. Up on the speakers' platform, representatives of a whole bunch of organizations were crowding around the microphone, eagerly awaiting their turn to address the crowd, to talk about their particular problems and demonstrate their support of the Movement. Representatives of the doctors out on strike at eight different hospitals had shown up that day to support our six-point student petition, and representatives from a number of small labor unions had shown up too: groups of parents, of grade-school teachers, of women's organizations, of railway workers, of peasants had also sent representatives. . . . There wasn't time for all of them to speak, but messages and letters and telegrams and greetings were read to the crowd, and the organizations that had come out in support of the Movement were announced.

Raúl Álvarez Garín, of the CNH

The blood that had spattered my blouse was red, bright red, and when I looked again it had turned coffee-colored. . . . I thought to myself, All this can't be true: I must be dreaming!

Cristina Fernández Ríos, social worker

"Can't you hear me?"

I kept shaking him, but he didn't answer one word. So I left him, and started running.

Antonio Llergo Madrazo, nine-year-old boy from the Tlatelolco housing unit

Just as we reached the foot of the stairway a very young girl wearing a big dark raincoat ran past, trembling with fear. She wasn't shouting or saying anything, just making very peculiar sounds, grunts, sort of. She kept running, so they shot at her feet too, but instead of heading in the other direction, she ran straight back toward where the bullets were coming from, over our way, and the only thing we could think to do was to grab her by the arm and get her in behind us and stay there at the bottom of the stairway where we were standing yelling for them to let us in. She began murmuring, "I'm going over to the Guerrero building . . . I have to get to the Guerrero building . . . I've got to get over there. . . ."

"You mustn't go anywhere," I said to her. "Just stay right here."

She ran in behind us then. I could see she was trembling and shaking from head to foot, not because she was cold but because she was scared to death, and she kept making those strange moaning sounds. We kept shouting to the men blocking the stairway, "Let us by! Our children are up there on the fifth floor! I live up there. Let us go upstairs! Our children may be hurt! They're all alone up there! Let us go upstairs, sir! They must be scared to death! Please let us go to our children! You can go up to the fifth floor and see for yourselves—if you don't find our children up there you can come down and shoot us on the spot!"

Then the security agent with the white glove who was in command of that particular unit decided that in order to shut us up, they'd either have to shoot us then and there or let us go upstairs. So he told his men, "Okay, let all these two-bit whores go on upstairs if they want to!"

Two agents went up with us. It was plain to see that they were more scared than we were; they were so terrified when I opened the door of my apartment, shaking from head to foot, that one of the men with a white glove escorting us closed the door in my face and said, "Take a look if you want to, but if you see that your kids in there are dead, don't start screaming." His tone of voice wasn't at all sympathetic or friendly: it was a threat, because he had his pistol aimed at my back as he said it.

We were horrified when we went inside: there wasn't a soul in there, the entire apartment was full of smoke and bits of fallen plaster, the floor was covered with rubble, the walls all had big holes in them, there were things strewn all over the floor, and there wasn't one single piece of furniture in its usual place. Despite having been warned not to scream, Margarita and I both started yelling at the top of our lungs, and just then my mother's helper stuck her head out of the bathroom door and said to me, "The children are in here with me, *señora*."

The police who'd gone upstairs with us were so terrified at that point that they shouted to us, "Get down on your hands and knees, all of you!"

They locked us up in the bathroom, searched the whole apartment, and took my maid off with them. We sat there on the floor in the bathroom, hugging the children in our arms, with the young girl we'd found downstairs, the one in the big heavy raincoat which probably didn't belong to her, sitting there on the floor beside us. When she took the raincoat off, a bunch of leaflets fell out of the pockets, and the poor child was so distraught that she dropped a CNH collection box on the floor and the coins in it rolled all over the bathroom, just as the police were searching the apartment. You can imagine how scared all of us, including the kids, were when that happened. If they'd heard all those coins falling on the floor, they would have taken it as certain proof that all of us were active in the Movement.

Margarita and I were so incensed we couldn't help blurting out,

"You little fool, you! How could you have been so stupid as to hold on to that collection box? Why didn't you get rid of it downstairs?"

And the girl, still half dazed, answered, with simply unbelievable naïveté, "You mean I should have thrown it away? Oh, I couldn't have done that—it's money that belongs to the CNH! It's their money—I couldn't possibly have thrown it away!"

We took the CNH label off the Mobil Oil can she'd been collecting the money in, opened it, and took the money out of it.

"Oh, no, don't do that! . . . that money belongs to the Movement. . . . It's money for the CNH—how can you possibly take it?" she moaned.

"Listen, it doesn't matter who the money belongs to. I promise I'll keep it for you and give it back to the Movement later. . . ."

And despite her protests, we emptied the can. Most of the coins in it were twenty-céntimo pieces; * as I remember, there were four-teen pesos altogether. Amid this terrible massacre, the bullets flying in all directions, the building on fire, the leaking gas mains, the broken water mains, the ambulance sirens that set our teeth on edge, the only thing that had mattered to this young girl was hang-ing onto her CNH collection box. We also set a match to her Move-ment handbills, because she simply didn't realize what terrible trouble she'd be in if she were found with leaflets like that in her possession.

We heard someone inserting a key in the lock on the bathroom door and turning it.

"They've gone, *señora!*" a voice said.

It was my mother's helper.

Mercedes Olivera de Vázquez, anthropologist

We ran behind one of the buildings and somebody opened a little chute of some sort leading down into a tiny tin shed in the base-ment. When we slid down that chute into that little room, we dis-covered that there were already other people down there, and soon many more people slid down the chute. . . . There were air holes between the floor and the roof, and an opening with a little grate over it. There was a stairway alongside the chute we'd slid down,

* A coin worth about one and one half cents. (Translator's note.)

and I stood right there beside it. I remember that a machine gun kept firing one round after another. None of us said one word. We were so weak in the knees we couldn't even talk. I thought about the kids on the fourth floor, and I was sure they'd all been killed. I remembered faces smiling at me, warm greetings we'd exchanged, people who had chatted with me. The shooting stopped for a few moments, and we heard people running, the footfalls of two or three youngsters doubtless trying to take cover in the stairwell there next to the chute.

I heard a voice call to them, "Come on, I'll get you out of here."

We could hear all sorts of noises from there inside the room. It was pitch black in there. I was sure that the man calling to those kids was going to double-cross them, was going to kill them. And in fact the tone of voice of whoever was calling to them suddenly changed completely: "Come on, you fool, here's your chance."

"No, I'm not coming out," a youngster's voice answered. "If I do, you'll arrest me."

The man who'd shouted to the boy apparently went away then, because I heard footsteps running again, but I never did find out what happened to those kids. It's very strange, you know. Down there in that room, I could suddenly tell the difference between the sound of youngsters' footsteps, women's footsteps, and children's footsteps. You notice that they all sound different, and when you hear people's footsteps later on, you remember and say to yourself, That's the footsteps of a woman, a man, a child. It's funny: a man walks faster than a woman, but a woman's heels make more noise, and children sound almost as if they're flying when they run!

The shooting stopped for a while then, and we heard the footsteps of a woman running in our direction. Someone began pounding on the door of one of the apartments and calling out someone's name, and a little girl answered in a terror-stricken voice, "No, I can't let you in, my mama's not here. . . ."

"It's Mama, darling. Open the door."

"No, you're not my mama. My mama's not here, and I can't open the door. . . ."

Someone there in that pitch-black room said, as though trying to send out thought waves to the little girl, "Let her in, little girl!" And the woman answered, "If you don't let me in, I'm really going to spank your bottom. . . . Open the door, you little dummy. . . .''

At that moment the shooting started again and something exploded just above that room there in the basement. One of the kids reached up and touched the ceiling and said, "It's red-hot. We've got to get out of here or we'll all be roasted like chickens on a spit." And then a big argument started as to whether we should all clear out of there or not. I have a very fond memory of one woman there in that room who had her three boys and her two girls with her. The others told the woman that she and her two girls should leave. She refused to go, and told them she'd never leave her three boys behind. A little baby about a year old burst out crying then. It made us feel very bad hearing him crying like that. We all would have done anything to get him out of there, out of danger. Everybody down there started dreaming up all sorts of harebrained schemes for getting that baby out—like going out and handing him over to a soldier or sending one of the women out with him, because the only person with that baby was his father, who kept sobbing, "Please, please, take him some place where he'll be safe, you people. I don't care what happens to me."

Finally the man who had the most common sense of any of us said that it was absolutely foolhardy for any of us to try to get out of there at that point, since we were sure to get hit, what with all that gunfire from all directions. When I heard that baby crying, I suddenly felt really scared. You feel that every nerve in your body is hypersensitive all of a sudden, that your skin is stretched as taut as a drum, that it's like very thin parchment, and for some reason your mouth and your tongue are suddenly bone-dry, and your every muscle tenses one minute and the next minute you're as limp as a dishrag. You realize then what nothingness, what absolute emptiness is, what it's like to have your life come to a sudden end . . . that's what sheer terror does to you, it seems to me. Suddenly you're deathly cold, you feel a chill breeze blowing through a stuffy room in a basement, and you think of your friends in the Plaza, of the meeting, and you're tempted to make your peace with the good Lord and pray that they're still alive, to beg Him please not to let anything happen to them; it's like in the movies, like a film in slow motion; though you try your best not to think, not to go to pieces, you keep seeing their faces, their hair, the things you've been through together, their jokes, their . . . I just can't put it into words. . . .

María Alicia Martínez Medrano,
nursery-school director

I have a friend who's a reporter for the *Nouvel Observateur,* Jean Francis Held. He was right there on the fourth floor, on the speakers' stand on the balcony, and he saw young people, very young kids, wearing white gloves and firing right at the crowd and shooting at people inside the Chihuahua building, and he thought to himself, Those students are absolutely out of their minds! Held had been in Vietnam and Israel, but he was dumfounded nonetheless: I've never seen anybody fire on a crowd like that! he thought to himself. The young people whom he took to be students made him take cover in an apartment swarming with cops. Youngsters wearing a white glove kept pouring into the apartment, and he heard one of them say, "We got orders twenty-four hours ago to come here, wearing something white on one hand, armed with pistols, with no sort of badge or identification."

As I stood there at one corner of the church of Santiago Tlatelolco, I saw that tanks had drawn up and surrounded the Plaza de las Tres Culturas, blocking off all the entrances. At just about that same time, the drizzle that had already begun to fall suddenly turned into a downpour. It was about seven o'clock by then, and it was raining cats and dogs. When it started to pour like that, I thought to myself, We won't hear the shooting now. But we could nonetheless still hear the gunfire above the heavy downpour. . . . I had been standing there in the rain getting soaked for three-quarters of an hour, and absolutely ridiculous little things kept popping into my mind. I remember thinking to myself, My hair is going to be a mess, getting it soaking wet like this—I won't be able to get a comb through it tomorrow! I also noticed that I'd lost the buckle off my shoe, and I thought, I wonder what happened to it? When did I lose it? I even began looking all around trying to find it. So as I said, all sorts of crazy little things kept running through my mind, yet at the same time I was aware of everything that was going on around me. I also remember that planes kept passing by overhead, big commercial airlines like Pan-American, the sort that make the run to New York, you know—and I thought to myself, Good Lord, the people up there in those planes don't have the slightest idea what's happening down here! Nobody in this world could persuade them that there's a massacre going on down here. And at the same time I thought, Oh, how happy I'd be to have a seat on one of those planes! All these thoughts kept running through my mind—which just goes to show you how strong the survival instinct is. . . .

> Claude Kiejman, correspondent for Le Monde,
> Paris; author of the book Mexico, le pain
> et les jeux [Mexico, Bread and Circuses].

Who's going to pay for all this blood? Who's going to avenge our dead?

> Mercedes Olivera de Vázquez, anthropologist

Most of the shots were coming from the September 16 building. The students later held a meeting at the corner of San Juan de Letrán and the Calle de Sol, begging the crowd to support them.

> Raúl Torres Duque, Mario Munguía, Ángel
> Madrid, Luis Mayen, José R. Molina, Silviano
> Martínez C., and Mario Cedeño R., in a piece
> entitled "Bloody Gun Battle in the Plaza de las
> Tres Culturas. . . . ," Ovaciones, October 3, 1968

Before that, around eight-forty-five p.m., Army troops had arrested about four hundred youngsters behind the Foreign Relations building and made them squat down on the ground. Another hundred had been loaded into Army transport vehicles.

Several hundred others were being held behind the Santiago church. In front of the right wing of the Foreign Relations building, a large square fenced-in area, the site of the Aztec ruins, was full of people who had been arrested, among them a reporter from a foreign news service.

At eight-twenty p.m., the panic-striken employees inside the Foreign Relations building were all evacuated. The soldiers covered the workers with their rifles as they came out of the building, as though they were troops on combat maneuvers.

The fire from the machine gun posted in the Social Security building and that from the sharpshooters on the roofs of the other nearby buildings was answered by the Army troops with FA machine guns, M-1 and M-2 .30-caliber rifles.

Raúl Torres Duque et al., in "Bloody Gun
Battle in the Plaza de las Tres Culturas"

I could no longer hear the chattering of the machine guns. . . . I could no longer hear the shouts and screams: all I could hear was the sound of chains rattling in my head. . . . Perhaps the machine-gunner had been blasted to bloody hell! Maybe all of us were going to be blasted to hell! Perhaps the whole world was going to be blasted to hell! I didn't care in the least, because once I saw all that happen, I couldn't believe in anything any more . . .

Gerardo García Galindo, engineering
student at ESIME, IPN

Several submachine guns were aimed straight at us. Before I came out with my hands behind my neck, I said good-by to one of my comrades from the CNH and wished him luck. We started filing out one by one. Two men armed with submachine guns stood there guarding the door, and two others went inside the apartment. They herded us all together on the landing, one on top of the other. They warned us we were not to talk or put our hands down for any reason whatsoever. As we came out of the building, the armed men frisked us and searched us and then shoved us over to the wall.

My clothes were soaked through and I was scared to death. I was shaking from head to foot and so ashamed of trembling like that that I tried my best to stop, but couldn't. A comrade behind me nudged me in the shoulder with his elbow and said, "Don't shake like that, pal—don't let those sons-of-bitches get you down." I immediately got hold of myself then and stopped trembling.

They escorted us to an apartment on the fourth floor, one by one, with our hands behind our necks.

"Olimpia Battalion here, coming down with a prisoner."

Eduardo Valle Espinoza (Owl-Eyes), of the CNH

They arrested me up on the fourth floor, where the speakers' stand had been set up on a balcony. When the shooting started, just as it was getting dark, they took us down to the ground floor, one by one. There was no electricity anywhere in the building, and the whole housing unit was flooded. I had no idea why there was water all over the place, but from what other comrades told me later, the main water boilers had been riddled with bullets and they had leaked all over. As you know, the walls of the apartments in the Chihuahua building are made of masonite. The first order they gave us when they entered the apartment was, "Take off your shoes, you sons of bitches!" and then they made us throw them into a room that I think must have been the kitchen of the apartment. I have no idea why they made us do that. The whole kitchen, or whatever it was, was full of men's and women's shoes. They arrested other comrades in an apartment on one of the floors above where they had sought shelter, and they were not taken down to the floor where we'd been, the fourth floor, till much later, after they'd taken the rest of us away. They all said the same thing had happened to them: they had found themselves in a pitch-black apartment, with the furniture all shoved in one corner, and a kitchen full of shoes.

When they took us out of the apartment there on the fourth floor, they escorted us down to the ground floor. By the time they took me downstairs, there were already a whole lot of kids there, all practically standing one on top of the other, with no shoes on and their pants down around their ankles, and most of them stripped of their shirts by that time, standing there in nothing but their undershorts. Their stripping us like that to prevent us from making a run for it was ridiculous. They no doubt did it just to humiliate us. When they read me the twenty charges against me, I remarked to the court secretary that there was one charge missing on the list of supposed crimes I'd committed: disorderly conduct, since I'd been forced to run around in public bare-ass naked. He didn't think my little joke was the least bit funny.

Luis González de Alba, of the CNH

As the gun battle was raging, all the members of the National Strike Committee were arrested, and were among the several hundred prisoners taken to Military Camp 1.

A number of the members of the CNH were stark naked.

"Terrible Gun Battle in Tlatelolco. The Number of Dead Not Yet Determined and Dozens Wounded"

The moment the flares appeared in the sky, a whole bunch of agents immediately piled out of an apartment on the fourth floor, as though the flares had been a signal, rushed out onto the balcony where the speakers' stand had been set up, tackled everybody out there, and threw them to the floor. Then they dragged them to one of the other apartments. If you weren't a cop, you had no way of defending yourself.

Arturo Fernández Gonzáles, student at ESIQIE, IPN

A couple of kids had .22-caliber pistols, but what good is a dinky little .22-caliber pistol against the M-1 rifles the Army troops are equipped with? . . . If I'd had a pistol, I'd have started shooting with it, I felt so enraged and so helpless seeing that slaughter. . . . Let's say that in a housing unit where thousands of people live, like the one in Tlatelolco, there happen to be forty guns or so, belonging to people who like to go hunting or trap-shooting or sport shooting, and so on: that's really a pretty small arsenal. And even if there were twenty .22-caliber rifles in the whole unit, what does that amount to, compared to all the weapons the Army and the police had?

Dionisio Santana, tenant in
the Tlatelolco housing unit

If any student had a pistol with him, he'd be a damned fool to hang on to it. The sooner he gets rid of it, the better.

Hesiquio de la Peña, student at ESIME, IPN

There were soldiers standing at the main entrance to the Chihuahua building, guarding barefoot citizens, identified by the Army as speakers at the meeting that ended in violence this afternoon, and making them lean their hands against the walls.

Two small children, who could not have been more than six years old, were standing sobbing on the stairway inside the Chihuahua building, alongside their mother's dead body. There were reports of a four-year-old girl with a bullet through her chest. Reporters from a number of news services counted twenty dead bodies of civilians.

At nine-fifty p.m. the Army was still besieging Tlatelolco.

Salvador Pérez Castillo, student at ESIME, IPN

We saw machine guns, .45's, .38-caliber pistols, and a number of 9-mm. weapons.

> *Miguel Ángel Martínez Agis, in a news*
> *story entitled "Chihuahua Building, 6 p.m.,"*
> Excélsior, *October 3, 1968*

Many soldiers must have shot each other, because as they closed in on the Plaza, bullets were flying from all directions.

> *Félix Fuentes, in "It All Began at 6:30 p.m."*

At certain times the confusion was so great that the police and the Army troops appeared to be shooting at each other. . . .

> *Philippe Nourry, in a news story entitled*
> *"Bloody Gun Battle Begins amid Mysterious*
> *Circumstances and Continues All Night*
> *Long,"* Le Figaro, *Paris, October 4, 1968*

None of us used any sort of firearms whatsoever, despite all the charges to the contrary that have been leveled against us.

> *From a manifesto signed by fifty-seven*
> *students imprisoned in Lecumberri, published in*
> El Día, *October 17, 1968*

Sócrates A. Campos Lemus told the newspaper reporters on October 6 that at a meeting of the CNH in the Faculty of Sciences at UNAM it had been decided that "security squads" would be organized: five security units, under the command of the following persons: Guillermo González Guardado, Jesús González Guardado, Sóstenes Tordecillas, Raúl Álvarez, and Florencio López Osuna. He said that these squads were really shock groups, that each of these units or shock groups was made up of six armed members of the Movement and headed by a leader or a commander responsible for it. That he knew the names of only a few of the members in these squads, among them José Nazar, Canseco, Cantú, Palomino, and a couple of others. That the reason such squads were organized was to protect those attending the meeting in Tlatelolco, and that these groups had been given orders that the moment the *granaderos* or Army troop arrived on the scene to break up the meeting, they were

to open fire on them, and that the prime target was to be units suspected of having among their numbers Army officers and riot-
squad officers. That to that end the aforementioned security squads
were provided with firearms, which as he recalled had been secured
through certain persons at the Chihuahua School of Agriculture:
twenty .38-caliber pistols; two M-1 rifles; two .22-caliber submachine guns; one 30.06-caliber rifle; and two .45-caliber pistols.

Anybody with an ounce of common sense realizes that it would
be ridiculous to try to fight the Army or the police with such an absurd arsenal.

Félix Hernández Gamundi, of the CNH

Gilberto put it in exactly the right words there in the camp: the only
arms we've ever had are our ideals. They were the only weapons we
had on the second of October. Only fervent desires and ideas,
which as the government sees it are much more dangerous than
bullets. A bullet kills a person. A revolutionary idea arouses the
conscience of hundreds or thousands of people.

Raúl Álvarez Garín, of the CNH

The Army found fifty-seven firearms, over two thousand cartridges,
and other war matériel in the buildings of the Tlatelolco Housing
Unit.

This matériel was found abandoned in various apartments, on
the rooftops, and in various other sites by those persons who last
Wednesday committed the criminal act of firing on the crowd from
the Chihuahua building, forcing the Army and police units to
intervene.

This impressive arsenal was shown to reporters last night in Military Camp 1, in the presence of one of the professors arrested on
that bloody night, Ayax Segura Garrido, who recognized a number
of the weapons.

The following matériel has been found: three submachine guns,
fourteen rifles, five shotguns, four carbines, thirty-one pistols of
various calibers, and a total of 2200 cartridges.

A cartridge reloader, a scale for weighing gunpowder, a small
crucible for melting lead, two karate sticks, a tamper, a gauge for

shell cases, several pairs of field glasses, and a portable Motorola sending-and-receiving radio set have also been found.

> *News story entitled "Arsenal Found in Buildings*
> *Surrounding the Plaza de las Tres Culturas,"*
> El Nacional, *October 7, 1968*

Ayax explained to us that they had shown him a photograph of his wife and kids and used it to force him to make the statement the Army wanted to get out of him. I think he was telling the truth.

> *Luis González de Alba, of the CNH*

The administration in power believes that when there is talk of revolution, we're talking about taking up arms: they're so convinced that that's what's happening that in order to fight back they're doing exactly what they've been accusing *us* of: engaging in all sorts of subversive activities.

> *José Revueltas, to Margarita García Flores, in*
> Siempre!, *no. 381, May 29, 1969*

SOLDIERS: CLASSROOMS ARE NOT ARMY BARRACKS

> *Banner at the meeting on October 2*

General José Hernández Toledo later stated that he ordered the Army troops not to use heavy-caliber arms so as to prevent greater bloodshed. His statement to this effect was published in *El Día* the following day, October 3. What a liar! The one thing missing there at the Plaza de las Tres Culturas was the Air Force, dropping a few bombs on the crowd—because there are big gaping holes from bazooka fire in the Chihuahua building, and lots of the kids there at the meeting can testify that they saw tanks shooting.

> *Juan Manuel Sierra Vilches, student at the Faculty*
> *of Commerce and Business Administration, UNAM*

The government's only proof of its contention that there were "sharpshooters" involved is the fact that General Hernández Toledo

was wounded during the "activities" that day. Nonetheless there
are a number of significant details that demolish this argument. In
the first place, General Toledo was wounded in the back, and if we
take into account the fact that he was passing just in front of the
Foreign Relations building, proceeding in the direction of the Plaza
de las Tres Culturas, when he was struck by the bullet, we may
conclude that the shot came from his own troops, either from one of
his own men in the rear guard, or from the helicopters that were
participating in the slaughter at that point, hovering overhead and
firing down at the crowd helplessly trapped in the Plaza. In the second place, this reconstruction of events is further substantiated by
the fact that the bullet which hit the General was of the same caliber
as an AR-18 rifle cartridge, this rifle being a brand-new weapon
which has heretofore been used almost exclusively by the United
States Marine Corps in Vietnam. Moreover, even though the precise
circumstances which led to General Toledo's receiving this bullet
wound have yet to be determined, the fact that the shots apparently
came from some nearby building, plus the fact that it has not yet
been determined what person or persons were doing the shooting,
leads one to suspect that the bullets were fired by one or several
special sharpshooters, who were undoubtedly very well trained and
able to hit their precise targets from the very first and provide perfect cover for the rear guard. All the apartments of the buildings
around the Plaza were carefully searched by the Army troops and
the police, and no weapons of the type mentioned were found anywhere. All this is further corroborated by the fact that the agents of
the Olimpia Battalion are known to have also fired on the troops
approaching the Plaza or already inside it at that particular
moment.

Gilberto Guevara Niebla, of the CNH

The Olimpia Battalion, which participated in the events at Tlate-
lolco, was made up of soldiers and young officers, members of the
Federal District Police Force, the Federal Judicial Police, the Federal
Security Agency, and the Federal Treasury Agency.

Valerio Ortiz Gómez, attorney

We arrived late and stood there down below the speakers' stand, on
the esplanade. As we were almost directly below the balcony where
it had been set up, we could see many members of the CNH up

there. One speaker said that there had been plans to march on to the Santo Tomás campus, but since there were many Army troops on the campus, the march was being canceled. "Go home now, all of you. Don't make any trouble! Just go quietly home now." It seemed to me that the meeting had broken up very quickly. Then suddenly we saw a flare in the sky and all of us turned around to watch it, and when I looked toward the speakers' stand again, I saw some men wearing a white glove on one hand standing up there next to the speakers. The leaders were shouting through the microphone, "Don't run; there's no danger," but one of the men in the white gloves started firing on the crowd or on the soldiers standing behind us. Then the crowd panicked and everybody started to run. I stood there trying to stop people: "Why are you running?" I asked them. When I finally realized what was happening, I was standing behind one of the big pillars supporting the Chihuahua building. I hadn't panicked and started to run because I wasn't afraid, I was merely angry. My daughter was the one who pushed me over behind the pillar. My daughter and I stayed there then, crouched behind the pillar, trying to keep under cover. . . .

I'd really gone to the meeting just to keep her company because my grandsons are high-school students who'd gone to several of the meetings. When we heard the first shots, I saw boys jumping off a wall and falling one on top of the other down below. They must have gotten badly trampled! The whole esplanade was being raked with machine-gun fire, and some youngsters started calling to us from some sort of store, a flower shop or a gift shop—I've wanted to go and see exactly what sort of shop it was, but it makes you feel bad to go back there. "Come on inside here, *señoras,*" they called to us. Since we didn't move—I just stood there gripping the pillar, as angry as could be—a boy came out and grabbed hold of me, put his arm around my neck, and dragged me into that shop, but there was another burst of machine-gun fire just then, and the next moment I felt just a slight prick in the leg, and it immediately began bleeding. Fortunately it was only a fragment of a dum-dum bullet, because if the entire bullet had hit my leg, it would have torn it right off. One of the youngsters took off his shirt, tore it into strips, and bandaged my leg above the knee. I felt no pain at all. I realized I was bleeding, but it was only a little trickle of blood.

My daughter was there beside me, and the youngsters said to her, "You ought to get your mother out of here—she's been wounded."

There were about a hundred people there in the shop—small children, teen-agers, middle-aged ladies—all lying there on the floor, and my daughter and I got down on the floor too. After we'd lain there for two hours like that, trying to protect ourselves—my leg seemed to have gone to sleep—some soldiers entered through the back of that shop there on the ground floor of the Chihuahua building. They pointed their rifles at us and everybody begged them not to shoot, because there were women and children in there. Then the soldiers ordered us to stand up and searched all of us. I know for a fact that no one there in that shop was carrying any sort of weapon. The soldiers didn't find a single one on anyone. They took us out of the shop then and separated the men from the women.

My daughter spoke up then and said to a corporal, "My mother's been wounded."

"I'll get her a stretcher."

"I can walk," I said.

I walked over and got into the ambulance.

When we got to the Red Cross hospital, there were no Army troops there, but ten minutes later they occupied the entire hospital, and the doctors were furious: "Those Army troops have no business being here!" The soldiers began taking statements from people and arresting them.

A doctor bandaged me all up, and then he said to me, "Take those stairs over there and get out of here. There's no reason why you should have to make a statement. If you stay here, they may arrest you. . . . Go see a doctor tomorrow and have him take care of you. You're all right for the time being. I've disinfected the wound. . . ." That doctor and lots of the others were furious at the soldiers for having invaded the Red Cross hospital. . . .

My daughter and I went straight home from the Red Cross, and I was indignant when the newspapers reported during the next few days that the students had been armed and had deliberately provoked the Army into attacking them. I'm morally certain that it's a lie that the students had weapons, because among the hundred or so persons in that shop where we were, not a one of them was carrying any sort of weapon.

Matilde Rodríguez, mother of a family

Look what's happening over there! They're shooting the whole place up!

A voice in the crowd

"Let me out! I want to go out!"
"Clear out of here! Get the hell out, I tell you!"

Voices on a tape recorded at Tlatelolco on
October 2 by Leonardo Femat

I'd seen things like that on the "Gunsmoke" series on television, but I never dreamed I'd see them happening in real life.

Matilde Rodríguez, mother of a family

There were six of them in the ambulance already. They wouldn't let me get in. A very tall doctor—what funny things stick in your mind at a time like that!—said to me, "You aren't hurt. Let some of the wounded have your place—there are lots of them who've been very badly injured!" But I had no intention of leaving my mother, so I just stood there by the Red Cross ambulance. Then another doctor appeared.

"Please let me go with my mother to wherever it is you're taking her," I pleaded. "I'll just sit in a corner in the back of the ambulance somewhere . . . please," I begged him, with tears streaming down my face. "I'll take up just as little room as I possibly can."

"Okay, get in the back there and don't move. But make it quick, climb in right now, this minute," he replied.

I curled up in one corner. There was a girl there inside the ambulance whose fingers had been shot off. She told us she'd gone to make a phone call and a soldier had shot her. Another youngster lying on one of the stretchers was moaning in the most pitiful way. He asked me for a pain-killer, but I'm not a nurse or anything, and all I could do to help was hold his hand. He'd been shot in the stomach. There was another youngster there in the ambulance, lying face down. He had a bayonet wound in his back and at that point he was more dead than alive. My mama wasn't in much pain during the ride, despite the wound in her leg. And that's how we got out of Tlatelolco.

When we arrived at the Red Cross hospital, they put my mother in the emergency ward immediately. I stayed there with her and watched everything that was going on. A soldier with a leg wound was brought in, and they refused to admit him, or maybe he asked them to take him somewhere else, because the Red Cross isn't a military hospital. I went outside for a while, but I was so worried about my mom that I went back into the emergency ward looking for her, and was very surprised to see that in all of the cubicles—nobody had bothered to draw the curtains at the door of any of them, there wasn't time, and nobody cared at that point whether anyone was looking or not—all the wounded, or at any rate the great majority of them, had been shot in the back, in the buttocks, in the backs of the legs. That's proof that they were all shot from behind, in the back. I imagine they'd all been shot down as they were trying to escape. My mom was wounded in the back of the leg too.

Ana María Gómez de Luna, mother of a family

The bodies of the victims lying in the Plaza de las Tres Culturas could not be photographed because the Army would not allow any pictures to be taken, and the soldiers threatened to take the photographers' cameras away from them if they tried to take any photos.
"Many Killed and Wounded Last Night"

The Red Cross attendants arrived and knocked on the door.

"Have you got any wounded in there? Where are the people who have been injured?" they shouted.

Meche and I opened the door, and you can't imagine how shocked we were when we saw that the attendant in the white uniform standing there was covered with blood from head to foot, even though I'm the wife of a doctor and went as far as the second year of med school myself, so I'm used to the sight of blood. We burst into tears and stood there screaming, with our four children clinging to our skirts, "We want to get out of here. Get us out, get us out, get us out, or we're going to jump off the balcony!"

The Red Cross attendant tried to calm us down but got nowhere.

"Sir, get us out of here, please, please, get us out of here!"

He realized we were absolutely desperate, and decided to help us get out: "Okay, I'll have the soldiers escort you out."

We started screaming even louder when we heard that. The kids were screaming too: "What do you mean, have the soldiers escort us out?—They're killing people!"

"No, you'll be better off if you leave with the soldiers. Come with me."

We started throwing things into a suitcase, and later we discovered that the only things we'd put in it were pajamas. We also had another problem on our hands because one of Meche's little girls, Ceci, suddenly broke out in hives all over. Every time Ceci heard more shooting, more huge red blotches appeared, like great big welts. She wasn't crying, just clinging to my dress and whining. We went downstairs then. The ground floor was crawling with Army troops.

The ambulance attendant went over to one group of them and said to one of the soldiers: "Listen, corporal, let me speak to the colonel."

The corporal went off, and at that moment there was a heavy burst of gunfire. Then the soldiers shoved us over against the wall and covered us with their rifles to keep us from leaving. In addition to the girl with the CNH collection box, there were also two very young girls there with us, who had immediately latched on to us and stuck right with us from then on.

When the shooting stopped again, a man came up, the colonel I suppose, and the ambulance attendant said to him, "Listen, sir, we have to get these two women out of here, because if we don't we'll soon have to take them out on a stretcher."

"What's the matter with you, anyway—running around answering calls from hysterical old biddies? Go pick up some of the wounded."

The colonel started swearing a blue streak, and since the ambulance attendant didn't budge, he shouted at him, "Stop picking up hysterical women and start taking away some of the wounded, the way you're supposed to! Didn't you hear what I said? . . . And you two women, go back up to your apartment this minute!" he ordered.

The four children began to cry.

"No, sir, you can kill us all right here on the spot if you want to, but we're not going back to that apartment up there. Listen, we've seen how you're killing people, how you're murdering them, look at all the blood, just look. . . ."

We began screaming again, and all four kids were howling—a terrible racket, in a word—you can imagine how hysterical we all were at that point.

Then the colonel said, "Listen, I'm doing you a favor letting you go back to your apartment. Don't you realize that if I turn you over to the *granaderos*, as it's my duty to do, they'll search you and haul you off to jail? You'd be much better off going up to your apartment."

"We're not going back up there to our apartment. You can kill us right here and now or do whatever you want with us, but we're not going back up there."

Then one of our little girls, Cecilia, saved our lives at that point, I think, because she piped up and said to me, "Margarita, where are the dead people? I don't want to see any dead people." And then she went on in a soft little voice, "I don't want to see any dead people. When we go past the dead bodies, will you please put your hand over my eyes, Margarita?"

I don't know exactly why it occurred to me to say to her, "Those weren't bullets, dear; they were fireworks. You've seen fireworks before, haven't you?"

Then the colonel said to us, "Okay, come with me, I'll see that you get out of here."

One of the soldiers grabbed the suitcase and all of us left the building: we three women, our four children, and the two young girls who'd tagged along with us. The colonel escorted us all the way across the esplanade to Nonoalco.

When we got there he said to some other soldiers standing there, "Let these women out."

We started across the street. It was blocked off by *granaderos*, and one of them shouted to us, "Where do you think you're going? Go on back across the street."

A whole bunch of riot police rushed up and surrounded us. Then Meche said to them, "What do you mean, go on back? If the police over there chase us this way, and you people order us to go back the other way, the only thing we can do is stay right here in the middle of the street."

"The soldiers let them out," somebody said to the *granadero*.

So then a couple of the *granaderos* stepped aside and let us through. We got home around eleven that night, and found that the students and professors from the Anthropology Department had already drawn up a plan that would enable them to go out searching systematically for their comrades. They immediately organized brigades, and we began to make lists of the ones who were still missing. My oldest son still hadn't come home.

Margarita Nolasco, anthropologist

The Red Cross attendants were behind the convent, deciding which of the wounded they were going to take out first, and separating them from the dead—we could see them because we were standing right there in front of the Chihuahua building—and then suddenly bullets started raining down on them too, and a nurse and one of the male ambulance attendants collapsed on the pavement right there in front of us. We saw all of this with our own eyes. It was awful, and the Red Cross people were furious.

Mercedes Olivera de Vázquez, anthropologist

Reyes Razo reported at approximately eight-fifteen p.m. that a Red Cross ambulance attendant, who has since been identified as Antonio Solórzano, had received several bullet wounds and was in serious condition when he was picked up. He died a few hours later in the Red Cross hospital.

"26 Dead and 71 Wounded; Sharpshooters Fire on
Army Troops. General Toledo Wounded"

The Red Cross also announced that after nine-forty-five p.m. it was no longer able to lend aid at the scene of the disaster, since squads of *granaderos* were preventing Red Cross ambulances from leaving the hospital. The agency was informed that these riot police had been posted around the hospital to protect it and to prevent any of the wounded from leaving it.

Doctors, administrative personnel, ambulance attendants, and others employed by this worthy institution protested what they termed an illegal invasion and interference with their activities. They stated that the Geneva accords, whereby the Red Cross had been formally recognized as a neutral institution, were thereby being violated.

Story entitled "Partial List of Dead and Wounded in the Gun Battle," Novedades, *October 3, 1968*

The Red Cross, which had suspended its emergency services at approximately nine p.m., following orders it had received from the General Staff of the National Department of Defense, resumed its services at eleven-thirty p.m., at which time a number of ambulances were dispatched to the Tlatelolco area.

The authorities explained that this suspension of services was necessary in order to avoid the presence of "intruders in the emergency ward" and in order to permit them to interrogate the wounded.

"Terrible Gun Battle in Tlatelolco," Excélsior, *October 3, 1968*

An ambulance! Please, I beg you as a fellow journalist, call an ambulance for me!

Oriana Fallaci, to Miguel Ángel Martínez Agis, as recounted in a news story entitled "Oriana Fallaci, Famous Reporter, Wounded in the Gun Battle," Excélsior, *October 3, 1968*

My boy friend and I ran up about ten flights of stairs to the roof, and I don't remember it being a hard climb at all. I heard people falling on the stairs, and when we reached the roof I saw a kid about fourteen or fifteen years old darting in and out of the utility rooms, and then I saw them run him through with a bayonet.

Enriqueta González Cevallos, normal-school teacher

At the morgue . . . the autopsies showed that most of the victims died . . . of bayonet wounds . . . others from gunshot wounds from weapons fired at close range. The doctors performing the autopsies were particularly struck by three of the corpses they examined: that of a youngster of about thirteen years of age who had died of a bayonet wound in the skull . . . that of an old woman who died from a bayonet wound in the back . . . and that of a young girl who had received a bayonet wound in her left side extending from her armpit to her hip. . . .

> *News story entitled "Heartrending Identification of the*
> *Victims,"* El Universal, *October 4, 1968*

Bayonets—the weapons of invaders—who ordered bayonets to be used against our children?

> *Banner of Vocational 7 at the August 27 demonstration*

Ambulances from the Red and Green Cross and from the Central Military Hospital began to enter Tlatelolco, approaching along several streets at once. They did not arrive until after eight-thirty.

According to reliable witnesses, the Army troops continued to attack any group of more than ten persons, charging them with fixed bayonets.

A journalist from AMEX * reports that around seven p.m. he saw a student fall to the ground upon being hit by a rifle bullet fired by one of the soldiers, whereupon the soldier finished him off by stabbing him to death with his bayonet. This particular incident occurred on the corner of Allende and Nonoalco.

> *Margarita García Flores, press secretary, UNAM*

The Army troops first appeared just as the meeting was ending, a few minutes after one of the leaders had announced to the crowd that "it has been decided that it is best to cancel the planned demonstration at the Santo Tomás campus."

> *Félix Fuentes, in news story, "It All Began at 6:30 p.m."*

There were the most shocking scenes, one for instance witnessed by this reporter on the fourth floor of one of the buildings. He heard a man shout, "My little girl is inside there in her playpen," and saw him run into one of the apartments. Then we saw him sink to the floor as a bullet hit him in the chest: a few moments later we managed to get the little girl out of the apartment unharmed and hand her over to her mother, who was so stunned by what had happened that she looked like a sleepwalker.

> *Jorge Avilés R., in news story, "Serious Fighting*
> *for Hours Between Terrorists and Soldiers"*

---

* A Mexican news agency. (Translator's note.)

"Why are you beating me, since I've already showed you my student-body card?"

"That's exactly the reason I'm beating you, you little bastard," was the answer.

I admit I was scared, because I'd never been beaten like that before in my life. I shouted to my brother, but he didn't answer and then that same soldier—a blond-haired guy with slanty eyes—asked me where our weapons were. I said I wasn't carrying any sort of weapon. He and another soldier shoved me against the wall with my hands behind my neck, in a whole line of other kids they'd nabbed and were searching.

Then the tow-headed soldier said to one of his buddies, "If any of these kids gives you any trouble, mow him down."

I decided to stick as close to the wall as I could, and not budge an inch.

Ignacio Galván, student at the San Carlos
Academy and the Ciudadela Ceramics Workshop

Joey eapon

I suddenly saw him as I had never seen him before. I saw his very pale hands, as white as wax, with blue veins, his little goatee that I had kept begging him not to shave off: "Leave it, please!"—because it made him look older than he really was, twenty-one; I saw his deep-set blue eyes (they've always had a very sad look in them), and felt his warm body next to mine. Both of us were soaking wet from the rain and from having fallen into so many puddles every time we flung ourselves down on the ground, yet his arm felt nice and warm around my shoulders. Then for the first time since we'd been going together, I told him yes, that when the Army troops let us go I'd live with him, that we were going to die some day, sooner or later, and that I wanted to live, that I was saying yes, yes, I love you, I really really love you, I'll do whatever you want, I'm in love with you too, yes, yes, I'm in love too, yes. . . .

María del Carmen Rodríguez, student of Spanish
literature, Iberoamerican University

As they began beating him, I heard my brother Ignacio call to me and I asked one of the soldiers, "Why is that soldier beating him like that? He's a student too."

And the soldier answered, "Well, what do you want me to do? Go stick up for him yourself. . . ."

When he said that, I almost laughed in his face. "What would I defend him with?"

"Hey kid, get your ass over here!" the other soldier shouted.

I went over and he grabbed me. I had a badge from the Russian Circus sewn on my sweater. He asked me what it was, and I said, "It's a badge from the Russian Circus."

He didn't say anything more about it but kept on asking me questions: "Okay, kid, tell me, what you were doing here at the meeting?"

I didn't answer, and he said, "Get down on your knees."

I got down on just one knee.

"No, get down on both knees, punk. And up with your hands."

The thought immediately crossed my mind: Is this cat trying to make me apologize, or what?

"Where would you like me to kick you? In the ribs?"

"No, man, you'd break 'em," I answered.

Then, with no further warning, he kicked me in the pit of the stomach. Then he hit me on the back with his rifle butt, and I doubled over in pain. He pulled me up by the hair. Every time we doubled over, they'd lift us up by the hair, then hit us in the belly, the chest, the back, the shoulders, with their rifle butts; they really gave it to us, and what hurt most was that the blows rained down so thick and fast. They kept shouting, "We'll see if you call us murderers again."

One of them, apparently the leader, said to some of the others standing around watching, "Come on, what are you waiting for?"

The only people they were beating up were us students, and the ones who were having the roughest time of it were the ones from UNAM and Poli. When they searched us they found leaflets in our pockets.

"How come you're carrying this stuff around with you?"

"They handed them to us just a few minutes ago."

"You're lying. You were going around distributing them. . . ."

If any of the kids begged them for mercy—"No, no, please don't beat me any more"— the soldiers just beat him all the harder.

They made us line up with our hands up, and took the ones with long hair aside. They made one kid kneel down and lopped his hair

off with a bayonet. I thought they were going to cut my brother Ignacio's hair off—he's an artist and wears it very long. Then they
told us to line up with the rest of the kids.

"Here's a little farewell present for you."

And they started hitting us as though they were breaking
piñatas.*

*Carlos Galván, student, School of
Library Sciences, UNAM*

They've nabbed everybody in the CNH!

Andrés Pérez Ramírez, student at ESIME, IPN

They laughed in a very nasty way and said, "So you're a student,
are you?"

Somebody smacked me so hard with a rifle butt that I thought I'd
go out of my mind, it hurt so, but then I pulled myself together,
because it occurred to me that if I collapsed I'd never be able to get
up again. They're going to kill me, I thought to myself, and some
sort of very strong instinct of self-preservation made me get control
of myself again. I said to myself, Why am I going to die like this?
The one thing I wanted was to see my brother and say good-by to
him. I was prepared to die, because I know that all of us are going
to die some time, but not like that, not that way. "Hey you, get
your ass over here, we're going to burn your hair off with gaso-
line," they said to me.

They loaded us in the riot squad's panel trucks, and once we
were inside, the sergeant, who was terribly pissed off at us, kept
saying to me and the other kids, "I know your kind—instead of
going out somewhere to have a cup of coffee with your folks or your
girl friends you keep running around stirring up trouble, like this
meeting today. . . . But it's your parents' fault, because instead of
bawling you out, they egg you on. 'Sure, go to the meeting; of
course, why not, go right ahead, kid.' They're the ones to blame.
But now that we've nabbed your leaders, we'll see what happens. . . ."

I couldn't see where they were taking us. That sergeant kept run-

---

* Clay figures of animals that children break open at birthday parties to get the
candy inside. (Translator's note.)

ning off at the mouth like that. What had apparently made him the maddest was, as he put it, "For two months now we've been confined to barracks because of all of you kids. We're going to get even with all of you." He got madder and madder as he sat there letting off steam, and finally he shouted, "And this is only the beginning, you fucking little punks. You're going to really get it when we get you to Camp 1."

He gave us a long lecture: he said that we were pretty thick between the ears if we thought we could overthrow the government, because they had machine guns too. "What have we done, anyway?" he asked. "How come you keep insulting us? You keep screaming 'You murderers' at us. . . . It's the government that gives us our pay: we have to defend it. They docked us a day's pay after what happened at the University." He also said that if it was really true that the government was bad, he and his buddies on the riot squad would be the first to join a movement such as ours. He told us all this as the panel truck drove on and on, and we had no idea where they were taking us. They parked it somewhere for about three minutes, and we noticed that we were in some very dark spot with nothing but trees around. I thought they were going to order us out of the truck, but they didn't; instead two other *granaderos* got in, the truck started off again, and the two of them who'd gotten in began talking together. We were piled up in there one on top of the other; we'd all been beaten up pretty badly, and they made us keep our hands behind our necks the whole way. We finally arrived at Military Camp 1, the one right next to the Cuatro Caminos bullring.

We didn't want to get out of the truck; we were all so scared we were shitting in our pants, but they shoved us out, and once we were inside the camp a lieutenant colonel said to us, "*Señores*, you may put your hands down; you're among gentlemen here. . . ."

Ignacio Galván, student, San Carlos Academy

I beg parents to restrain their children, so that those on both sides may be spared the pain of mourning dead loved ones. I believe that parents will understand this appeal that we are making.

General Marcelino García Barragán, Secretary of
National Defense, as reported by Jesús M. Lozano

*in a news story entitled "Freedom Will Continue
to Reign: the Secretary of National Defense Is
Studying the Situation,"* Excélsior, *October 3, 1968*

They rounded us all up—I think there were more than five hundred
of us there in that little recess on one side of the church of Santiago
Tlatelolco—and ordered us to put our hands behind our necks and
walk around to the front of the church. Then a colonel told all of us
women who were carrying umbrellas to throw them down and
made all the men take off their belts. We all threw these articles
down on the ground, and then they left us standing there for a long
time. After an hour or so, people began to get tired, and some of
them sat down on the ground without even asking permission. Fortunately there were two peanut vendors who had also been taken
into custody there with the rest of us, and we bought all their wares
because we were famished. It was nine p.m. by then and it had
been raining hard.

People started striking up conversations with each other, trying
to figure out why the whole thing had happened; they spoke of
repression and began discussing their problems, and when they
realized that I was a foreigner, they told me, "They're bound to let
you go, but they're going to throw *us* in prison." Then they all
began giving me their telephone numbers, with instructions that
when someone answered at the other end, all I should say was,
"Pablito's all right. . . ." "Paco's all right. . . ." "Marisa's all
right. . . ." "Juan's okay. . . ." "Rosa's okay. . . ." "Eduardo's
okay. . . ." We realized, because it was taking them such a long
time to get them all out of the Plaza, that there were a great many
dead and wounded. Later, around three o'clock in the morning, I
heard an Army doctor say that they'd found more than seventy
dead thus far, and then he added, "I'm certain we'll find many
more."

Claude Kiejman, correspondent for Le Monde, *Paris*

Don't spirit my son's dead body away, the way you have all the
rest! You can't do that to me! Even if he's been killed, even if he's
here among the dead somewhere, I want to see him!

Elvira B. de Concheiro, mother of a family

Around two a.m. this morning, the families of two persons who had been killed in the Chihuahua building refused to allow the ambulance attendants to remove the bodies.

> *Raúl Torres Duque* et al., *in news story, "Bloody Gun Battle*
> *in the Plaza de las Tres Culturas"*

Leobardo López Arreche, whom we all called "Cuec"—a comrade whose death enraged me—and I were among those being held on the east side of the church of Santiago Tlatelolco. They kept us there until five in the morning, and then they took us to Santa Marta Acatitla and put us in dormitory ward 4. . . . At six o'clock that evening, October 3, some agents went down the line to see if they could identify any of us locked up there in the ward, and by eight o'clock we'd been taken to Military Camp 1. We were held there incommunicado for thirteen days. They put me in solitary, and I was glad I never once saw a soul, because it makes me nervous to have to talk to people. It's better to be by yourself: it gives you a chance to think. But being in solitary often has a very bad effect on people. I was never in solitary long enough for it to affect me. . . . Thirty days after I arrived at Military Camp 1, I was transferred to cell block H in Lecumberri.

> *Raúl Álvarez Garín, of the CNH*

I found out that the warden of Santa Marta Acatitla Penitentiary had asked the authorities not to send him any more prisoners, that there was no room for them, that he had no place to put any more of them. . . . And then along came seven hundred students and there was simply no place to put them. Four or five days before October 2, they cleared all the prisoners out of ward 4, which proves that the attack on the Plaza of Tombs was all planned beforehand, in the most underhanded way, in cold blood. . . . Even so, they arrested so many youngsters that there was no room for them anywhere!

> *Demetrio Vallejo, prisoner in Santa Marta Acatitla*

> They took the dead away—heaven only knows where.
> They filled every jail in the city with students.
> > *José Carlos Becerra, "El Espejo de Piedra"*
> > *["The Stone Mirror"]*

I'd never seen him cry before, and I was shocked to see how much older his face suddenly looked, his eyes as red as blood, all bloodshot, with bags underneath, dark circles under them in that dawn that reeked of gunpowder. . . . I think he must have cried all night long without my noticing, or without my being really willing to accept the fact that he was actually shedding tears. . . . I had heard his stifled sobs, but I was so ashamed for him, so unwilling to admit to myself that I'd heard them, that I pretended that it was someone else sobbing like that. . . . It was five in the morning; I looked at the reflecting pools; the soldiers seemed to be trying to avoid us now; they kept going by there in front of us, pretending not to see us. It was a bright, clear morning, as mornings usually are in October. I looked at him again. Big tears were streaming down his cheeks, which I suddenly noticed had very deep wrinkles in them. "There, there, Papa, don't cry! Don't be upset," I said to him.

Elba Suárez Solana, political science student

No, no, I'm not going to grant anybody an interview, not after what happened to me: they shot me, they stole my wristwatch, they left me lying there bleeding on the floor of the Chihuahua building, they refused to allow me to make a phone call to my embassy. . . . I would like to see the Italian contestants withdraw from the Olympics: that's the very least they can do. I'm going to present my case to the Italian Parliament; I'm going to let the whole world know what's happening here in Mexico, what kind of democracy you have in this country—everyone in the entire world is going to know! What a bunch of savages! I've been in Vietnam and I can assure you that there are barricades, foxholes, trenches, holes, and things like that you can take cover in during machine-gun barrages and bombings. (And they use flares in Vietnam, too, to mark out the areas that are to be bombed.) But here there was absolutely nowhere to take cover. On the contrary, I was lying there face down on the floor and when I tried to cover my head with my handbag to protect myself from the shrapnel, a policeman pointed his pistol at me, just an inch or so from my head, and said, "Don't move." I could see the bullets imbedded in the floor of the terrace all around me. I also personally witnessed how the police were dragging students and young people around by the hair and hauling them away. I saw many wounded, and lots of blood: I was wounded myself, and lay there in a pool of my own blood for forty-five minutes. One student next to me kept saying, "Chin up, Oriana, chin up." The police paid no attention when I begged them, "Please phone my embassy, please phone my embassy." They all refused to make the call, and then finally one woman said to me, "I'll get word to them for you."

I've called my sister, who's taking a plane here today; I've called London, Paris, New York, Rome. When they took me to be X-rayed this morning, some reporters asked me what I was doing in Tlatelolco. What was I doing there! I was doing my job, for heaven's sake! I'm a professional journalist. I've been in touch with the leaders of the National Strike Committee because the Student Movement is the most interesting recent development in your country. The students talked to me at my hotel on Friday and told me that there was going to be a big meeting in the Plaza de las Tres Culturas on Friday, October 2, at five p.m. Since I'd never seen the Plaza, and knew that it was an archaeological site, I thought I'd combine the two things. That's why I was there. Ever since I arrived in Mexico, I've been impressed by the students' efforts to put a stop to police repression. I'm also amazed at the stories in your newspapers. How bad your papers all are—so afraid to speak out, so afraid to express any sort of indignation! To hell with the Olympics and all the rest of it. As soon as they let me out of this hospital, I'm leaving.

Oriana Fallaci, correspondent for L'Europeo,
patient in the Hospital Francés

Within minutes after the beginning of the gun battle, the wire services started sending teletypes out from one end of the world to the other reporting what was happening—stories that were quite exaggerated, thereby causing irreparable and incalculable damage to our country's reputation.

"26 Dead and 71 Wounded; Sharpshooters Fire on
Army Troops. General Toledo Wounded"

Another hour went by. The lights in the buildings had gone out, and there wasn't a soul to be seen at any of the windows. Oh, yes, there was one woman who for some strange reason was cleaning the windows of her apartment on the fifth floor. I found out later that many apartments were full of people who had fled from the gunfire and were lying stretched out on the floor in the dark. We saw many prisoners go by in front of us there on the esplanade—young kids, for the most part, with their hands behind their necks, being herded along by the soldiers, who were clubbing them in the back with their rifle butts. Many of these youngsters were stark naked and the police and the Army troops were forcing other youngsters to stand stark naked on the terraces on the rooftops. There were dead and wounded, many of them children, all over the Plaza de las Tres Culturas. Strangely enough, I wasn't really very scared; the one thought in my mind was that it would be absurd to die like that. That same thought was running through so many of our minds at that very same instant.

Claude Kiejman, correspondent for Le Monde, *Paris*

They lined both the boys and the girls up against the walls and made them take all their clothes off. Then they loaded all of them, stark naked, into paddy wagons and panel trucks to take them to Military Camp 1.

Rodrigo Narváez López, student at the
School of Architecture, UNAM

I would have liked to kill the guy, or at least cut off his fingers gripping the trigger of that machine gun. I'll never forget the ear-splitting chatter of that machine gun. For days afterward, as I walked down the streets, all I could hear was the tracatracatracatraca of that machine gun.

Jaime Macedo Rivera, dentistry student, UNAM

Behind the church of Santiago Tlatelolco
thirty years of peace
plus some thirty more years of peace
plus all the iron and the cement used for
the fiestas of this dreamlike country
plus all the speeches—all this
poured out of the muzzles of the machine guns

José Carlos Becerra

We sat there like that, waiting, and at ten that night they started shooting again, but we couldn't tell exactly where the shots were coming from. It seemed as though they were firing at us from behind the church and from other buildings farther away, either the November 20 or the September 16 unit, I'm not sure which, and there we all were, with no sort of cover at all. There was another moment of panic then, because the bullets were much more likely to strike us there in front of the church than they were around the corner of it, where we'd been before. The women were terror-stricken, and began screaming for them to open the door of the church so they could take shelter inside: "Open the door of the church, they're going to kill us, they're going to shoot us. . . . Open up . . . we're Mexicans too!" They never did open the door of the church. I was scared to death too, because it occurred to me that if the Army was firing on the crowd, there was no reason why they wouldn't shoot at us, too. There has been a great deal of talk about sharpshooters. Maybe there were some, but I didn't see a single person shooting from any of the windows, nor did I ever see any groups that might lead anyone to suspect that Tlatelolco was a guerrilla headquarters. But since people were firing in every direction, and bullets were whizzing every which way, there was a very good chance that we'd be wounded. I saw youngsters with a white glove on one hand who went back and forth all over the square without the police or the Army troops ever stopping them; that was why I took particular notice of them.

There were thousands of people in the square: eight or ten thousand perhaps—it's difficult to estimate how big the crowd was. But I never once saw anybody trying to get rid of a pistol he might have had on him. Perhaps there were people in the buildings who grabbed their rifles or pistols when they saw that they were being attacked, that's quite conceivable—wouldn't any of us do the same if a thief or a marauder were attacking us?—but there really weren't any armed guerrillas inside the Tlatelolco housing unit. The very manner in which the Army troops conducted the attack, closing in on the square from all sides at once, and therefore shooting at each other, is quite sufficient in and of itself to account for the large number of soldiers killed.

This second barrage went on till about eleven p.m., and we were detained there in front of the church till three in the morning. Then at three a.m. they ordered us to put our hands behind our necks again, and took all of us inside the old convent next to the church. They herded us all in there like animals, and people kept saying that everybody was going to be arrested, including all the women, but that since I was a foreigner, they'd let me go.

I told an Army doctor who came in to have a look at us, "I happened to be here by sheerest chance. I was on my way to the Railway Workers' Theater, just around the corner, to see *The Magic Lantern*. I was to meet one of my relatives there. Would you be so kind as to phone my house so they won't worry about me?"

I also told him that I was a journalist and thought the authorities might not like it very much that I'd been there and seen everything that had happened. I also asked him to phone the French Embassy for me, and he told me that it was not necessary for me to contact my embassy, and that he would get in touch with my relative—which he did, I hasten to add—and what's more, I think it was because he intervened on my behalf that I was allowed to leave Tlatelolco at seven the next morning.

As we left, we passed by the other side of the church and I realized that there were many, many people still in custody there. I thought that those in our group were the only ones who had been taken into custody, but near a pond or a reflecting pool I saw that there were many more people who had been arrested. The Army doctor was escorting me. Even at that late hour, we could still hear shots from time to time, all over the place, more or less. The Avenida Nonoalco was full of tanks, but on the other streets traffic seemed to be completely normal, and since all the lights were still off in the Plaza de las Tres Culturas and all the buildings around it, and it was pitch-black everywhere in the square, doubtless people passing by had no idea that five or ten thousand people were still trapped in there. A friend of mine went to the Secretariat of Foreign Relations searching for somebody who had gone to the meeting. He was told that there was nobody in the Plaza, that everybody had gone home, so he had no idea what terrible things were happening.

When I got in the Army car, it seemed incredible that everything was just the same as always. It was as if the entire Tlatelolco incident had never happened. The driver asked me where I wanted to go; there were people along the streets who didn't even turn around to watch as we drove by, there were cars honking, taxis cruising the streets, bicyclists pedaling along, as though nothing at all had happened.

Claude Kiejman, correspondent for Le Monde, *Paris*

The way people were going about their business as usual outside, quite normally and peacefully, was like a slap in the face to me.

Elvira B. de Concheiro, mother of a family

When we left Tlatelolco, life was going on just as usual—everything was so normal it was horrible, insulting. It simply wasn't possible that everything could just go on as peacefully as before. But people were going about their business as though nothing at all had happened, and there we were, filthy dirty and feeling like fools. We rode along in the taxi and when we got to Bellas Artes we saw that they'd set a trolley bus on fire and a crowd had gathered to watch, as always happens whenever there's a little excitement. I was suddenly overcome then with a kind of fit of hysteria, and began to scream at the top of my lungs, "They're shooting a whole bunch of people in Tlatelolco!" and who knows what else. My screaming like that scared the taxi driver, who put his foot to the floor and told us that if we were going to behave like that he was going to make us get out on the next corner.

Margarita Nolasco, anthropologist

We were riding along in the car, taking the girls we'd picked up back to where they lived, when Margarita braked to a halt at a stop sign when she saw a man selling papers standing there. She reached out of the window, grabbed the newspaper vendor by the shirt, and asked him, "Does it say anything in your paper about the massacre that's going on in Tlatelolco?"

"No, *señora*, it doesn't say anything about it, and it's not going to. You don't expect them to report a thing like that in the papers, do you?"

"Well in that case, it's your duty to spread the news to everybody that comes along. . . ." And then she stuck her head out of the car window and started shouting, "They're killing people by the hundreds . . . in cold blood!" This was on the corner of Tacuba and San Juan de Letrán, and she hadn't noticed that just behind the man selling papers there were four or five soldiers closing in on a trolley bus that was on fire on the corner. . . .

It's useless to do things like that, I agree, but there are times when you can't help doing them. We just couldn't calm Margarita down. I realized what she was going through, because I had all my children right there with me and she didn't.

Mercedes Olivera de Vázquez, anthropologist

I went back home and sat down and thought to myself, Tomorrow the people are going to rise up in arms! When they find out what's happened tomorrow, there'll be a revolution. And when I saw that everything was going on just as usual, that nothing was about to happen, it was the greatest shock I've ever had in my life.

Enrique Vargas, student at ESIQIE, IPN

What's going to happen now, pal? Where do we go from here?

Eulogio Castillo Narváez, student, Vocational 1

The only explanation for what has happened in the Plaza de las Tres Culturas is the need for the ruling class to remain in power. But even though there is a logical explanation for Tlatelolco, this does not make the situation that it has given rise to any less absurd. What is even more senseless than the slaughter is the desire that has suddenly arisen to prove that the whole thing never really happened, that nobody was really responsible for it and that nobody can possibly be held accountable for it.

Carlos Monsiváis, in an article entitled
"Conjectures and Reassessments," in
Siempre!, *no. 453, October 14, 1970*

Emery told me afterward that he had also been in the Plaza when the Army occupied it. Bullets landed inches from him, and they kept firing round after round straight at him, but he threw himself to the ground right next to the dead body of a young boy. They kept shooting at him, but all the bullets hit the other boy's dead body.

Raúl Álvarez Garín, of the CNH

I opened the front door.

"What about Carlitos?" I asked.

"He hasn't turned up yet. We've no idea what's happened to him." Then the worst night in my entire life began.

Margarita Nolasco, anthropologist

Upstairs there on the speakers' stand, the confusion soon became utter desperation. It was all quite clear then: this was a sneak attack on us. The Olimpia Battalion had their firearms trained on us. And they had begun firing at will at the crowd fleeing in panic down below. The sound of rifle and machine-gun fire, and the screams from the crowd and those of us there on the speakers' stand, were really deafening.

"Get upstairs! Run for it!" some of us shouted as we looked around for some way to get off that big wide balcony on the fourth floor of the Chihuahua building from which the speakers had been addressing the crowd.

Eventually some of us found an apartment where we could take shelter for the time being. Others who weren't as lucky were already lying dead or wounded from the deadly hail of bullets, or were about to be.

The Army troops were shooting in all directions. It was impossible even to show our heads in that apartment. The bullets were flying about everywhere, imbedding themselves in the walls after having shattered the windowpanes and torn big holes in the curtains. Bits of plaster and other objects were raining down on our heads all over the place.

That was where the agents arrested me: there in that apartment on the sixth floor of the Chihuahua building.

Pablo Gómez, economics student, UNAM, and member
of the Communist Youth

On the eleventh floor of one of the buildings in the Tlatelolco unit with an entrance on Constantino I saw the corpse of a man who'd been shot in the head. . . . I ran downstairs to report what had happened, and there in the street I met a girl who said her name was Georgina Henríquez. Tears were streaming down her cheeks. She'd gone to Tlatelolco just for the fun of it, and they'd shot her in the left leg. I think she'd somehow managed to phone her family, because they came and picked her up in a car, which then took off like greased lightning. . . . Everybody there at Tlatelolco was trying to get in touch with their families before the Army troops started arresting people. . . . I was scared then, and decided not to report that man with a bullet through his head. He was past help by that time—as dead as a doornail.

Manuel Pacheco Hinojosa, student at the Faculty
of Philosophy and Letters, UNAM

I saw a bloodstain on the wall opposite, a great big one dripping down the wall. I reached my hand out and touched it, and got my hand all sticky. And then, for some reason, I felt terribly nauseated and almost vomited.

Sofía Bermúdez Calvillo, student at the School of
Commerce and Business Administration, UNAM

Who gave orders to do this? Who could possibly have ordered such a thing? It's cold-blooded murder.

Voice on a tape recorded by Juan Ibarrola, amid
the barrage of gunfire

I can take it okay when they club me with their rifle butts, but what I can't take is when they spit in my face.

Mauricio Sabines Cándano, student, Vocational 1

Up against the wall, you mother-fuckers, we're going to give you a taste of the revolution you've been agitating for!

One of the "White Gloves," to members of the CNH

Don't turn around or I'll blow your head off! Don't turn around! Keep your face to the wall!

A "White Glove," to Luis González de Alba, of the CNH

Get down, get down, I tell you!

Voice recorded by Juan Ibarrola

There are a number of bullet holes in the walls of the Secretariat of Foreign Relations. It was not possible to evacuate everyone from the offices. Only a few employees on the night shift were able to get out of the building, with the help of the police and Army troops.

The only precautionary measure possible was to turn out all the lights in the building. The employees who were unable to leave kept away from the windows and crawled across their offices on their hands and knees to answer incoming telephone calls. The motorcycle courier of the Secretariat of Foreign Relations, Manuel Landín, received a bullet wound.

Report to the AMEX News Service by Adolfo
Alanís, clerk in the Secretariat of Foreign Relations

The body of a fifteen-year-old boy who had received a fatal head wound was removed from apartment 615 of the Chihuahua building in the Tlatelolco housing unit.

Augustina Román de Falcón, tenant in the
Tlatelolco housing unit

"Stand up, *señora*," I said.

The woman tried to get to her feet, but was unable to.

"Are you a paralytic?" I asked her.

"No, no, I don't know what's wrong with my legs. I can't move them all of a sudden."

"I'll help you up. . . ."

"No, young man, you'd better not . . . I'm so embarrassed . . . I'm a mess, my skirt is filthy . . . please don't look. . . ."

"Don't worry, *señora*, I won't look. . . . That's the least of your troubles. You can't stay here . . . please try to get up . . . I promise not to look. . . ."

The old woman tried to get up on her knees, to stretch one leg out and to get to her feet. . . . That was when I noticed that both her legs were all bloody, way up past her knees.

"*Señora*, you've got shrapnel wounds in your legs! I'm going to go get a stretcher-bearer for you! Please bring a stretcher over here: there's somebody who's been hurt over here!" I shouted.

And it was only then that that woman began to cry. She was over seventy.

Ricardo Esteves Tejada, student, UNAM

I am attached to the Fourth Infantry Battalion, a sergeant second class; my commanding officer is Colonel Ramón Arrieta Bizcarra. At approximately seven p.m. I received orders to get into a military transport, which brought me to the Tlatelolco housing unit. When the transport arrived there, I got out and headed toward one of the entrances to the unit; I don't recall exactly which one it was. As I was walking along, I heard several bursts of gunfire coming from the tops of various buildings; they were firing at me and the other men in my unit, so one of my buddies and I started to run for cover in a zigzag pattern, but as I was running my rifle suddenly went off and wounded me in the right foot. An ambulance picked me up later and took me to the Central Military Hospital. . . . I made an official statement reporting what had happened, Deposition number 54832/68, which has been filed with the Division of Investigations.

Jesús Marino Bautista González, sergeant second
class, quartered in the Fourth Infantry Battalion
Military Barracks

The woman was sobbing as though her heart was breaking.

Carlos Lemus Elizondo, clerk, Canadá Shoe Store

It makes me boil when I hear people say that the students looted abandoned stores and shops and commercial establishments in the Chihuahua building. They weren't the ones who robbed them at all; it was the agents in the white gloves and Army troops who broke the windows of these shops and filled their own pockets. I know that for a fact, because I was right there and saw it with my own eyes.

Angelina Rodríguez de Cárdenas, mother of a family

Alberto went to the meeting with his friend Emilio. They were standing on one corner of the esplanade listening to the speakers and watching the crowd. There were young kids riding their bicycles around the square and other youngsters playing with each other—children who doubtless lived right there in the housing unit. They seemed to be paying no attention to the speakers—or at any rate the meeting hadn't kept them from going on with their games and having fun. Alberto and Emilio had gotten there early. They noticed that the sound equipment had already been set up, because people were testing it, the way they always do: "One, two, three, testing. . . ." The two of them hung around for a while, but they soon got bored, and were even thinking of leaving. Then suddenly the shooting started, and all the demonstrators flung themselves on the ground. Emilio landed on top of Alberto, and the two of them lay there like that. When the noise of the guns going off stopped, Alberto said to his friend, "Come on, get up, you're like a ton of bricks on top of me, come on Emilio, get up—let's get out of here." Alberto scrambled to his feet and as he did so Emilio's body rolled over onto the ground. Emilio was stone-cold dead.

Alberto had never been interested in politics one way or the other. But he was so shocked and so angry when Emilio was killed like that, when they murdered all those people in Tlatelolco, that he wants to be active in politics now to help organize demonstrations and meetings, to protest.

Gabriela Silva de Guerrero, mother of a family

Beneath the posters, beneath the rain-soaked banners, there were two dead bodies.

Rosario Acevedo, psychology student, UNAM

May the victims of last night recover, may they return to their homes, may we make amends to them by setting them free. . . .

María Luisa Mendoza, writer, journalist, and resident
of the Cuauhtémoc building, Tlatelolco housing unit

You know what? The soldiers fired the moment they saw people peer out of one of the windows. . . . So when Margarita leaned her head out to look for Carlitos, they immediately fired a hail of bullets at the window of her apartment. . . . So then she put a dark-colored silk scarf over her almost platinum-blond hair and felt a little bit safer when she leaned her head out of the window.

Mercedes Olivera de Vázquez, anthropologist

Many people who lived there in the Tlatelolco unit wanted to organize rescue brigades, but it was hard to do very much of anything because we were still in such great danger ourselves. . . . Every so often we could hear the shooting starting again. . . .

Cecilia Carrasco de Luna, resident of the
Tlatelolco housing unit

Just as it was getting light, four more corpses were carried into the headquarters of the Third Police Precinct, bringing the number of dead who had been taken to this particular police station to around fourteen to eighteen. Those who have been identified thus far are: Leonardo Pérez González, an employee of the SEP; Cornelio Caballero Garduño, from Prep 9; Gilberto Ortiz Reynoso, a student at ESIQIE; Luis Contreras Pérez; José Ignacio Caballero González; and Ana María Reyes Touché. A child who had received a bullet wound and been evacuated from apartment 615 of the Chihuahua building was also brought to this police station.

There are rumors that there are four dead in the Rubén Leñero Hospital, one of whose corpses was thrown out of a car, immediately in front of the hospital.

Ovaciones, *October 3, 1968*

Approximately fifteen thousand bullets of various calibers were fired during the exchange of gunfire in Tlatelolco.

An officer

Unlike previous occasions, the hundreds of Molotov cocktails thrown by the demonstrators are of a remarkably high quality this time.

An officer

After what's happened, I'm resigning my commission in the Army. It's getting worse and worse for both sides. The situation has become much more serious since we occupied CU. Heaven only knows where we're all going to end up.

A lieutenant in the Parachute Troops

The situation is very delicate. We are unable to fire at will, because we've had orders to shoot only in self-defense. We've been shot at continually with heavy-caliber weapons ever since we arrived here. . . . Life's hard, you know, and you have to earn your daily bread somehow or other. Unfortunately we have to obey orders, because if we retreat a single step, our own buddies plug us.

A sergeant in the Nineteenth Infantry Battalion

Here in the Plaza, if we move one inch they shoot us. There are sharpshooters all around. A convoy of civilian ambulances should be sent here to see if they'll let them come in. They should drive up with their sirens on full blast to show they're ambulances.

Miguel Ángel Martínez Agis, in news story,
"Chihuahua Building, 6 p.m."

Armed troops with machine guns were shooting at anybody who moved, especially people at the windows in the nearby buildings. A platoon of soldiers grabbed a sixty-year-old man who'd been wounded right out of our hands. We have no idea where they took him. We were enraged at that.

Lorenzo Calderón, Alfonso García Méndez, and
Vicente Orozco, tenants in the Tlatelolco housing unit

Quiet words, an announcement: "We should like to inform everyone that the demonstration that has been scheduled has been canceled. We repeat: there will be no march on the Santo Tomás campus. This march has been canceled. In a few moments we shall all go our separate ways, because there is not going to be a march on the Santo Tomás campus," and the spontaneous chants of a tense but peaceful crowd were suddenly met with bursts of machine-gun fire and death-dealing bayonets.

We do not speak that sort of language. The language we have used has always been entirely different. When our struggle took on national proportions, our banners, on more than one occasion, suddenly appeared in the Zócalo, demanding political freedom, an end to repression, the right to strike, and the release of political prisoners.

We were united and we had right on our side.

The authorities could have granted these demands, but faced with the choice of giving in to our demands and murderous repression, they chose the latter.

Pablo Gómez, student and member of the Communist Youth

The headquarters of the Third Precinct was surrounded by police; they were not allowing anyone in, but my husband went over and asked to speak to one of the men in charge because he had suddenly remembered that one of the officers in this particular police precinct had been a patient of his at the Social Security hospital. The authorities sent for him, and they recognized my husband, who then explained that we were very worried because our son had gone to the movie theater in Tlatelolco and we hadn't heard from him, and also told them that he knew there were many dead bodies in that police station and asked the officer to let him in to see if our son was among them.

"All right, I'll see if I can arrange it." The police officer came back in a little while and said, "It's okay, you can go on into the morgue, you two." But when he saw how upset I was, standing there with tears streaming down my face, the officer changed his mind and said, "On second thought, you go in alone, doctor, since you're used to this sort of thing."

My husband came back after a while, his face deathly white.

"What is it? Is he one of the dead in there?"

"No, he's not in there. . . ."

"Did you take a really good look?" I asked.

"Good Christ, of course I did! Come on, let's get out of here."

We left, and once we were outside my husband told us that he'd counted twenty-two dead bodies lying there on the floor. It said in the paper later that there were twenty dead. Among the dead bodies he'd seen was the corpse of a pregnant woman. He went over to see whether the baby was alive, and the anthropology student who was with us remarked, "Sir, she's no doubt been dead for more than five hours!"

"I realized that when I went over to examine her, but that was my first instinctive reaction," my husband said to me. At one o'clock in the morning we tried to get back into Tlatelolco; but the only way you could get through was on the Avenida de la Reforma side, and one of the policemen standing on the corner in front of the Cuitláhuac Monument told us, "They've arrested lots of people and taken them to Military Camp 1. . . ."

We went there to the camp and the guards outside denied that there were any prisoners there. Both at the main entrance and the side entrances the soldiers told us, "There are no prisoners here, not a single one. . . ."

Margarita Nolasco, anthropologist

The Leñero Hospital reported that it was literally impossible for people who wanted to see their friends or relatives to enter the hospital, because the police were barring the door.

"Partial List of Dead and Wounded in the Gun Battle"

The lieutenant colonel and other officers began counting us off in groups of sixty to put us in the wards. I turned out to be number 60, with my brother there in line right next to me. So the two of us were separated, and he got put in a different ward with another group of sixty. They went down the line taking our names down one by one and asking how old each of us was. Almost all of us were in our teens or early twenties, although there was one man with his wife and his little girl there; four young children; three foreigners—I think they were newscameramen, because they had movie cameras and a tape recorder with them—and three teen-age girls, thirteen to fifteen years old, all scared to death.

Each dormitory ward has two rows of fifteen cots, but they're big double iron cots, so there was room in there for sixty kids. I was the first one in, and I asked a soldier sweeping the floor in there—a military prisoner—where the lavatory was, and the very first thing I did when I went into the john was to tear my student-body card up and flush it down the toilet, because I'd been told that they'd be roughest on students. We all started talking there in the ward, and since I'm the nervous type I kept going about from group to group, eavesdropping on first one conversation and then another.

Then they brought in a woman who was in hysterics because she'd been separated from her children: "My kids are locked up in the car, my kids are locked up in the car, they made me leave my kids behind. . . ."

A lieutenant colonel came in then and said to us, "Please, everyone, calm down. Nothing's going to happen to you here. I want each of you to settle down on a cot and make yourselves comfortable."

The woman went on screaming. The officer told her to pull herself together, that all the women were going to be taken to the infirmary. . . . When they heard that, the older man's wife and daughter and the three girls with their textbooks still under their arms all burst into tears. I asked the three girls what school they were from, and they said they were students from some academy—I don't remember now which one they said they were from. A chubby kid who was there in the ward with his fiancée hugged her in his arms, but they started separating out all the women: the wife, the three girls, and the fiancée.

"I want all the ladies to come with me to the infirmary, please," one of the officers said.

The husband demanded an explanation, and the colonel said something about "offending people's sense of decency"—I don't remember his exact words. "They can't stay here," he said. The women didn't want to go, and clung to their loved ones in tears, but they were all eventually taken to the infirmary where the rest of the women were.

After a while the officers came back to ask which of the men there had been with the older lady and the girls, and took them away. They also took the foreigners away. We never found out what happened to them.

"Are they going to let the rest of us out now, too?" we asked the soldiers.

They just laughed in our faces.

"Aren't they going to come for us, too?"

"Sure they are—they're going to come and give you a nice little warmup."

One of the soldier-prisoners said to me, "They're going to bring you all mattresses in a while."

I believed him, but all they brought us was a few cardboard boxes, not nearly enough to go around. They lined us up and shouted, "Here you are—here're some 'box springs' for you."

I didn't get any of the boxes. In the lockers next to the lavatory we found some newspapers and comic books and grade-school textbooks. We latched onto the textbooks to use for pillows and grabbed the newspapers for blankets. That first night I was so sore from the beating I'd gotten I couldn't sleep. Around midnight a chubby little second lieutenant with a mustache came in to talk to us. We asked him what was going to happen to us and when they were going to let us out.

"Don't worry. If you youngsters don't have anything to do with the Movement you're not going to have a hard time of it—they won't even hold you here. The ones who are really going to have a rough time of it are the members of the National Strike Committee—they're going to shoot them for treason," he told us.

More officers came in and we all got up off our cots, thinking they were going to let us out, but they just lined us up and took a roll call and then left again. Along about four in the morning the door opened and I saw them come in and beat up six other kids. They got a worse beating than the one we'd gotten. One of the kids had the whole left side of his face covered with blood and his eye was swollen shut; the others had all been bloodied; the soldiers had stripped them naked and they'd stood there in the rain with their hands on the napes of their necks for four hours, and then later, after the pipes there in the Tlatelolco housing unit had been riddled with bullet holes, they had put them in a room where more and more water kept pouring in. We all began trading stories of what had happened to us. Most of the kids had been robbed; some of them had had everything they had on them stolen by the soldiers, and others had had all their money swiped by the secret agents. Some of them said the cops had been quite decent to them, that it hadn't been the police but the Army troops who had beaten them; but others said just the opposite, that it wasn't the Army troops who had mistreated them but the cops. That's why I think those in our group had a worse time of it than anybody else—because we fell into the hands of both the Army and the police; both the soldiers and the cops beat us. At seven a.m. they lined us up to take roll call again, and around ten o'clock some officers and the same military prisoners we'd seen before came in with big kettles to pass out breakfast. They made us form a line that went the whole length of the ward, and as we filed by one by one they handed us a plate of food and a cup.

That night officials from the Public Prosecutor's office came. They asked us what school we were from, took both our thumbprints and our photographs full-face and in profile: in other words they made out police records on each of us, and when they'd finished they locked us up again and said, "You can rest some more now."

Carlos Galván, student at the School
of Library Sciences, UNAM

They denied everything at Military Camp 1. Around two in the morning we went to one of the side entrances—number 3, I think it was, one of the ones farthest towards the back anyway, and pleaded with the soldiers there: "No, please, if they've brought any prisoners here. . . . You know they're in there . . . you can get a message in to them. . . . Please, tell us whether they're here." But the troops on duty there wouldn't tell us a thing. What's more, every time any sort of vehicle approached, the soldiers cocked their rifles and kept them at the ready.

All of a sudden a military transport drove up, and a man dressed in civvies stepped out and said, "I'm from the Olimpia Battalion. Clear all these people out of here, because we're bringing in the others."

"All right, clear out of here this instant, all of you," the soldiers barked at us.

"Why do we have to leave, pray tell, if we're just standing here quietly on a public thoroughfare?"

Then they pointed their guns at us and said," We've got rifles, that's why."

We got back in the car and left. I know now that the Army troops were bringing in more prisoners and didn't want us to see what they were up to. From there we went to the Attorney General's office, where they informed us that around eight o'clock the next day they were going to announce the lists of names of those who had been arrested. Since it was past four a.m. by that time, we decided to go back home and wait it out there till eight o'clock.

At six that morning, our son still hadn't come home, and we hadn't heard one word about him. All I knew was that he apprently wasn't among the casualties, because we'd gone to the Red and Green Cross hospitals and given them a photograph of him, and they'd checked to see whether he was among the dead and wounded. What's more, my husband had kept in touch with other doctors. Since my son apparently wasn't among the dead and wounded, I was afraid he'd been arrested. At seven that morning I went back to the military camp and was told once again that there were no prisoners there. At eight o'clock we went back to the Attorney General's office to see if the lists of people arrested had been posted, but there wasn't a one. They told us there at the Attorney General's office that there were no prisoners there, we'd been told at the military camp that there were no prisoners being held there, and at the district police headquarters they also told us there was no one detained there. So according to the authorities nobody was being held in custody anywhere. Then we went back home to leave word where we were going next; it had occurred to us that we should perhaps go to the Defense Department, but my daughter met me at the door and said that a youngster had phoned to say that my son was hiding out in any empty apartment in the Chihua-hua building. We rushed over there, and Meche pretended she wanted to see the state her apartment had been left in; she showed her papers and they let my husband and Meche and me in. It must have been about nine in the morning when we arrived there at the Chihuahua building. It was full of Army troops, but we started knocking on one door after the other anyway. We had no idea which one my son was in, and we knocked on every door, on one floor after the other.

I kept shouting, "Carlos, Carlitos, Carlitos, where are you?" I got more and more desperate: "Carlos, answer me, Carlitos, it's me . . . it's me, Carlitos. . . ." Three or four soldiers kept tagging along after me, but by that time I was past caring; I thought to myself that the best I could hope for now was just finding him alive.

Margarita Nolasco, anthropologist

Margarita was absolutely beside herself. We spent the entire night looking for her son, and her fit of hysteria reached its peak, so to speak, the next day, when they phoned us that he was in one of the apartments in the Chihuahua building, though they couldn't tell us exactly which one he was in. Then I witnessed really awful scenes, because it wasn't only Margarita who was searching, but lots of other people, lots of other mothers looking for their children, lots of whom were very young, a couple of them only two years or so old, though others, like Margarita's boy, were high-school kids. Margarita was more or less out of her mind by that time and was going from door to door shouting, "Carlitos, it's me, Mama! Let me in!" It was all straight out of Kafka. Obviously, her son wouldn't have opened the door for anyone.

Mercedes Olivera de Vázquez, anthropologist

. . . The defenseless creatures running back and forth in a panic trying to get out of the line of fire, the mute cries of the hundreds of people who had been arrested, the heroism of those who lived in the Nonoalco-Tlatelolco housing unit as they rushed out to help, passing out coffee, bandaging the heads of those who had been in-jured, taking the wounded into their apartments at the risk of their

own lives, and then, in the gray light of dawn, with not a drop of
water coming out of the faucets, after the endless sleepless night
. . . a mother . . . a mother sobbing and calling "Carlitos, Carlitos!" along all the corridors and up and down the stairways, searching for her son and asking everybody if they had seen him. . . .

María Luisa Mendoza, writer and resident
in the Tlatelolco housing unit

Around five that morning, the entire family started organizing. My
husband began making the rounds of the various offices of the Attorney General, Pepe went to all the police stations, Chelo and I
went to the Red and Green Cross hospitals and all the other hospitals and morgues where there were dead or wounded. The twins,
Rubén and Rogelio, went off to work, waiting for us to get in
touch with them the minute we had any news.

At the Red Cross hospital, they asked me if I was brave enough to
go down to the morgue in the basement. (The Red Cross hospital is
on Ejército Nacional, opposite Sears.) I replied, "Don't you think a
mother is automatically brave enough to do a thing like that?"

One of the hospital employees went down with me in the elevator. My daughter didn't go in with me: "Wait here for me outside,
Chelo," I told her. Once inside the morgue, the hospital employee
pressed a switch and began to pull the drawers out. In the first one
he pulled out there was the corpse of a youngster about sixteen
years old; his skin had already turned a deep purple. Since part of
his face was missing, I tried to identify him by looking at his teeth
and seeing if he had any moles on his face, since all my children
have them. The only thing left of this cadaver's face was the jaw-
bone and a couple of teeth. When I saw this youngster's dead body,
I was sure it was Pichi, because every one of the corpses I saw
seemed to be one of my children; every dead body I saw seemed to
be one of my boys; but in order to make sure I opened whatever
was left of their lips and looked at their teeth, and none of them
was Pichi, because there is a big gap between my son's front teeth
and the teeth of all these corpses were very close together, and my
oldest son has gold caps on his. . . . They produced other corpses
that had been brought in from Tlatelolco, but none of them was
Pichi. Lots of them were women's bodies, but I didn't pay much attention to them because what I was looking for was bodies of dead

boys. I only remember one of the women's bodies—a woman about forty-five years with henna hair, dressed in an orange blouse.

We went upstairs again, and I asked the hospital attendant where he thought we should look next.

"Go over to the emergency clinic at Balbuena," he told us.

On the way over there Chelo and I didn't say one word to each other. The only ones they'd brought there to the clinic were people who'd been wounded; they wouldn't let me in to see them, and none of them fit the description I gave. I was absolutely beside myself, and asked again where else they might have taken people who'd been injured. They said that a number of them had been taken to Rubén Leñero Hospital, but that they would refuse to answer any questions there because everyone who had been brought to Leñero was under arrest. I found out later that they'd taken fifty-eight students who had been wounded there, but none of the dead.

I gave an official from the Public Prosecutor's office photos of my sons and he came back after a while and said to me, "No, they aren't here. None of the ones we have here look like these photographs you've given me."

People were going all over the city searching for their dead or wounded. I went to the headquarters of the Third Police Precinct in Lagunilla then. When I arrived, the streets were full of smoke, as though there were a heavy fog, because they'd set a bus on fire and it was producing great clouds of smoke.

I asked the cops there if I could go inside the police station, and one of them said it was okay: "Go on in if you want to, it'll teach you a lesson."

They'd made everybody who wanted to go in form a line, so we walked over and stood in it. They were admitting people in groups of five.

"Wait for me out here, Chelo, don't go in," I said to my daughter.

When they let me in, I walked down a hall and was ushered into a room that was freezing cold—it seemed even colder than the one at the Red Cross hospital. The first thing I saw in there were seven corpses of youngsters about twelve to fifteen years old, but these particular bodies had already been identified. That's why they'd been separated from the rest. Since these seven bodies were the only ones I noticed at first, I thought they were the only ones there, but then I began looking around the room and saw three stone slabs with three dead bodies of railway workers on them, with their heads half blown off by dum-dum bullets. I realized they were railway workers because they had bandanas around their necks and were dressed in coarse blue cotton work shirts. The other corpses were underneath them. The first one I caught sight of was a woman about to give birth: the fetus's head was showing because the bullets had ripped her belly all to pieces.

Later I asked Cosme, my husband, "How come her belly was ripped apart like that?"

"Because they were dum-dum bullets," he answered.

A little farther on I saw the body of the Olympic Games hostess, a very pretty girl with long dark hair, lying there with a peaceful expression on her face. Her whole bosom was bare, like a flower that had opened, and I thought to myself that she must surely be even colder than I was, so I took my sweater off and put it over her. She was naked from the waist up and it made me feel bad seeing her lying there with her breasts exposed like that, so that everybody could see. There were other dead bodies there—twelve more of them—all railway workers, piled up one on top of the other, and I asked the policeman, "How come there are only railway workers' bodies here? What about the students who were killed?"

"They didn't bring any of them here," he answered.

"Well, where are they then?"

"You might take a look out at Military Camp 1."

And when I asked there in the police station how I could get to Military Camp 1, a lieutenant colonel told me, "It's no use going out there, *señora*. They won't tell you a thing. It's no use trying out there."

I was really in a state when I left the police station, because it had all been such a terrible experience. I walked and walked, and it all seemed like a nightmare that had made me break out in a cold sweat. I walked on and on down the entire length of the Paseo de la Reforma, hugging the walls. I wasn't even aware of Chelo walking along there beside me. We didn't say one word to each other. She didn't ask me one question. We turned off the Reforma then and headed home. The others came back then, one by one.

"I haven't found out a thing," Cosme reported.

"I couldn't find out a single thing," my son Pepe reported.

It was two weeks before I had any word at all. I remember that I sat for hours at a time at the window waiting. I felt sick to my stomach the whole time. I was as limp as a dishrag and felt as though I were at the end of my rope. And I'm a strong woman. For two weeks I never sat down to a meal, I was so upset. I hardly ate a bite, really; I just drank liquids every once in a while. We never sat down together at the table from then on. Two weeks later I found out that Pichi had been in cell block H in Lecumberri, and I went to pick him up the day they let him out because they couldn't prove the charges against him. We found out where Eduardo was when my son Rogelio got word at the place where he worked that he was in Military Camp 1. He was alive! I was terribly distraught, I admit, but it would have been hard not to be upset. When they transferred Eduardo to Lecumberri, his fiancée and I went to see him.

They would only let one of us into cell block H to see him, and said to me, "You go in, *señora.*"

Everything that all of us had been through made me very brave, because when I saw Eduardo stumbling down the stairway from his cell block like a mole, clinging to the banisters, and only recognizing me because he could hear my voice as I shouted to him "Eduardo, over here! I'm over here!"—well, it's something I'll never forget. He had to crawl downstairs like that, clutching the banister, because they'd beaten him within an inch of his life and he'd lost his glasses. All he had to guide him was my voice. He's had to wear glasses for the last four years and can hardly see without them; they're glasses with a very strong correction, with thick thick lenses—that's why everybody calls him Owl-Eyes.

The whole thing made me terribly depressed, and I began writing a great many poems to give vent to my feelings. Read this one, for instance:

PRISON BARS

Move the prison bars even closer together
As close as you possibly can
Because however close together you place them
You will never be able
To trap the desire for freedom behind them.
And I suggest that you also
Erect bars shutting out the sky

So that people's thoughts cannot escape
And cause you trouble.

One morning when I read in the papers that Díaz Ordaz was going to have an operation on his eye, I wrote an epigram for the occasion:

The doctors are doing their best
To give light to a person who plunges others in darkness.
Wouldn't it be more proper
To give him a little dose of hemlock?

I am going to hand my poems over to you—not so that you'll try to get them published or anything like that, but just to see what you think of them. Write my name down, go ahead, write it down; after all the things I've been through, could anything worse possibly happen to me? What more can they do to me now that they've got my son there behind prison bars?

Celia Espinoza de Valle, grade-school teacher,
mother of a family

They brought several bodies to Military Camp 1. A friend of mine who's also an accountant went to claim his mother's body, and they told him they'd give it to him on one condition: he would have to sign a statement that his mother was a dangerous agitator. He signed everything they asked him to. Everything. His mother was a little old lady who had been there at Tlatelolco by the sheerest chance.

María de la Paz Figueroa, public accountant

The police station in Tacuba—the headquarters of the Ninth Police Precinct—reported that the body of a fifteen-year-old student from Vocational 1, Guillermo Rivera Torres, had been brought there. The detective on duty stated that the young man had still been alive when he was brought to the Central Military Hospital, but had died there, and that his corpse had subsequently been taken to the Ninth Precinct morgue.

At two-ten a.m. the Third Police Precinct reported that thus far a total of eighteen dead bodies had been brought to police head-quarters in that precinct.

The Third Police Precinct headquarters also reported that the following dead had been identified: Leonardo Pérez González, an employee of the Secretariat of Public Education; Cordelio Garduño Caballero, a student at Preparatory 9; Gilberto R. Ortiz Reinoso, a fourth-year student at the School of Chemical Engineering, IPN; Luis Contreras T.; José Ignacio Caballero González, a thirty-six-year-old office clerk; and Ana María Touchet.

The Red Cross hospital reported that they had seven dead there, among them two young boys; an ambulance attendant, Antonio Solórzano García; and an unidentified woman.

The Balbuena first-aid station reported one fatality, Cecilio León Lorres, who had been picked up by their ambulance in the vicinity of Tlatelolco.

At eleven p.m. fourteen dead had been brought to the Third Police Precinct morgue by Red and Green Cross ambulances. Among them were three women: a young girl of about twenty-three years of age, a pregnant woman about thirty-five years old, and another woman of about forty years of age. At the headquarters of this precinct there are also bodies of two men over thirty, and nine bodies that appear to be those of students. Only three or four of these dead have been positively identified thus far, and no names of any of the dead will be made public until the proper legal procedures have been complied with, according to this detective. (Later four more dead bodies were brought in.)

The Secretariat of National Defense announced one fatality: Corporal Pablo Pinzón Martínez, of the 44th Infantry Battalion. As of twelve-forty-five a.m. this morning, the reports received by our newsmen indicate that there are a total of twenty-five dead and more than seventy wounded as a consequence of the tragic events at Tlatelolco.

"Partial List of Dead and Wounded in the Gun Battle"

THE DEAD:

Red Cross: Manuel Telésforo López Carballo, Antonio Solórzano Gaona, and three unidentified persons, a woman of approximately fifty-five years of age, and two young men, about eighteen and twenty-five years old.

Central Military Hospital: Corporal Pedro Gustavo López Hernández.

Rubén Leñero Hospital: Carlos Beltrán Maciel, though this body has not yet been positively identified. It was thrown out of a car at the entrance to the hospital.

Balbuena: Cecilio de León Torres.

Headquarters, Third Police Precinct: Eighteen bodies, none as yet identified.

Story entitled "Bloody Encounter in Tlatelolco,"
El Heraldo, *October 3, 1968*

Ambulances 3, 4, 6, and 9 of the Red Cross, plus ambulance 71 of the Green Cross and another from the Mexican Social Security Institute, last night picked up the bodies of fourteen persons who had died of gunshot wounds in the Plaza de las Tres Culturas.

These bodies are being held in the morgue at the headquarters of the Third Police Precinct until they are identified by their families.

These persons were apparently innocent victims of gunfire from various groups of professional sharpshooters, who fired indiscriminately on the crowd below from the Chihuahua building of the Nonoalco-Tlatelolco housing unit.

Only five of these victims have thus far been identified. The names of the dead positively identified to date are: Ana María Regina Teucher, approximately twenty years of age, a first-year medical student, either at the IPN or at UNAM; Gilberto Reinoso Ortiz, approximately twenty-four years of age, a fourth-year student at the School of Chemical, Industrial, and Electronic Engineering, IPN; Cornelio Caballero Garduño, a student at Preparatory 9; Luis Contreras López; and José Ignacio Caballero González, thirty-six years of age.

There were no identification papers found on any of the other bodies.

Military Hospital

At midnight, the Central Military Hospital reported one fatality: Private Pinzón Martínez, who was struck by a bullet that entered the left occipital area and exited in the right temporal area. This wound was apparently caused by an expansive .38-caliber bullet. Private Pinzón Martínez was a member of the 44th Infantry Battalion.

News story entitled "29 Dead and More Than 80 Wounded; Casualties on Both Sides; 1000 Arrested," El Universal, *October 3, 1968*

The hostess's name was Regina; she was a very pretty young girl, wearing that striped uniform they had dressed all the Olympic hostesses in.

Socorro Lazcano Caldera, grade-school teacher

There was beauty and a bright glow in the souls of these dead youngsters. They wanted to make Mexico a land of truth and justice. They dreamed of a marvelous republic free of poverty and deceit. They were demanding freedom, bread, and schooling for those who were oppressed and forgotten, and were fighting to do away with the sad expression in the eyes of children, the frustration of teen-agers, the cynicism of older people. In some of them there were perhaps the seeds of a philosopher, a teacher, an artist, an engineer, a doctor. But now they are merely physiological processes come to a sudden end inside skins cruelly ripped apart. Their death has wounded each and every one of us and left a horrible scar on the nation's life.

The pages recorded in history that night are admittedly not glorious ones, but they can nonetheless never be forgotten by those who are mere youngsters today but who tomorrow will write the story of these fateful days. So perhaps it is still possible to realize the dream of these young people, the dream, for instance, of the pretty girl who was a first-year medical student and an Olympics hostess felled by the hail of bullets, whose dead body lay there on the ground with empty eyes staring into space and lips which spoke four languages that were now forever silent. Some day a votive lamp will be placed in the Plaza de las Tres Culturas in memory of all of them. Other young people will keep it burning brightly.

José Alvarado, in an article entitled "Lament for the Youngsters Who Died," Siempre!, *no. 799, October 16, 1968*

Among the fatalities were a young man, Antonio Solórzano, reportedly a Red Cross ambulance attendant, although he was not on duty when he received the wounds that cost him his life; a woman, as yet unidentified, around fifty years of age; a young man between the ages of seventeen and twenty-two, apparently a student; and another man who has not yet been identified.

News story entitled "The Student Situation. Shots Fired from the Chihuahua Building, According to Cueto. Cueto Also Reports Three Secret Service Agents Wounded, Two of Them Seriously," El Día, October 3, 1968

Moreover, according to information furnished by the Red Cross, fifty-four wounded were treated in the hospital of that institution; of these fifty-four wounded, four subsequently died. Thus far only one of these four dead has been identified: Antonio Solórzano Gaona, a thirty-six-year-old ambulance attendant, killed in the line of duty. This ambulance attendant was just about to evacuate one of the wounded when he was struck by a burst of machine-gun bullets.

News story entitled "Sharpshooters Fire on Army Troops in Tlatelolco. One General and 11 Soldiers Wounded; 2 Soldiers and More Than 20 Civilians Killed in a Terrible Gun Battle," El Sol de México, October 3, 1968

Regina, the [Olympics] hostess, was engaged to be married. Her father is a doctor, did you know that? I think he's from a German family. That's why Regina learned so many languages, because of her father. And that's why she was chosen as one of the hostesses. She was so happy that day!

María Inés Moreno Enríquez, student, Iberoamerican University

The Red Cross hospital reported that it had admitted forty-six patients with injuries, almost all of them the result of bullet wounds, a number of which were very serious. The Red Cross also reported that four of the wounded who had been brought to the hospital of that institution had died after being admitted. These four dead have not yet been identified.

> *"Terrible Gun Battle in Tlatelolco. The Number of Dead Not Yet Determined and Dozens Wounded"*

The next day and during the days that followed, people became more and more apprehensive. There were thousands of persons who had suddenly disappeared without a trace. Alarming, contradictory rumors that went the rounds made people even more enraged and distraught. There were huge throngs at the hospitals day after day, around the clock: people kept scrutinizing the lists of wounded and making the rounds of all the morgues in the city to see if their friends or relatives were among the dead, and spent endless hours waiting at the gates of the prisons and the various courts for the lists of prisoners to be posted. People were not only grief-stricken and worried; they were also angry at the government's repressive policies, and the situation was further aggravated by the insolent behavior of the police toward those who came to them to inquire after their friends and relatives. After eleven days with absolutely no news as to what had happened to Raúl, my husband and I paid to have a petition addressed to the Attorney General of Mexico inserted in the newspaper.

> *Manuela Garín de Álvarez, mathematician*
> *and professor at the School of Engineering and*
> *Faculty of Sciences, UNAM*

> A barefoot woman
> with a black shawl over her head
> is waiting for them to hand over the dead body:
> a boy twenty-two years old, a student at Poli
> with a red hole in his side
>   made by a regulation
>   M-1 rifle.

> *Juan Bañuelos*

We would not like to find ourselves in a situation which would require measures that we do not wish to take, but we shall take such measures if necessary. Whatever our duty requires us to do, we will do. We shall go as far as necessary.

Gustavo Díaz Ordaz, President of Mexico, Fourth Annual Message, September 1, 1968

Recovering what was lost during that dark night of Tlatelolco is vital to the country. Recalling the soldiers to their barracks, emptying the jails of prisoners, and purging souls is what is needed in this dark hour. Nobody is winning in this bitter fight in which Mexico is foundering.

Francisco Martínez de la Vega, in an article entitled "Where Is Our Country Headed?" El Día, *October 8, 1968*

We all thought we would be out in seventy-two hours and began to give up hope when they didn't release us. We spent ten days and nights there in jail. I was so nervous and so scared that I slept very badly. There was one man—a worker at the Pepsi-Cola plant—who had happened to get assigned a cot right next to the door; he didn't sleep much either, and he told me that around three a.m. every morning officers would come in with flashlights and go from cot to cot looking for people who belonged to the CNH. Since they had already photographed all of us, I suppose they showed our pictures to the members of the Committee that they'd already nabbed—I can just see them asking them, "Okay, you guys, tell us, which of these kids do you recognize? Which of them had anything to do with the Movement?" One time they took all of us into the john and turned the lights in the dormitory ward off, leaving just the one light on there in the lavatory where the officers were. They took us in one by one and one of the officers began asking questions:

"Where were you picked up?"

"In Tlatelolco, of course."

"And what were you doing there?"

"Just attending the meeting. . . ."

"When did they pick you up? Before or after the shooting?"

"Er . . . well . . . let's see . . . after."

"Have they given you a paraffin test?"

"No."

"Okay, go back to bed. . . . We'll give you one tomorrow. You should have been given one along with all the others."

They took us all in the lavatory and questioned us like that, one by one. But a rumor went the rounds later that Sócrates was standing there by the john, in the dark, watching us as we filed in one by one to see if he recognized any of us. When we went into the lavatory, one of the officers grabbed us by the head and made us turn our faces first one way and then another, and when a teacher from Vocational 5 went in, they kept him there quite a while. "Wait a minute, sir, let's see, you're . . ."

"You're a member of the Teachers' Coalition, isn't that right?" one of the other officers said.

"No," the man answered. "I don't know a thing about it."

"Have you gone to any of the demonstrations, to any of the meetings?"

"Yes, some of them."

"And did you meet any of your colleagues there?"

"Of course I did—it's only natural that I'd have run into a number of them."

"And how do you know one of them didn't squeal on you?"

"I don't have any idea what this is all about . . . there must be some mistake."

"Well, go back to your cot and get some rest. But if you hear your name called out during the night, you'd better start saying your prayers, because they're going to bump off anybody they find that belongs to the Coalition."

The teacher then gave an engineer who was there in the ward with us a photograph of his daughter and told him that if anything happened to him to please get word to his family. There was nothing he could do then but lie down and try to get some rest. But every time they opened the door of the ward after that we sat up on our cots to see what was going to happen. But that teacher just lay there on his cot trying to rest so as not to go to pieces.

Ignacio Galván, student, San Carlos Academy

I realize that the government could not possibly permit the student disturbances to continue since the Olympic Games were scheduled to begin in a few days. The eyes of the entire world were focused on Mexico. They had to stop the students any way they could, at whatever cost! Many visitors from European countries who had planned to come to the Olympics began canceling their reservations; the students' acts of bravado and the turmoil they were causing were threatening to ruin the Olympic Games; they were attempting to exploit an international event for their own personal ends, to further demands having to do with a purely domestic situation. The presence of foreign correspondents who are always on the lookout for sensational news and lurid stories made them behave all the worse; it encouraged them to stir up even more trouble. They had to show the foreign journalists that they were real *machos*; they invited them to their demonstrations and got them to take part in their meetings. . . . I understand very well why the Mexican government reacted as it did, and if I had been in the authorities' shoes, I would perhaps have been obliged to behave in precisely the same way.

Daniel Guian, director of an insurance company
and Olympics visitor from France

When one is so alarmed and so painfully disturbed by the repeated bloody episodes that have occurred during the student conflict, one cannot help wondering whether the government is not being two-faced, whether there is any sports event that is worth the death of Mexican citizens, and whether the celebration of an international event promoting the cause of peace can be held when the country is in the grip of the cruelest sort of violence.

Alberto Domingo, in an article entitled "Bloody
Wrath Held Its Own Celebration," Siempre!,
no. 799, October 16, 1968

What happened was that students wanted to steal the spotlight from the Olympics.

Lola d'Orcasberro, Olympics visitor from France

If they're killing students so they can have their Olympics, it would be better not to hold them at all, since no Olympic Games, or even the Olympics as a whole, are worth the life of a single student.

An Italian athlete, member of the Italian team
competing in the Olympic Games, as quoted in
Ovaciones, *October 3, 1968*

Everything was so carefully planned, such enormous sums of money were spent, that not a single detail was overlooked; even the tickets for each event had been designed with the greatest good taste; and the same is true of the signs, the brochures, the printed programs, the uniforms of the hostesses, the advertisements, and even the balloons; and every event has begun exactly on time. It was all beautifully organized, and that's why it makes me sick at heart that the Nineteenth Olympic Games are stained with blood.

Beatriz Colle Corcuera, graphic arts designer and artist

Once the shooting started, the Army acted as if it were putting down an armed insurrection rather than stopping a meeting of students. There were more than fifteen hundred people arrested, and the treatment of the prisoners afterward was even more outrageous and severe: many persons—of both sexes—were stripped naked, thrown against the wall, and made to stand for hours with their hands up. A photograph in one of the morning papers on Thursday, October 3, shows a group of soldiers grinning from ear to ear as they cut one young prisoner's long hair off, an act that is both completely unjustified and most disturbing.

Alberto Domingo, in "Bloody Wrath Held Its
Own Celebration"

People should wash their dirty linen in private. The students wanted to wash theirs in full view of the Olympic contestants, who had come to Mexico from all over the world, and to take advantage of their being there to get them involved in the country's domestic politics.

Douglas Crocker, museum curator and Olympics
visitor from the United States

We never claimed we wanted to boycott the Olympics. On September 14 the head of the Department of Internal Affairs informed us in a written statement that if it was our intention to apply pressure on the government by causing disturbances that might prevent the Games from being held or to interfere with them in any way, the authorities would take advantage of every legal recourse available to them to ensure that the Olympics went ahead as planned.

We still maintain that we were not against the Olympics. As a matter of fact, on August 29 we drew up a manifesto that was published on the thirtieth in *El Día*, declaring that our Movement had no connection whatsoever with the forthcoming Olympic Games, and that we had no desire to disrupt an event that was international in scope.

Gilberto Guevara Niebla, of the CNH

One time, when we were all exhausted (we've already told you that the CNH sessions sometimes went on for as long as ten hours at a time), Ayax Segura Garrido pulled a manifesto out of his pocket and proposed that it be published the next day in the papers. He said that his school would pay for it. We asked him to read it—it was five in the morning by that time, let me add—and as soon as he'd read the first few sentences we told him he needn't read the rest of it and approved it for publication. The text had to do with a previous position the CNH had taken, one we'd discussed at length and approved weeks before: it was an announcement to the public that we were not against the holding of the Olympic Games in Mexico City. But Ayax had added other things to this text, paragraphs promising that we would sweep the city streets, serve as guides, wash windows, and even shine people's shoes, practically. That was the part we hadn't heard. And the reason we hadn't was that I had gotten up after he'd read the first few sentences and said, "Comrades, we approved this manifesto three weeks ago, so let's not start discussing it all over again. Let's publish it." So the others agreed. When I read the text in the papers the next day, my hair stood on end. I arrived at the meeting that day fully prepared to get my ass chewed out. And of course that's exactly what happened! The rank-and-file Movement people were furious—and they had every reason to be. I thought at first I'd dream up some sort of story, invent some sort of fancy explanation; but in the end I decided to simply lay it on the line and tell the people at the meeting how the session of the Strike Committee had gone on and on till the wee hours of the morning and how we had happened to give our stamp of approval to such a terribly stupid announcement. If they believed me, okay, and if they didn't, too bad. But after hearing me out, they accepted my self-criticism.

Luis González de Alba, of the CNH

We weren't against the Olympics as a sports event, but we *were* against what the Games represented economically. We're a very poor country, and the Olympics meant an irreparable drain on Mexico's economic resources, despite what anyone says to the contrary. López Mateos* was responsible for getting Mexico City chosen as the site of the Nineteenth Olympics, but he made this commitment simply to make a big splash, to enhance our country's outward image, which had nothing at all to do with the country's real situation.

Gustavo Gordillo, of the CNH

It will perhaps be of some interest . . . to note all the lectures which the students who demonstrated their discontent received from their naturally meddlesome and officious advisors and mentors. These complacent, sour adults, who are so solidly behind the rule of law and order, even if it is indiscriminately enforced by the most violently repressive means, who are so touchingly imbued with a sublime spirit of patriotism, have neglected, as was only to be expected, to acknowledge the policy that the Student Movement and its leaders, who had been badly beaten and assaulted, adopted with respect to the Olympics. These lily-white Catos who have been most eager to point out the errors and excesses committed by the students and their docile compliance with directives from "obscure foreign interests" have not said one word about these youngsters' willingness to declare a "truce" during the Olympics so as not to appear to be irresponsible "spoilsports."

Francisco Martínez de la Vega, in an article
entitled "The Peacefulness of the Rebels," El Día,
October 23, 1968

Being sensitive to the pressures being brought to bear by the 25,000 American businessmen and technicians present in Mexico, the Mexican government decided to use force to remedy the situation. It did not occur to the authorities that they were running the risk of emptying the Olympic stadium when they filled the jails.

Albert Paul Lentin, in an article in Le Nouvel
Observateur, *Paris, October 7, 1968*

---

* Adolfo López Mateos: the president of Mexico immediately preceding Gustavo Díaz Ordaz, elected in 1958.

Is that how you people in Mexico have a dialogue? By firing bullets at each other? You'd almost think Pancho Villa was still around, shooting up the town!

Andrew Fulton, American businessman and
Olympics visitor

It is my opinion that the dialogue has already begun, and that in his Annual Message the President of the Republic discussed in detail each of the six points contained in the petition drawn up by the so-called CNH, as well as other subjects of fundamental interest and transcendent importance. Surely the most important of the problems confronting us is the restructuring of higher education in Mexico.

Thus the dialogue has already begun, for the president's remarks were delivered from the highest tribunal in Mexico, amid great solemnity, and reached as large an audience as possible, for his Annual Message was heard not only by those present but was also broadcast over the radio and the television networks and later published in the national press. Thus the president has now taken part in the dialogue, answering each of the points raised in the petition.

Luis Echeverría Álvarez, Secretary of the
Department of Internal Affairs, as reported in a news story by
Rubén Porras Ochoa entitled "According to the
Secretary of the Department of Internal Affairs,
the Dialogue with the Students Has Already Been
Initiated by Díaz Ordaz in his Annual Message on
September 1," La Prensa, *October 3, 1968*

Leaders of the CNH died in Tlatelolco, you say? It's even worse when entirely innocent people are killed.

Álvaro Monroy Magaña, cabinetmaker

The Tlatelolco incident led those who sincerely believed that great improvements had been made in our democratic institutions, and that the political and social system of our country was basically sound except for certain minor failings and mistakes, to re-examine all their most cherished beliefs.

Elena Quijano de Rendón, normal-school teacher

A kid in bare feet asked one of the soldiers imprisoned in Military Camp 1 whether he could get him some shoes to wear, and the soldier hunted him up a pair of boots, but was asking a lot of money for them. We all chipped in to buy the kid the boots, because he didn't have a cent in his pockets.

Then the boy said, "You're real pals, all of you, and to show you how grateful I am to you, I'm going to dance the 'Jarabe Tapatío' for you."

We all began humming the melody: Tarara, tarara, tarara, tarara, tarara, tarara. . . . and he did the "Mexican Hat Dance" for us.

Ignacio Galván, student, San Carlos Academy

The clearest proof that our educational system is in a profound state of crisis is that all of our government officials, the majority of whom are university graduates, are incompetent and ignorant.

Raúl Álvarez Garín, of the CNH

"I only went to the meeting out of curiosity. . . ." "The only reason I went was because I was curious. . . ." You idiots—that's all you know how to say. You see where your curiosity got you!

An officer, to sixty prisoners in the dormitory
ward in Military Camp 1

They'd lined us up to take our fingerprints, and since there were lots of us waiting, I started rapping with one of the soldiers.

"Listen, you guys don't know what you're talking about," he said. "I suppose you'd like to have a government like Che Guevara's? I suppose you'd like to see Che Guevara President of Mexico?"

"No, of course not."

To keep on the good side of him, I pretended to more or less agree, and, like a fool, I started talking politics with him.

"No, listen, you people are all wrong. How come you want to see Che Guevara president?" he asked.

I thought to myself, It's obvious this guy doesn't even know that Che Guevara's dead. Apparently they don't give soldiers any sort of education.

Carlos Galván, student at the School of Library
Sciences, UNAM

How pigheaded those cops are! They even made paraffin tests on corpses!

Ramón Ceniceros Campos, student

As a matter of fact, there were hardly any public protests after October 2. The authorities may have shut people up. Or perhaps most people were too frightened to speak out. On October 3, teachers and students who had been at the meeting in Tlatelolco inserted a paid announcement in *Excélsior,* stating that they merely wished to express their profoundest indignation as human beings, that the sole persons responsible for what had happened were the forces of law and order, both those in uniform and those in plainclothes, and that there had been no provocation of any sort on the part of ordinary citizens attending the meeting: students, workers, peasants, families, and the general public. Also in *Excélsior* the Bloc of Resident Physicians on Strike in the Hospitals declared on October 4 that they wished their names to be added to those expressing their indignation at this unconscionable attack on the people who had peacefully gathered together in Tlatelolco, and stated that they were still determined to continue their all-out strike in support of the National Strike Committee indefinitely, until such time as the CNH's conflict with the government was resolved to the complete satisfaction of the Committee. . . . On October 5, a protest signed by the Congress of Intellectuals, Artists, and Writers was also published in *Excélsior.* . . . But the organizational framework of the National Strike Committee had been weakened, and there were already clear signs that it was falling apart politically. The police were hunting down and attacking those "on the outside." For these reasons, the general indignation and the popular discontent could not be properly channeled into political acts in response to the repression. After the Committee unilaterally declared the so-called "Olympic truce," a great many sectors of militants were isolated and brutally attacked by the authorities, for they had practically no means of defending themselves. In a word, it was one hell of a mess!

Félix Lucio Hernández Gamundi, of the CNH

The massacre on October 2 was "justified" by every sector of the government—the most shameless authorities made brazen public statements and the others responded with a total silence that made them accomplices in the repression. Not a single official voice was raised in protest against the murder of students, with one exception: outside the country, Octavio Paz submitted his resignation as Mexican Ambassador to India.

Raúl Álvarez Garín, of the CNH

I do not believe that images can ever lie. . . . I have seen the newsreels, the photographs. . . .

Octavio Paz

I have the impression that people were taken completely by surprise, and have remained more or less petrified. They still don't understand what the whole thing was all about. Why? What was behind it all? Who is responsible?

What struck me most was that a week afterward, the Olympic Games began amid at least the outward appearance of perfect calm, as though nothing at all had happened. . . . What in any other country in the world would have been quite enough to unleash a civil war has resulted here in Mexico in nothing more than a few tense days immediately following the events of Tlatelolco.

I am so appalled by Tlatelolco that I sometimes wonder if the whole thing ever happened at all. I am not making any sort of moral judgment with regard to Tlatelolco: the only thing I can say is that I don't understand it. What was the reason for it? Nor do I understand why everyone has remained silent. Personally speaking, from what I have seen, it would seem to me that the system here has enormous shortcomings. A professor from the University said to me one day, "You must never forget that all of us are government employees." Apparently they are all caught up in the system, and as I see it, this is one of Mexico's major problems.

Claude Kiejman, correspondent for Le Monde, *Paris*

It's a shame, but there's nothing that can be done about it!

José Vázquez, owner of a small corner grocery
store, La Norteñita

Oh, there's one other thing! Finally, just after they'd lined us all up to take us away, the top-ranking officer there gave us a lecture: he told us we should be grateful to General Marcelino García Barragán for not wanting to see so many people suffering needlessly, that what had happened should be a warning to us not to stir up any more trouble and that we were more than welcome in the Plaza de las Tres Culturas: "You can come here to play soccer whenever you like, you can come here and exercise whenever you please, you're more than welcome here," he said, plus a lot of other stuff like that. But who's going to want to come play games there in the Plaza after what's happened? Then everyone began applauding—most of them, of course, were clapping so that they'd be let out of the military camp—but I refused to applaud and a kid behind me shook my hand and said, "Good for you! Right on! I'm happy to see you're not like the rest of these sheep."

"I've got no reason to applaud what that guy over there said; I don't go along with what he said at all," I replied.

I didn't approve of what he said because I don't see things his way at all: I'm all for freedom, myself. I talk about freedom in the songs I write. I'm resigned to things as they are, I admit, but at the same time I still hope to accomplish something, though most of my songs are about total failure, about how hard life is. I also remember one other thing. When they were taking us back to the city in trucks after they'd released us there at the military camp, some of the kids were fooling around, and it made one kid mad: "Listen you guys, don't get rowdy, or they'll take us all back there," he told them. Those kids were in very good spirits still, but most of us were scared to death; we were terribly demoralized after they let us go.

Ignacio Galván, student, San Carlos Academy

The only concerted protest came from the very militant Bloc of Resident Physicians on Strike in the largest hospitals in the city. The most severe repressive measures taken by the government were naturally directed against those sectors that had gone on fighting. On October 12, this bloc announced that the Secretariat of Public Health had sent a notice around that no residents on strike would receive their stipends as medical trainees; and at the same time the police began searching for the leaders of the bloc, a number of whom had gone into hiding, among them Mario Campuzano.

Félix Lucio Hernández Gamundi, of the CNH

The reaction on the part of a number of professors and students was one of outright fear and trepidation.

Dr. Paula Gómez Alonzo

Not since the military uprising against Madero led by Victoriano Huerta in 1913 had there been anything that had damaged our image as much as Tlatelolco/October 2, that had so defiled us, that had so stunned us, that had filled our mouths with the taste of blood, the blood of our dead.

Isabel Sperry de Barraza, mother of a family

I don't approve of what the students have been doing, but in all frankness the authorities went too far.

Jorge Olguín Andrade, bank clerk

All of us were reborn on October 2. And on that day we also decided how we are all going to die: fighting for genuine justice and democracy.

Raúl Álvarez Garín, of the CNH

After Tlatelolco I've changed a lot, though I don't know whether it's for the better or for the worse. Whatever sort of person I am after Tlatelolco, that's the way I'm going to be till I die.

Manuel Cervantes Palma, student at ESIQIE, IPN

I shall never forget, as long as I live, the hours of Tlatelolco.

Luis Gutiérrez Lazo, student at ESIQIE, IPN

I didn't used to be interested in politics. But I am now, because I'm enraged at what's happened.

Enrique Zúñiga Flores, student, Vocational 9

Furthermore, since we have asked the students time and time again to quiet down, let us now insist that the authorities too leave us in peace. Our entire country was wounded at Tlatelolco.

Francisco Martínez de la Vega, in an article
entitled "Where Is Our Country Heading?" El Día,
October 8, 1968

So going back to the Chihuahua building the next day was like . . . like . . . I can't describe it . . . something so vague and indefinable that I can't put into words; returning to my apartment and finding it riddled with machine-gun bullets, turned upside down, still reeking of gunpowder, with soldiers at the door, with police watching your every move, searching through everything you have with you, and the floor with bloodstains all over it. . . .

Well anyway . . . I'm living there in that apartment in Tlatelolco again because the bullet holes have been filled in, the walls have been repainted, and everything looks very nice again and nobody remembers anything about what happened. . . . On the contrary: we receive absolutely priceless messages every day telling us we must all come demonstrate against the students at the Secretariat of Education, that we must all sign petitions demanding that the schools in Tlatelolco be closed down because they're a threat to society.

Mercedes Olivera de Vázquez, anthropologist

The municipal sanitation workers
Are washing away the blood
On the Plaza of Sacrifices.

Octavio Paz

We women have never in our lives shed as many tears as we have in recent days. It's as though we were trying to wash all of Tlatelolco—all the images, all the walls, all the curbs, all the stone benches stained with blood, all the traces of bodies bleeding to death in the corners—clean with our tears. But it is not true that images can be washed away with tears. They still linger in your memory.

Perla Vélez de Aguilera, mother of a family

For days afterward, going to Mercedes's apartment just to try the soldiers' patience became almost an obsession on our part. We made up all sorts of reasons why we wanted to go up there, that we were coming so as to . . . well, we invented all sorts of excuses. We really had it in for those Army troops. We would see them reading, and say to them sweetly, "My goodness, you know how to read, do you? Isn't that nice!"

Once when we went downstairs to make a phone call we saw a whole bunch of them lined up outside the phone booth at the corner of the building, and we said to them in that same simpering tone of voice, "Please, may we ask whether we civilians are allowed to use this phone, or is it reserved for policemen and soldiers?"

I'm not certain whether they realized we were making fun of them, because they merely answered that we could use it too. We got in line and when the soldier right in front of us put his call through, we suddenly realized that these Army troops were human after all, because he said something like, "Listen, darling, I can't come home, I have no idea when they're going to let us out of here. . . . Listen, put him on the phone; come on, have him say a few words to me." We realized that he was talking to a child on the other end because he said to him, "How have you been, son? Have you been a good boy? This is Daddy," and all the other silly little things we all say to our kids. That was when Meche and I realized that those cops were people just like us, because on October 2 in Tlatelolco they hadn't seemed at all like us.

Margarita Nolasco, anthropologist

I don't want to live here in Tlatelolco any more, even if they repair everything, even if they clean it all up—I don't want to live here, no matter what they do. I went back there, and I don't mind telling you I could taste blood in my mouth; I walked along the esplanade with the warm, salty taste of the blood of all the dead choking me. . . . I know that the blood is drying up now, that it's turning black, but it seems to me that it's soaked right down through the cracks between the paving stones in the Plaza de las Tres Culturas, that it's encrusted in the *tezontle*.* You know, even the *tezontle* seems like blood trampled underfoot. . . . That's why I can't live here. . . . My daughter and I walked around the Plaza and she kept saying, "Look, Mama, here's where the tanks were. . . . Look, here's where the dead bodies were. . . . The bullet holes have been repaired and the walls have been painted over. . . . The elevator's working again. . . ." and I answered, "Dear, I can't bear Tlatelolco one minute more, let's get out of here, let's go far far away."

Catalina Ibarrola de Cabera, tenant in
the Nonoalco-Tlatelolco housing unit

---

* A porous stone.

The whole country reeks of blood.

Eulalio Gutiérrez, appointed Pro Tempore
President of Mexico by the Aguascalientes
Convention, serving in that capacity from
November 1, 1914, to January 20, 1915

Thank God I bought my apartment here in the Nonoalco-Tlatelolco housing unit rather than just renting! I'm never going to leave it, even if General Marcelino García Barragán shows up in person, with all his gold stripes, and troops armed with bazookas to try to get me out of here. This is my own little bit of breathing space, my trench. . . . Oh, no, listen, don't put down that I said it was my trench, because they'll think I've got a stock of bombs and hand grenades in here, when even my kitchen knives are so dull they won't cut!

María Luisa Mendoza, writer

THE PARISH POOR

I went to the Franciscan Brothers of the Tlatelolco parish and told them that I had come as a representative of a group of mothers of youngsters who had been killed and wounded on October 2, and that we would like to have a requiem mass said for them there in Tlatelolco.

The reply was, "We're very sorry, but there aren't any priests available to celebrate a requiem mass on the day you've requested. Our list of masses that day is already full up."

"We've been saying the Our Father for them, Padre, but we would like to have a mass celebrated for them here on the second of November, because this is where our children lost their lives, you see."

"But we just don't have time on our schedule," was the Padre's answer.

"In that case this is doubtless the only church in Mexico that has every minute of its time booked up, because usually there aren't enough priests to fill the . . ."

"No, the church is entirely booked that day."

"Well, in that case, it doesn't necessarily have to be a requiem mass; you could say matins for them or whatever you wanted—just something in honor of our dead."

"I'm sorry, but we just can't do anything for you."

"Well then, let us erect a memorial altar that day in one corner of the church."

"I'm sorry . . . we can't permit that either."

"But this group of mothers wants to come here and erect an altar. We've been trying to dissuade them, but they insist that that's what they want to do. If anything happens on the second of November, it's going to be your fault."

"We're terribly sorry. We can't grant your group permission."

"All right. Since you say it's impossible, I'm going to bring these mothers to see you, because they're all devout Catholics, even though I'm not one, and if I don't they're going to say that it was my fault we didn't get your permission because I'm not a Catholic. They'll say that I'm just one of those people who spread stories about how bad the priests are, so it's best that you explain to them personally your reasons for refusing."

"Very well. Bring them here and we'll try to convince them."

The next day a delegation of thirty of us in all went to talk to them again: the mothers of two dead students, the brothers of the two dead boys, other members of their families, and a number of students. We took them all to the Franciscan prior and he began to explain how he didn't have time and how it was impossible to grant permission for an altar to be erected in a church such as Santiago Tlatelolco, because the smoke from the tapers would make smudges on the wall, the walls of the church were four hundred years old, and so on—the same old story. Those of us who had gone there prepared to have it out with the priests suddenly shut up and didn't say a word because one of the mothers started to moan in a very strange sort of way, a plaint that started as a kind of quiet lament and ended in a shrill scream that gave us all goose pimples. She said that even the Church was turning its back on them, that it was more than she could bear if they wouldn't say a prayer for her son, and at that the Franciscan finally took pity on us and said, "I can't celebrate a special requiem mass for your dead, but we usually say four masses during the day for the poor of the parish, and if you like we might consider those dead youngsters poor people of the parish."

We agreed at once: we said we would be very happy to have them considered poor people of the parish.

"Well then, you must write the name of each poor person on an envelope and put one peso inside as alms."

Since we were furious at the way the Franciscans had treated us, we wrote the names of the dead on the envelopes and put exactly one peso, not one centavo more, in each of them. We wrote down only the names of the dead that had been published in the newspapers—thirty-four dead, among them women, students, and children, without making out any envelopes for the unidentified corpses that all the papers had mentioned. . . . Unfortunately a complete list of all those killed on October 2 in Tlatelolco has never been made public.

We took a notice around to all the newspapers, and asked them to publish it on November 2. In it we said that we remembered with the most profound grief those who had died on October 2 and listed their names. That was all our notice said.

It eventually reached the desks of the editors-in-chief of all the papers, and every last one of them refused to publish it.

On November 2, a woman with bright blue eyes who's absolutely fearless approached one of the Franciscans of Santiago Tlatelolco and told him that her labor union had given her a wreath in memory of her son, and whether he approved or not, she was going to place it there for him, no matter what. She had no sooner placed it against the wall when people suddenly popped up from all over, even from beneath the gravestones it seemed like, and began to light votive candles. They made little altars all over the Plaza de las Tres Culturas, with flowers and candles. As I came to the square with my *cempazúchitl* flowers, I saw that there were *granaderos*, armed to the teeth, not only in the Plaza but all over the housing unit. There were cars full of secret agents in front of the Secretariat of Foreign Relations! And others were patrolling the area with walkie-talkies. On the ground were a number of cards placed there in memory of the dead: "To the martyrs of Tlatelolco, murdered in cold blood." We saw a very pretty green cross from the Union of Women with a card that said, "To our martyrs of October 2," and next to the cross a large square of bristol-board with a drawing of a youngster impaled on a bayonet.

Margarita Nolasco, anthropologist

They've killed my son, but now all of you are my sons.

> *Celia Castillo de Chávez, mother of a family,*
> *to students on the esplanade of University City,*
> *at the meeting on October 31, 1968*

On the eighth we buried Jan. After the funeral, during that endless trip back that was not taking us anywhere, my mother looked out of the car window and saw a helicopter in the sky. I'll never forget her face and the fear in her voice as she exclaimed: "My God! A helicopter! There must be a demonstration going on somewhere."

> *E. P.*

That helicopter circling just a few feet above our heads frightened me. It seemed to be a great ill-omened bird.

> *María Elena Cervantes, grade-school teacher*

Some four thousand students and parents gathered today at five-fifteen in the Plaza de las Tres Culturas in Tlatelolco to begin their march on the Santo Tomás campus.

Armored vehicles, light Army assault tanks, had been patrolling the Plaza de las Tres Culturas and nearby areas.

Agents of the Federal Police, the Judicial Police of the Federal District, and the Secret Service have also been keeping a close watch on developments in this area.

The tension between students and police in civilian clothing is evident, but thus far there has been no active intervention or any sign of violence on either side.

> *Press bulletin*

At six-ten p.m. a helicopter fired several green flares. The Army moved in then and blocked off all the exits.

> *Raúl Álvarez Garín, of the CNH*

Four green flares shot off at six-ten p.m. were the signal for troops attached to the Olimpia Battalion, dressed in civilian clothes, to open fire on the students and workers demonstrating in Tlatelolco that afternoon.

> *Margarita García Flores, press secretary, UNAM*

Two helicopters kept circling the church. I saw several green flares go off in the sky. I stood there like a robot, listening to the familiar sound of bullets whizzing past. . . . The gunfire became heavier and heavier, and then Army troops appeared, as though somebody had pushed a button. . . .

Rodolfo Martínez, press photographer,
in "The Gun Battle as the Press Photographers
Saw It," La Prensa, *October 3, 1968*

Don't be frightened, don't run, they're trying to stir up trouble, don't try to escape, comrades, keep calm, everybody, don't run, keep calm, comrades. . . .

Eduardo Espinoza Valle (Owl-Eyes), of the CNH

They're dead bodies, sir. . . .

A soldier, to José Antonio Campo, reporter for El Día

Chronology

Events Mentioned by the Students in Their Tape-Recorded Testimony

JULY

Sunday, July 22

Students from Vocational 2 of the IPN and from Isaac Ochoterena Preparatory, one of the high schools affiliated with UNAM, have a violent confrontation. The reasons for this skirmish between the students of the two schools are not clear; rumor has it that it was the result of friction between two gangs frequenting the Cuidadela district, "The Cuidadelans" and "The Spiders." The buildings of Isaac Ochoterena, where the fighting takes place, are damaged.

Friday, July 26

Two public meetings take place: one organized by the FNET to protest the police intervention at Vocational 6; and another organized by leftist groups to celebrate the anniversary of the Cuban Revolution. The first demonstration is completely orderly, according to its organizers, except for one incident at the Monument to the Revolution, where a group blocks the marchers' way and attempts to force them to turn off down the Avenida Juárez. The marchers continue on to Santo Tomás, where a group of students urges those present to proceed to the Zócalo to draw wider attention to their protest. The demonstrators march down the Avenida Hidalgo and then continue on down San Juan de Letrán and Madero. The first confrontation with the police takes place at the corner of Palma and Madero. The fighting then spreads throughout the main downtown section of the city. According to a number of students, among them Luis González de Alba, of the Faculty of Philosophy and Letters, by some curious coincidence (or perhaps sheer happenstance) there were stones in the litter containers along the street, right there at hand should some charitable soul wish to make use of them. Since when have the residents of Mexico City been in the habit of throwing stones into litter containers?

Saturday, July 27

Eduardo de la Vega Ávila and other members of the Communist Party protest the invasion by the police of the headquarters of the party's Central Committee, which has occurred the day before. De la Vega and his companions are arrested in the Communist Party headquarters at 186 Mérida, and have been in prison ever since.

Sunday, July 28

Student representatives of UNAM and the IPN meet at the IPN School of Economics to discuss the possibility of organizing a strike, which is to continue until the following demands are met:

—The dissolution of the FNET, university rightist groups backed by the government, and MURO.
—Expulsion of students who are members of these groups and of the PRI.
—Indemnities to be paid to the students who have been injured and to the families of the dead.
—Release of all students being held in custody.
—Disbandment of the Corps of Riot Police [*Granaderos*] and other repressive police units.
—Repeal of Article 145 of the Penal Code.

Thursday, July 29

Students from Preparatory 8 block the Avenida de la Viga and seize two policemen.

Students from Vocational 7 capture public buses and block the main streets.

Preparatory 1 votes to go out on strike indefinitely in support of the Movement. Vocational 2, 4, and 7 follow suit.

Tuesday, July 30   why ?

The forces of law and order launch a bazooka attack on the San Idelfonso Preparatory School. Many students from Vocational 2 and Vocational 5 are wounded, and mass arrests are made. The Secretary of Defense, Marcelino García Barragán, declares, "The Army appeared on the scene at 0.40 hours. The troops immediately proceeded to cordon off the entire area and arrested a number of students, the majority of whom were injured. At approximately two a.m. the Army had the situation completely under control." Attorney Echeverría, the Secretary of the Department of Internal Affairs, holds a press conference at three-thirty a.m., at which he declares, "The extreme measures that have been taken have been aimed at preserving the autonomy of the University and shielding it from efforts on the part of petty and naïve, extremely naïve, interests which are attempting to keep the Mexican Revolution from continuing on its ever upward course. The ever upward course of the Mexican Revolution which so irritates these naïve militants is slowed down when there are unrest and interferences with the rule of law and order. Mexico is endeavoring to maintain a rule of freedom that is almost without parallel in any other country, by contrast with what happens in dictatorships of whatever political persuasion, or in nations in which chaos and violence rule. The CNED is the group that is behind these incidents."

In an interview in the Federal District Headquarters Alfonso Coronal del Rosal, Regent of Mexico City, declares to the leaders of the FNET, "We are all aware that there are many agitators who are not bona fide students. I have made it plain to you that we are the first to disapprove when a regular police officer or a *granadero* invades an educational institution. They have been expressly forbidden to do so and will continue to be prohibited from so doing; the government does not have the slightest interest in wounding the feelings of students who want the police to stay out of their schools.* "

---

* The powerful FNET is more or less controlled by the PRI. Its efforts to serve as a mediator and its attempts to foster dissension within the Movement were condemned by the CNH.

AUGUST

Thursday, August 1

The outstretched hand: The President of the Republic declares in Guadalajara, "Peace and calm must be restored in our country. A hand has been extended; it is up to Mexican citizens to decide whether to grasp this outstretched hand. I have been greatly pained by these deplorable and shameful incidents. Let us not widen the gap between us; let us all refuse to heed the promptings of our false pride, myself included, naturally."

Monday, August 5

At a meeting of the entire faculty, the professors at the IPN vote for the creation of the Committee of IPN Professors for Democratic Freedoms, the aim of which is to ensure that science and culture will be passed on by teachers within a society of free men. The Committee also demands the immediate release of professors, students, and citizens being held in custody; the repeal of Article 145 of the Penal Code; the punishment of those responsible for repression; the disbandment of the Corps of Riot Police; no further invasions of educational institutions by the forces of law and order. At this meeting of the entire faculty, the FNET was also censured for having fostered dissension among the students.

Thursday, August 8

Formation of the CNH, representing UNAM, the IPN, the Normal Schools, the College of Mexico, the Chapingo School of Agriculture, the Iberoamerican University, the Lasalle University, and the national universities in the provinces. The CNH makes public the students' six-point petition.

Tuesday, August 13

The first mass demonstration in the Zócalo, attended by a crowd of 150,000 people made up of students, IPN, UNAM, the Normal

Schools, Chapingo, schoolteachers, and the general public. The march begins at the Santo Tomás campus and the demonstrators proceed to the Zócalo. The Teachers' Coalition heads the groups of marchers, and the demonstration is an orderly one. The demonstrators demand the release of Vallejo and the political prisoners, and there are shouts of "Being an honest leader means becoming a political prisoner!"

Thursday, August 15

The University Council supports the students' demands, and appoints a committee of twenty-one as a liaison group. According to a statement by Dr. Ricardo Guerra (*Siempre!*, no. 793, September 4, 1968), this meeting of the Council was an epoch-making session in the history of UNAM.

Friday, August 16

"Lightning meetings," brigades organized to pass out leaflets, etc. The Congress of Artists and Intellectuals joins the Movement.

Thursday, August 22

Attorney Luis Echeverría, Secretary of the Department of Internal Affairs, proposes a "frank and peaceful dialogue which will lead to the clarification of the origins and the development of this deplorable problem."

The CNH requests that these talks be public: conducted with representatives of the press, television, and radio present.

Friday, August 23

Professors and students again insist that they are willing to accept the offer to hold a dialogue with the government, with the one stipulation that the talks be broadcast live over the radio and television networks and that journalists be present. They suggest that these talks be held either in the National Auditorium, on the esplanade of University City, on the esplanade of Zacatenco, or in any other suitable place on the grounds of UNAM or the IPN, including Vocational 5 and the Santo Tomás campus.

Saturday, August 24

The SME* declares, "We stand behind the students when they protest against any sort of foreign infiltration (whatever the political line it is attempting to further), that of the CIA for instance, which is endeavoring to create the myth that Mexico is swarming with Communists." The members of the SME state in their declaration that there is a pressing need for "the authorities and bona fide students to cease refusing to compromise and sit down at the conference table together."

Tuesday, August 27

A huge demonstration. Three hundred thousand people march from the Museum of Anthropology to the Zócalo. The youngsters carry banners with pictures of Juárez, Pancho Villa, Zapata, Hidalgo, Ernesto Guevara, and Vallejo.

Sócrates Amado Campos Lemus proposes that the public dialogue with the government begin on September 1, the day of the President's Annual Message, in the Zócalo, at ten a.m. A red and black flag is raised to the top of the flagpole in the Zócalo. Campos Lemus suggests that a brigade of student guards remain behind to guard the Zócalo. At one a.m. Army troops, police, and firemen clear the Zócalo.

Wednesday, August 28

Large numbers of government employees are transported to the Zócalo for a ceremony organized by the Department of the Federal District to make amends for the students' insult to the national flag.

Thursday, August 29

Heberto Castillo, professor of engineering and member of the Teachers' Coalition, declares after having been brutally beaten, "The violent attack on my person is a grave error on the part of those who gave orders for such an attack on me. . . . I have no weapons save ideas. . . . Respect for the Constitution must be restored."

---

* Sindicato Mexicano de Electricistas (Mexican Union of Electrical Workers).

SEPTEMBER

Sunday, September 1

The President of the Republic, Gustavo Díaz Ordaz, delivers his Fourth Annual Message. He declares, "Culture is the splendid fruit of freedom . . . ," a statement he had made on a previous occasion, at the University of Guadalajara in 1964.

Saturday, September 7

A meeting called by the CNH in Tlatelolco is attended by twenty-five thousand people.

Monday, September 9

The Rector of UNAM calls for the resumption of classes at the University. He states, "In his Annual Message the president answered the students' demands in a satisfactory manner."

Friday, September 13

THE GREAT SILENT DEMONSTRATION

Sunday, September 15

Professor Heberto Castillo gives the *"grito"* celebrating Mexican Independence on the esplanade of University City. There is also a celebration at the IPN.

Tuesday, September 17

The CNH agrees to a dialogue in written form if the texts are widely disseminated by the news media, but the Movement has become a genuine social struggle on the part of the people, seeking not only to register their protest, but to restore the rights guaranteed them by the Constitution.

Wednesday, September 18

Army troops invade University City.

Thursday, September 19

The Rector of UNAM, Engineer Javier Barros Sierra, officially protests: "The military occupation of University City represents an excessive use of force that our scholarly institution has not deserved."

Tuesday, September 24

The Army occupies the Santo Tomás cámpus, after a long and hard-
fought battle between students and police on the campus. There are
many dead and wounded, and many arrests.

OCTOBER

Tuesday, October 1

The CNH refuses to agree to the reopening of UNAM. The Army
departs from University City. The CNH announces that an important meeting will be held in the Plaza de las Tres Culturas in the
Nonoalco-Tlatelolco housing unit.

Tuesday, October 2

TLATELOLCO

Saturday, October 5

Sócrates Amado Campos Lemus makes public statements naming
politicians and intellectuals whom he claims were involved in the
Movement.

Wednesday, October 9

Conference attended by a number of members of the CNH in the
Casa del Lago, a cultural center affiliated with UNAM. There are no
demonstrations or violent incidents during the "Olympic truce" the
students have agreed to observe between the twelfth and the
twenty-eighth of October.

Saturday, October 26

Sixty-seven students being held in Military Camp 1 are released.

Thursday, October 31

First meeting at UNAM after Tlatelolco. The mother of a dead student addresses the crowd of seven thousand people.

DECEMBER

Wednesday, December 4

Classes are resumed.

Friday, December 13

Since this date, some five hundred persons have been arrested, in various places, among them Tita, Nacha, and Rodolfo Echeverría of the Communist Party, the latter for having served as defense attorney for Gerardo Unzueta.